Of

CRIME &
CRIMINALITY

TITLES OF RELATED INTEREST FROM PINE FORGE PRESS

Criminal Justice: Readings by George S. Bridges, Joseph G. Weis, and Robert D. Crutchfield

Crime: Readings, Second Edition by Robert D. Crutchfield, George S. Bridges, and Joseph G. Weis

Juvenile Delinquency: Readings by Joseph G. Weis, Robert D. Crutchfield, and George S. Bridges

The Politics of Injustice by Katherine Beckett and Theodore Sasson

Crime and Everyday Life by Marcus Felson

Profitable Penalties: How to Cut Crime by Nathan Glaser

Sociology: Exploring the Architecture of Everyday Life, Third Edition by David M. Newman

Enchanting a Disenchanted World by George Ritzer

The McDonaldization of Society, New Century Edition by George Ritzer

Social Statistics for a Diverse Society, Second Edition by Chava Frankfort-Nachmias and Anna Leon-Guerrero

Exploring Social Issues Using SPSS for Windows, Second Edition by Joseph F. Healey, John Boli, Earl Babbie, and Fred Halley

Investigating the Social World, Second Edition, by Russell Schutt

OF
CRIME &
CRIMINALITY

Sally S. Simpson
Editor

The
Use of
Theory in
Everyday
Life

PINE FORGE PRESS
Excellence and Innovation for Teaching

For information:

Pine Forge Press
A Sage Publications Company
2455 Teller Road
Thousand Oaks, California 91320
(805) 499-4224
E-mail: sales@pfp.sagepub.com

Sage Publications Ltd.
6 Bonhill Street
London EC2A 4PU
United Kingdom

Sage Publications India Pvt. Ltd.
M-32 Market
Greater Kailash I
New Delhi 110 048 India

Printed in the United States of America

Library of Congress Cataloging-in-Publication Data

Main Entry Under Title:
   Of crime and criminality: The use of theory in everyday life / edited by Sally Simpson.
        p.   cm.
   Includes bibliographical references and index.
   ISBN 0-7619-8638-3 (pbk.: alk. paper)
   1. Criminology. 2. Crime. 3. Criminal behavior. 4. Criminal Justice, Administration of.   I. Simpson, Sally.
   HV6018   .O3 2000
   364—dc21   99-050677

This book is printed on acid-free paper.

00   01   02   03   04   05   06   7   6   5   4   3   2   1

Acquisition Editor:	Stephen Rutter
Editorial Assistant:	Ann Makarias
Production Editor:	Sanford Robinson
Editorial Assistant:	Karen Wiley
Typesetter:	Tina Hill
Indexer:	Molly Hall
Cover Designer:	Ravi Balasuriya

■ About the Editor

Sally S. Simpson is Associate Professor of Criminology and Criminal Justice at the University of Maryland. In her research on corporate offending and gender and crime, she has applied and/or tested several criminological perspectives including rational choice, shaming, neo-Marxian, and feminist theory. Current research projects include a book on corporate crime control and a collaborative investigation of women's experience of violence (as offenders and victims).

■ About the Publisher

Pine Forge Press is a new educational publisher, dedicated to publishing innovative books and software throughout the social sciences. On this and any other of our publications, we welcome your comments.

Please call or write us at:

Pine Forge Press
A Sage Publications Company
31 St. James Avenue, Suite 510
Boston, MA 02116
Phone: (617) 753-7512
E-mail: sdr@pfp.sagepub.com

Visit our World Wide Web site, your direct link to a multitude of on-line resources: www.pineforge.com

CONTENTS

    The theory asserts that delinquency occurs as a consequence
of exposure to antisocial definitions that will vary by
priority, frequency, duration, and intensity. Giordano and
Rockwell explore whether chronic delinquency among
females can be explained by this perspective.

PART 2: Traditional Criminological Theory Updated

PART 3: New Directions in Theory: New Ideas, Applications, and Issues

adolescent limited versus life course persistent typologies—account for the developmental dimensions of drug-using careers.

MARCUS FELSON

Routine activity theory is an opportunity theory in that it explains crime as resulting from the convergence of three elements: a motivated offender, a suitable target, and the absence of a capable guardian against crime. Felson explains that individual, community, and societal crime patterns can be understood by exploring the relationships among these elements.

SALLY S. SIMPSON

Many things are uncertain in academic life, but the one thing that has been fairly consistent and predictable is how undergraduate students feel about theory. Typically, most find it obtuse and irrelevant to their everyday lives. This is particularly true for more traditional theories which students tend to find overly simplistic and noninclusive (that is, based in the experiences of the white working class or males). Students often suggest that the social circumstances that gave rise to these theories no longer exist. Consequently, they fail to see how the ideas, explanations, and predictions developed in the past are relevant to life at the dawn of the new millennium.

The purpose of this book is to give some life to the mordant theories of previous eras while also providing you with examples of more recent theoretical developments in the field. Thus, the eleven chapter contributors were asked to identify a current criminological problem and to show how theory could make the problem comprehensible. The contributors were also asked to draw up a set of policy recommendations in line with the theory.

The introductory chapter, by Don C. Gibbons, gives you a preview of the ideas, social events, and theorists who influenced how we currently think about crime. Woven into his review is a discussion of how the work in this volume relates to earlier themes. Once you finish reading the chapters, see if you agree with his prognosis about the future of the criminological enterprise.

Following the introduction, the book is divided into three sections that are grouped by common themes. In the first section, contributors challenge the focus of mainstream theory for what it ignores (females) and what it over-emphasizes (crime by young black males) while in the second grouping, older theories have been modified to account better for crime in contemporary society. Newly emerging theories and issues confronting theory development are grouped together in the last section.

For instance, in the first section, original theories are applied to one of the most obvious facts about crime in contemporary society; the inequalities in the commission of crime and how that has affected theory development and policy. In Chapter 1, Peggy C. Giordano and Sharon Mohler Rockwell explore whether the traditional theory of differential association is generalizable to the criminal careers of chronic female offenders. In other words, do both male and female offenders tend to be exposed to deviant lifestyles? Jody Miller, in Chapter 2, also focuses on female delinquency, but she uses a more contemporary explanation as a guide. For Miller, crime is a resource for doing gender (i.e., accomplishing masculinity or femininity) within a social system stratified by gender and race. The theme of stratification also guides the work of Katheryn K. Russell (Chapter 3) in her discussion of critical race theory and "racial hoaxes" as well as that of Katherine Beckett and Theodore Sasson (Chapter 4) who apply a neo-Marxian framework to the war on crime. But the two chapters present different visions and recommendations, influenced by the theoretical lenses through which the authors view crime. Russell addresses the social and economic costs of focusing on race and the limitations of current legal remedies. Beckett and Sasson focus on how race and class have shaped the "war on crime."

The chapters in the second part of the book reformulate traditional theories. Robert J. Bursik, Jr., in Chapter 5, describes how systemic theory, which is an extension of classic social disorganization theory, can predict the relationship between neighborhood characteristics (and local crime rates. The recent spate of highly publicized school killings are the subject of Chapter 6, in which Robert Agnew applies strain theory. He suggests that individuals who are exposed to negative experiences or who fail to achieve positively valued goals are more likely to feel anger and frustration and thus trigger some students to act criminally. Students who have negative relations with peers, who dislike their teachers, and who receive poor grades have a higher risk of crime than other students. Agnew also suggests that some schools are also more likely than others to make students feel angry and frustrated. Finally, in Chapter 7, Ruth Triplett updates labeling theory. She describes how society has shifted from defining acts as evil toward defining actors as evil and concludes that a generalized labeling effect now leads society to view all juveniles, but especially urban African American males, as dangerous.

The final section of the book introduces you to a newer set of ideas about crime and crime control. As you will see, the effort to test and apply a theory often creates new ideas, which may refine, strengthen, or call into question the original theory. In Chapter 8, which I wrote with coauthors Lyn Exum and Craig Smith, we explore whether shaming and reintegration, a crime control policy derived from social control and labeling theory, will diminish participation in corporate illegality among a group of managers. In another evaluation of theory, in Chapter 9, Jeffrey Bouffard, M. Lyn Exum, and Raymond Paternoster assess the role of emotion and emotional arousal (the thrill of taking risks) in explanations of crime. They go on to discuss how a theory based in "rationality" (rational choice theory) can incorporate these ideas without sacrificing its main assumptions or concepts. Paul Mazerolle's chapter on drug use (Chapter 10) raises the important question of whether static criminological theories can fully explain changes an individual's use of illicit drugs over time. He advocates developmental theories which recognize that factors related to one's first experimentation with drugs may be quite different than those that result in escalated use or the cessation of drug use. He finally suggests that drug use patterns over time may differ from drug to drug. In Chapter 11, Marcus Felson describes routine activities theory. The three main elements, this theory says, are a likely offender, a suitable target, and the absence of a capable guardian against crime. Felson claims that by placing the crime incident at the center of theory (instead of trying to predict what an individual is going to do next), this theory meets the standards of scientific theory better than any of the other theories reviewed in this volume. I shall leave it to you to agree or disagree with this provocative assertion.

As you can see, the chapters in this volume reflect the diversity of ideas in the field of criminology about what causes crime, how to control it, and whether existing theory can accommodate the wide range of offenders and circumstances involved in crime. In addition, the chapters show how several distinct methodologies can be used to explore research questions that grow out of theory. Interviews, surveys, analysis of crime records, and the application of theory to observed phenomena are all useful techniques to test or build theoretical models.

It is my hope that this brief glimpse into the craft of theorizing about crime and exposure to the wide array of interesting subjects that can be explored with theory will stimulate you to become more involved in research and debate, in both an academic setting and in the public arena. Criminological theory has been deemed boring and irrelevant for far too long.

Criminology, Criminologists, and Criminological Theory

DON C. GIBBONS

This introductory chapter presents a brief and incomplete account of the growth of the criminological enterprise during the 20th century and, in particular, of the twists and turns in criminological theory development over this period.[1] But first, I need to lay out some metes and bounds around this topic.

What is criminology? Sutherland and Cressey's (1978) widely cited definition declares that criminology is "the body of knowledge regarding juvenile delinquency and crime. It includes within its scope the processes of making laws, breaking laws, and reacting to the breaking of laws" (p. 3). Few criminologists would quarrel with this definition.

What is the *criminological enterprise*? This term draws attention to the fact that the production of criminological knowledge is carried on by flesh-and-blood living persons; that is, it is a collective human endeavor. Following Sutherland and Cressey's (1978) definition, the criminological enterprise has to do in considerable part with discovery of the causes of lawbreaking, principally through an interactive theory-research process.

Now, however, the plot thickens. For one thing, it is not only professional criminologists who think about and formulate explanations of lawbreaking. Both media gurus and ordinary citizens often put forth "theories" or "explanations" for criminality, many of which are wide of the mark. In short, causal thinking is not restricted to social scientists.

A more important point is that whereas a large share of the serious scholarly work on criminological questions during the 20th century has been by sociologically trained American criminologists, criminologists and criminology have become firmly established in a number of other nations as well—England, Germany, Australia, and Japan, among others.

I spoke in the preceding paragraph of "a large share of the serious scholarly work" to emphasize an even more crucial fact, namely that it is not solely professional criminologists who staff the criminological enterprise. Starting with the biological positivists in Italy around the turn of the 19th century—Lombroso, Ferri, and Garafolo, in particular—biological investigators have produced a large research literature on biological and sociobiological influences on lawbreaking. Although it is fair to say that many sociological criminologists have been disinterested, at best, in these findings, as I have noted elsewhere (Gibbons 1994), the evidence from modern sociobiological studies is sufficiently compelling that "sociological criminologists are going to have to become more biologically informed" (p. 132).

Criminological contributions have come from another quarter as well. Psychologists and psychiatrists have had much to say about mental pathology and personality differences among individuals that can contribute to criminality (Gibbons 1994:132-48). Moreover, whereas sociological criminologists traditionally have regarded the claims of psychiatrists and psychologists with suspicion, there has been considerable cross-fertilization during recent years in which the theories of some criminologists have become more "psychological" at the same time as psychiatrists and psychologists have become more sociologically informed.

Economists, political scientists, historians, and other social scientists also engage in criminological research and theorizing.[2] Clearly, we need to cast our nets over a vast and varied stock of knowledge if we are to be criminologically informed.

Finally, how do we know when we are looking at a criminological theory? Most criminologists and most readers of this book probably agree that a theory is some type of statement, usually written, regarding the presumed causes of lawbreaking, but they agree about little else (Gibbons 1994:79-94). A few criminologists, and most notably Gibbs (1985), have argued that most of our theories are discursive, which *Webster's New World Dictionary* defines as "wandering from one topic to another; rambling; digressive." The theories are loosely argued, contain propositions or claims that are implicit rather than explicit, and commingle propositions with illustrative material, all written in the conventions of everyday language. Gibbs's (and my own) preference is for the *formal mode* of theory construction, which results in more rigorously stated arguments.

However, many criminologists are ecumenical with regard to what they are willing to label as "theory." I suggest elsewhere (Gibbons 1994:79-94) that some of our arguments are more properly called *general perspectives*— broad viewpoints that suggest some of the concepts and propositions that might be included in a more detailed and explicit argument. I already have described *discursive theories. Semiformal theories* lie at some point between discursive and formal theories.

These four categories are, of course, points along a continuum, with spe-cific instances of "theory" falling at various locations along that continuum. As for some of the arguments in this book, I concur with Russell (Chapter 3), who describes critical race theory as a perspective, and I would so identify some of the other viewpoints in this book as well. Also, the writings of Tannenbaum, Lemert, and Becker, which Triplett (Chapter 7) identifies as labeling theory, also seem to me to be instances of a broad perspective. By contrast, differential association theory, discussed by Giordano and Rockwell (Chapter 1), is closer to a semiformal theory, as is the modern version of social disorganization theory in the chapter by Bursik (Chapter 5). Finally, Braithwaite's theory, presented in the chapter by Simpson, Exum, and Smith (Chapter 8), is a mix of discursive and semiformal theorizing. There are few, if any, formal theories in criminology.

These metes and bounds identify the outer boundaries of the criminologi-cal enterprise. The remainder of this chapter focuses on the development of *sociological* criminology and the theoretical products that have been pro-duced by contemporary criminologists and their criminological ancestors. Also, from this point onward, I employ the term *theory* in a relaxed or inclu-sive fashion.

■ The Origins of Modern Criminology

□ Premodern European Criminology

Who created criminology, and when did they do it? Clearly, a number of persons contributed to the gradual emergence of criminology over a long historical period. Drapkin (1983) reaches back into prehistoric times and identifies the Code of Hammurabi as a precursor of modern criminology, whereas Reid (1976:21) notes that Topinard, an early anthropologist, should be given some credit for coining the term *criminology*. However, most textbooks agree that the important names in European premodern criminology include Cesare Beccaria and Jeremy Bentham, major figures during the 18th century school of thought, which held that criminals were rational beings who made willful decisions to violate the law. Also, as I have noted, Lombroso, Ferri, and Garafolo were important 19th-century scholars who argued for the scientific study of crime and criminals. Some commentators have claimed that American criminology has ties to these figures and their works as well as to the contributions of other European scholars during the 1800s, but if so, then the ties are fairly tenuous.

■ American Criminology: The Early Years

□ *The Rise of American Sociology*

Because criminology in this country is the progeny of sociology, a few words are required on the genealogy of the parent field. Publications dealing with sociological topics began to appear in some number in the United States during the 1800s, and sociology courses began to pop up in college curricula during the 1890s. But whether its birth occurred in 1880, 1890, or the early 1900s, the infant discipline showed little resemblance to the field that developed during the second half of the 20th century.

The rise of sociology was part of a broader sweep of events during the first two decades of the 20th century, which historians have identified as the Progressive Era. Progressives were principally middle class citizens from various walks of life who were concerned about the harsh social consequences of industrialization and urbanization that were overtaking the nation. They also spoke out for rehabilitation of criminals, assistance to the poor, and humane treatment of the insane.

The emergence of American sociology is located against this background of Progressive thought. But there is more to the story including the prominence of persons from rural and religious backgrounds in the ranks of college professors of sociology during the first three decades of the 20th century. Most of these persons gave short shrift to the sociological theories that had emerged in Europe during the late 1800s and focused instead on social problems of one type or another, which they viewed as pathological byproducts of urbanization and industrialization.

□ *The First Stages of American Criminology*

Books dealing with crime and delinquency in America began to appear in some number around 1895. Most of them emphasized Lombrosian hypotheses about congenital criminality and biological and evolutionary theories of criminality. The first true criminology textbook was authored by Parmelee (1918). Its overall tone was that criminality is an abnormal and pathological form of behavior. This book, and nearly all of the others during this period, presented a potpourri of biological influences and social conditions that were said to play some part in causation.

The appearance of Sutherland's (1924) *Criminology* was a signal event in that it presented an incisive critique of most of the popular hypotheses of the day including those that emphasized physical or mental pathology on the part of offenders. Moreover, it contained a number of hints of the theory of differential association that would appear in subsequent editions.

□ *Criminology: 1930 to 1945*

Sutherland's book eventually helped to turn criminology away from mindless eclecticism and biological arguments and toward sociological analysis. Also, sociology had taken firm root in the United States by about 1930, due largely to the efforts of figures such as W. I. Thomas, Robert Ezra Park, and Ernest Burgess. The sociological fraternity had expanded noticeably by 1930 from the handful of persons involved in it at the beginning of the century. Criminology was part of this expansion.[3]

Clifford Shaw and Henry D. McKay: Delinquency as a Social Phenomenon

It would be hard to overestimate the significance of the delinquency studies carried on by Clifford Shaw and Henry D. McKay in Chicago and certain other cities from 1929 through the 1930s, for their inquiries generated much of the intellectual capital on which criminologists continue to draw, even to the present day (see Bursik's chapter in this book [Chapter 5]). In one set of studies (Shaw and McKay 1931, 1932), they indicated that juvenile court referral rates were highest in neighborhoods of rapid population change, poor housing, poverty, adult crime, and other social ills. They also reported that these high rates, usually found near industrial areas and deteriorated neighborhoods near the city centers, had remained consistently high over a 30-year period, even though the area populations had completely changed over this period. These findings led them to the view that delinquency was a cultural tradition in some urban neighborhoods.

Shaw and McKay also examined the processes through which youths became lawbreakers in these areas, principally through studying life history documents on offenders (Shaw 1930, 1931; Shaw, McKay, and McDonald 1938). They concluded that delinquents were normal youngsters who became involved in misconduct as they came under the influence of criminogenic conditions in their communities.

Shaw and McKay's studies remained extremely influential long after their publication during the 1930s. For one thing, their findings about normal youths learning delinquent traditions from their peers were an influence on Sutherland's thinking that culminated in differential association theory. These data also played more than a little part in the development of "subcultural theories" about delinquency that arose during the 1950s and 1960s. Then, too, as Bursik indicates in his chapter, their observations on the crime-generating influences of community conditions live on in contemporary theorizing and research on social disorganization, community conditions, and criminality. Finally, one can detect the influence of their work in a host of broader perspectives that identify a variety of "criminogenic social conditions" in American society that are said to be implicated in lawbreaking (see, e.g., Messner and Rosenberg 1994).

Sutherland's Contributions

Sutherland's theory of differential association is the focus of the chapter by Giordano and Rockwell (Chapter 1). The embryonic idea of differential association turned up in the 1934 edition of Sutherland's book, whereas the final version appeared in the 1947 edition and subsequent editions. His thesis was that criminal behavior occurs when persons acquire enough sentiments in favor of law violation to outweigh their prosocial or anticriminal conduct definitions. The formulation enjoyed great popularity in American criminology because it was a *sociological* perspective that asserted that individuals are the product of social experiences that provide them with beliefs and standards of conduct to guide their behavior. As such, it was a giant step away from eclectic "multiple-factor" orientations that were little more than long lists of specific variables that might play some part in lawbreaking.

Sutherland and Cressey (1978) also created a version of the criminogenic social conditions perspective alluded to earlier. Their "differential social organization" argument endeavored to limn the conditions under which criminality is more or less likely to be learned through differential association.

Other Contributions

A full chronicle of events during this period would include some other important developments, such as Sellin's (1938) theorizing about culture conflict and crime and Merton's (1938) influential essay on anomie and deviant behavior. These and other figures were involved in the construction of the skeletal structure of "mainstream criminology," which dominated in the criminological enterprise during the subsequent period of development, from about 1945 to 1970.

■ Criminology: 1945 to 1970

The post-World War II period, and in particular the years from 1945 to the mid-1960s, were extraordinary ones for the nation as a whole and for sociology and criminology in particular. Television journalist Tom Brokaw captures something of these times in his book about the returning veterans of World War II, whom he terms "the greatest generation" (Brokaw 1998). Americans during these years were infused with the belief that the possibilities for economic and social progress in the country were virtually unlimited.

Colleges and universities during this period quickly became filled with veterans-turned-students funded by the G.I. Bill. These and other funds supplied by the government resulted in large-scale increases in the size of educational institutions and student populations. These were halcyon days for sociology as students flocked to sociology and criminology. What ultimately emerged out of these events was a dramatically enlarged field of sociology and a much expanded corps of criminological theorists and researchers.

As I already have indicated, most of the criminology during this period was "mainstream" work. What is meant by mainstream? First, most of the criminologists of this era were neopositivists (although some of them might not have seen themselves in this way) because they took for granted that there is a stable reality that can be directly observed, described, and theorized about. In other words, they assumed without question that it is possible to zero in on verifiable social facts, including crime and criminals, and to submit them to scrutiny.

Mainstream criminologists, then and now, also hold that crime is a reflection of social structure and that criminal behavior is learned in some way or another. Then, too, their allegiance is to the view that it is possible to mend rips and tears in the social structure, reform the criminal and juvenile justice systems where necessary, and rehabilitate delinquents and criminals. In short, mainstream criminology is liberal and positivist in form.

Overall, criminological work during the period from 1945 to 1970 can be described as consisting of incremental steps to push the field further along the pathways that had been scouted by Sutherland and others. The investigations of "hidden" or self-reported delinquency conducted during this period were a case in point (Gibbons and Krohn 1991:41-48). Another important body of theorizing and research, having to do with gang delinquency or what often was termed *delinquent subcultures,* was stimulated by Cohen's (1955) *Delinquent Boys* and included Cloward and Ohlin's (1960) *Delinquency and Opportunity* and Short and Strodtbeck's (1965) *Group Process and Gang Delinquency.* Hirschi's (1969) influential book on control theory also appeared during this period. These are only a few samples of the considerable theoretical and research output of criminologists during this period, for I am forced to slur over a great many other contributions, most of which have been reviewed in textbooks (see, e.g., Gibbons 1992; Gibbons and Krohn 1991).[4]

■ Criminology: The Last Three Decades and Beyond

Although the warning signs were at first fairly feeble, and although the changes of which they warned were gradual, rents and tears began to appear in American society during the late 1960s. Feelings of disquiet, alienation, and the like, some of which were inchoate and others of which were given strong expression (especially by university students), began to appear in the United States. One of these had to do with the persistence of racial discrimination, another with continuing economic inequality, and still another with the war in Vietnam. Then, too, many have argued that the assassinations of President John F. Kennedy, Robert Kennedy, and Martin Luther King, Jr., contributed to the sense that "things are out of whack" that began to gnaw on increasing numbers of citizens, whereas others have contended that the Watergate affair and President Richard Nixon's resignation in disgrace played a significant role in the growing feeling that political leaders were not to be trusted. I cannot provide a more detailed account of the coming apart of American society here, nor can I identify all of the various events that led to this state of affairs, but it is palpable that these broad changes had a profound impact on sociology and criminology.

Still, most of these societal changes, and those in sociology and criminology as well, were gradual ones. Mainstream "scientific" sociology continues to be prominent, and mainstream criminology still is well represented. Even so, more and more persons have come forth in sociology during recent years, holding that the center cannot hold, that is, that the discipline no longer has a "central idea"; instead, it has become highly fragmented.[5] Growing numbers of criminologists also have become at least a bit dismayed about the balkanization of their field.

Next, I offer a few additional comments about the mainstream directions that have continued to the present, after which I draw attention to some of the "new criminologies" that have grown up. Finally, I provide a hint or two as to what might lie ahead in the 21st century.

□ *Ongoing Work in Mainstream Criminology*

The *control* thesis that lawbreaking often is the result of the failure of individuals to rein in their deviant impulses and/or of others to exert pressure to conform on potential miscreants was voiced by Bentham and Beccaria during the 18th century. A number of considerably more sophisticated versions of it have appeared in recent decades including Hirschi's (1969) book, which emphasizes the controlling influence of ties to parents and schools. Gottfredson and Hirschi (1990) offer a retooled version that argues that persons who are deficient in self-control are most likely to engage in deviance and criminality. Finally, Tittle's (1995) intellectual tour de force ties the notion of control to a number of contingencies and intervening variables. There is good reason to predict that control notions are going to be around for some time.

Elements from the *labeling* perspective are much in evidence in contemporary criminology as well, as both Triplett (Chapter 7) and Simpson, Exum, and Smith (Chapter 8) indicate in their chapters in this book. Then, too, *differential association* theory, particularly the social learning revision of it by Akers (1985), continues to draw considerable attention.

In their chapter, Bouffard, Exum, and Paternoster (Chapter 9) allude to *rational choice theory* in which it is argued that offenders frequently make deliberate and reasoned decisions to engage in lawbreaking (Cornish and Clarke 1986; Gibbons 1994:122-24). Drawing on Katz's (1988) ruminations about the psychic rewards of offending, they suggest that rational choice notions need to take emotional factors into account.

Developmental theory is still another theme with roots in ideas that were touched on but not explored in great detail during earlier decades. For example, Sutherland hinted at developmental notions when he drew attention to "behavior systems" in lawbreaking. Also, I attempted to identify a number of criminal "careers" and behavioral pathways in my book, *Changing the Lawbreaker* (Gibbons 1965). However, as Mazerolle indicates in his chapter (Chapter 10), developmental theory has emerged in a much more mature form during recent years in works such as Sampson and Laub's (1993) *Crime in the Making.* Still, it is worth noting that their book grew out of studies of delinquents that were produced by Sheldon and Eleanor Glueck during the 1940s and 1950s.

I already have mentioned the *structural* theories of Sutherland and Cressey (1978) and Merton (1938). This line of activity has continued, as reflected in the writings of Hagan and his associates (1989). Also, the "routine activities" approach of Felson and Cohen, discussed in the chapter by Felson (Chapter 11), is properly identified as a structural formulation.

Although contemporary mainstream theorizing has ties to the work of earlier generations of criminologists, the other side of the coin also needs to be underscored, namely that this work has grown markedly in sophistication over the decades.

☐ *Radical Marxist Criminology*

An implicit theme throughout the preceding comments is that few, if any, truly original theories have been developed by criminologists. Instead, scholars most often have taken existing arguments and revised and reshaped them into "new" theories. The conflict perspective is a clear example. Its central proposition is that crime often reflects social divisions, power relationships, class relations, and the like. Parmelee's (1918) textbook contained a few paragraphs that centered on conflict, and more recently, Vold (1958) and Turk (1969) have explicated this view in detail.

These older conflict perspectives identified a variety of social divisions, interest group conflicts, and the like that were thought to be related to lawbreaking. However, a new brand, most often referred to as radical Marxist theory, appeared on the scene during the late 1960s and early 1970s. One of its central propositions was that most, if not all, criminal laws are created to serve the interests of the ruling class, that is, corporation heads and other "movers and shakers" in society. The agents of the ruling class, the police, employ the criminal law as a means of keeping the oppressed working class under control. This was a profoundly pessimistic view of crime and American society, for it led to the conclusion that nothing short of a revolution and the collapse of capitalist society can bring about a major reduction in crime.

I can provide only a terse and markedly incomplete account of the twists and turns taken by radical Marxist theorizing in criminology here (but for many of the details, see Gibbons 1979:156-86). Among other things, a number of variants of this perspective were produced during the 1970s. Some of the initial formulations were said to be instances of "one-dimensional," "vulgar," or "instrumental" Marxism because they were filled with bombast and hyperbole, presented an oversimplified view of political and economic power, and were defective in a number of other ways. Later, some other, more finely grained "structural" Marxist arguments were put forth.

Why did radical-Marxist views arise when they did, or for that matter, why did they arise at all? The basic answer is clear. The radicalization of some segment of the criminological fraternity was part of the broader sweep of events that began during the late 1960s that challenged many of the taken-for-granted assumptions about American society.

What can be said about the eventual fate of radical Marxist criminology? First, a considerable number of mainstream criminologists simply chose to disattend to the strident pronouncements from advocates of this viewpoint. Still, many criminologists were, to some extent, "radicalized" by it in that they became sensitized to some of the flaws of American corporate capitalism, injustices being visited on some unfortunate citizens by the so-called criminal justice system, and other societal flaws about which radical Marxists had railed. However, the radical Marxist perspective never was more than a minority viewpoint in criminology, and much of the air eventually went out of it, largely because of the ending of the war in Vietnam, the broad movement toward conservative government in the United States, falling crime rates, and other factors that resulted in a good deal of criminological ennui. Even so, a number of criminological scholars, including Beckett and Sasson (Chapter 4) in this book, continue to find valuable insights in this body of theorizing (see also Colvin and Pauly 1983; Messerschmidt 1986).

☐ *Critical Theory and the "New Criminologies"*

At this point, I move into treacherous waters in that I am obliged to provide a few paragraphs regarding a very complicated and multifaceted topic, namely "critical theory," which, according to Henry and Milovanovic (1991), involves four somewhat related lines of inquiry that have appeared during the last decade or so: left realism, socialist/feminist theory, peacemaking criminology, and a postmodernist structuralist perspective (see also Ross 1998).

What is meant by "critical" as applied to these perspectives? These four viewpoints are critical in that all of them, in varying degrees, attack mainstream criminologists for their "scientistic" pretensions, that is, their assumptions about an objective and stable reality that can be captured by mainstream theories, conventional quantitative methods, and the like. In short, criminologists of a critical persuasion claim that a large share of mainstream criminological "knowledge" is fatally flawed. A correlative feature of critical criminology is the emphasis placed on uncovering various structural features of American society including economic, racial, and gender inequality and discrimination, which are some of the major "root causes" of lawbreaking, and also on differential and discriminatory treatment of many offenders who have been caught up in the juvenile or adult justice system.

Not surprisingly, critical theories also are properly described as radical in thrust. The research agenda for critical criminologists goes beyond "getting the facts"; rather, it centers on uncovering and attacking social inequalities in our society, many of which have been hidden behind various "social fictions" such as those that Russell discusses in her chapter in this book (Chapter 3).

Two other points should be made about critical criminology. First, it should be obvious that a good many of the themes that characterized earlier radical Marxist theorizing also are apparent in critical criminology; indeed, large parts of the former have morphed into the latter. In addition, critical criminologists often contend that their views have been inspired by postmodernist theorists (Gibbons 1994:157-60).

Postmodernism is a very large subject, but briefly described, it is a loosely connected body of thought that had its origins in the writings of a number of European philosophers and social critics. As an intellectual movement, postmodernism denies the existence of a stable reality that exists apart from the symbols by which it is described. Much of the writing of postmodernist theorists is "heavy going," owing to the strange and/or unfamiliar terms, odd linguistic constructions, and the like that appear in it. And, regrettably, a good share of the critical criminology literature is of the same character.

So much for the general outlines of critical criminology. I now flesh out this sketch with some details regarding the component arguments that make up critical criminology.

The Feminist Movement and Feminist Criminology

As Miller indicates in her chapter (Chapter 2), although the feminist movement in the United States during the past several decades has not been all of one stripe (nor has feminist scholarship in criminology), there still is a core of shared ideas that constitute feminist thinking and distinguish it from traditional forms of inquiry (Gibbons 1994:166-68). The feminist movement, both within criminology and in American society as a whole, has had salutary effects. The attack on sexism (i.e., male superiority and institutionalized discrimination against women in American society) was long overdue. Within criminology, the effects have been twofold: important insights with regard to gender relations and lawbreaking have been produced, and many criminologists have become sensitized to the long-standing neglect of gender in criminological inquiry. In this sense, many criminologists have become feminists.

Left Realism

Left realist criminology was largely the creation of a group of erstwhile British radicals in response to criticisms that had been leveled at some of the hyperbole in radical Marxist views. Left realism is a point of view that urges criminologists to "take crime seriously" and to "take crime control seriously" (Gibbons 1994:168-70). In my opinion, it more closely resembles mainstream arguments than it does radical ones.

Peacemaking Criminology

This is a perspective that is loosely tied to Marxist theorizing and argues for a dramatically altered social order in which pain, injustice, and the like that are experienced by both offenders and victims would be replaced by a new sense of communitarianism (Gibbons 1994:172-74). Although this is a laudable goal, there are serious doubts about the viability of the peacemaking project. At any rate, this version of new criminology has relatively few subscribers.

Constitutive Criminology

This brand of critical criminology has been proposed by its creators, Henry and Milovanovic (1991, 1994, 1999), as an overarching perspective that would amalgamate the several strains of critical thought. Although their exposition is a bit off-putting due to the postmodernist cant they employ in it, with a bit of effort it is possible to restate much of their argument in more familiar terms. Moreover, a considerable share of what they have to say appears to border on being "old wine in new bottles." At the same time, a number of criminologists have claimed that they found important insights in constitutive criminology (Henry and Milovanovic 1999). Thus, the ultimate fate of this perspective still is unclear.

□ Criminology in the 21st Century

As I have indicated, criminology in the United States began as a small family-owned business conducted by a handful of sociologists, but in the second half of the 20th century, it has become a much-enlarged multinational enterprise. Even more important, it is clear that contributions to criminological knowledge now are being made by persons from a variety of disciplines. Although criminology has yet to become a coherent interdisciplinary field, it surely qualifies as multidisciplinary in nature. It now is impossible to sustain the argument that criminology is simply a specialty field within sociology.

This brief review has drawn attention to a number of "tensions" in contemporary criminology, one of which has to do with the role played in criminal behavior by sociobiological factors, which is part of a larger dialogue regarding genetic and other biological influences in human behavior more generally. Whereas geneticists, molecular biologists, and kindred investigators undoubtedly will continue their investigations of lawbreakers, it is less clear whether their findings will be synthesized with those of sociological criminologists.

In addition, mainstream and critical variants of criminology probably will continue to exist in a somewhat uneasy relationship, although if the past is any guide, then some of the "taking of sides," as between feminists and other criminologists, probably will diminish.

I made brief mention earlier of the growing prominence of psychologists in criminology. A parallel development has been the infusion of microeconomic perspectives, including rational choice notions, into criminology. It would be tempting to argue that criminological inquiry has moved away from a focus on structural forces in lawbreaking and toward a greater focus on early learning experiences, immediate family influences, and the like because of a "sea change" in American society in which citizens' perspectives on crime and delinquency (and on many other social ills as well) have shifted away from an emphasis on structural flaws and toward individual deficiencies and the like. However, this is a line of conjecture for which firm evidence is lacking. Still, it would not be too much of a stretch to argue that this "individualization" of criminological analysis is likely to continue.

Finally, this review suggested that theoretical work in sociological criminology during the decades ahead will continue to move in a variety of directions, with the result that students of criminology in the 21st century will continue to be confronted with an even larger panoply of separate theories.[6]

NOTES

1. A large share of this introductory chapter has been adapted from my two books dealing with criminological theory (Gibbons 1979, 1994). Also, I have examined a large share of the research evidence bearing on various criminological theories in my criminology and juvenile delinquency textbooks (Gibbons 1992; Gibbons and Krohn 1991).

2. My criminology text discusses a number of important pieces of historical research on crime and reactions to lawbreaking. Two recent significant cases of historical research of interest to criminologists are Escobar (1999) and Schneider (1999).

3. Of course, not much happened in American criminology between 1941 and 1945 because many criminologists, and most "budding criminologists," were serving in the military during this period.

4. The period from 1945 to 1970 involved a large body of other criminological work in addition to theory building and research on causal questions. For one, criminologists devoted a good deal of attention to the study of lawmaking processes and to public attitudes toward criminal statutes. Also, criminologists engaged in a number of organizational studies designed to throw light on the workings of police agencies, jails, correctional institutions, and the like.

5. Gibbs (1989) has nominated control as a candidate for sociology's central notion, but that suggestion has not taken hold.

6. There has been considerable interest voiced in recent years regarding theoretical integration, that is, efforts to combine a number of separate theories into a single formulation. The basic argument for theoretical integration is a "bigger bang for the buck" argument or the idea that a theory that combines ingredients from a number of lines of argument might account for a greater share of lawbreaking behavior than would any of the separate theories. Although the idea of theoretical integration is easy enough to articulate, implementation of the idea appears to be much more difficult to accomplish. Most of the theoretical integrations produced so far have been restricted to only a sampling of criminological theories and variables (see, e.g., Braithwaite 1989; Tittle 1995). Barak (1998), on the other hand, proposes that the theoretical and research products of all the disciplines that contribute to criminology ought to be integrated. My response to that suggestion is "Good luck!"

REFERENCES

Akers, Ronald L. 1985. *Deviant Behavior.* 3rd ed. Belmont, CA: Wadsworth.

Barak, Gregg. 1998. *Integrating Criminologies.* Boston: Allyn & Bacon.

Braithwaite, John. 1989. *Crime, Shame, and Reintegration.* Cambridge, UK: Cambridge University Press.

Brokaw, Tom. 1998. *The Greatest Generation.* New York: Random House.

Cloward, Richard A. and Lloyd E. Ohlin. 1960. *Delinquency and Opportunity.* New York: Free Press.

Cohen, Albert K. 1955. *Delinquent Boys.* New York: Free Press.

Colvin, Mark and John Pauly. 1983. "A Critique of Criminology: Toward an Integrated Structural Marxist Theory of Delinquency Production." *American Journal of Sociology* 89: 513-51.

Cornish, Derek B. and Ronald V. Clarke, eds. 1986. *The Reasoning Criminal.* New York: Springer-Verlag.

Drapkin, Israel. 1983. "Criminology: Intellectual History." Pp. 546-56 in *Encyclopedia of Crime and Justice,* vol. 2, edited by Sanford E. Kadish. New York: Free Press.

Escobar, Edward J. 1999. *Race, Police, and the Making of a Political Identity.* Berkeley: University of California Press.

Gibbons, Don C. 1965. *Changing the Lawbreaker.* Englewood Cliffs, NJ: Prentice Hall.

———. 1979. *The Criminological Enterprise.* Englewood Cliffs, NJ: Prentice Hall.

———. 1992. *Society, Crime, and Criminal Behavior.* 6th ed. Englewood Cliffs, NJ: Prentice Hall.

———. 1994. *Talking About Crime and Criminals.* Englewood Cliffs, NJ: Prentice Hall.

———. 1996. "Taking Stock of American Criminology: 1900-2000." Paper presented at the annual meeting of the American Society of Criminology, Chicago.

Gibbons, Don C. and Marvin D. Krohn. 1991. *Delinquent Behavior.* 5th ed. Englewood Cliffs, NJ: Prentice Hall.

Gibbs, Jack P. 1985. "The Methodology of Theory Construction in Criminology." Pp. 23-50 in *Theoretical Methods in Criminology,* edited by Robert F. Meier. Beverly Hills, CA: Sage.

———. 1989. *Control: Sociology's Central Notion.* Urbana: University of Illinois Press.

Gottfredson, Michael R. and Travis Hirschi. 1990. *A General Theory of Crime.* Stanford, CA: Stanford University Press.

Hagan, John, with Celeste Albonetti, Duane Alwin, A. R. Gillis, John Hewitt, Alberto Palloni, Patricia Parker, Ruth Peterson, and John Simpson. 1989. *Structural Criminology.* New Brunswick, NJ: Rutgers University Press.

Henry, Stuart and Dragan Milovanovic. 1991. "Constitutive Criminology: The Maturation of Critical Theory." *Criminology* 29:293-315.

———. 1994. *Constitutive Criminology.* London: Sage.

———, eds. 1999. *Constitutive Criminology at Work.* Albany: State University of New York Press.

Hirschi, Travis. 1969. *Causes of Delinquency.* Berkeley: University of California Press.

Katz, Jack. 1988. *Seductions of Crime.* New York: Basic Books.

Merton, Robert K. 1938. "Social Structure and Deviant Behavior." *American Sociological Review* 3:672-82.

Messerschmidt, James. 1986. *Capitalism, Patriarchy, and Crime.* Totowa, NJ: Rowman & Littlefield.

Messner, Steven F. and Richard Rosenberg. 1994. *Crime and the American Dream.* Belmont, CA: Wadsworth.

Parmelee, Maurice F. 1918. *Criminology*. New York: Macmillan.

Reid, Sue Titus. 1976. *Crime and Criminology*. Hinsdale, IL: Dryden.

Ross, Jeffrey Ian, ed. 1998. *Cutting the Edge*. Westport, CT: Praeger.

Sampson, Robert J. and John H. Laub. 1993. *Crime in the Making*. Cambridge, MA: Harvard University Press.

Schneider, Eric C. 1999. *Vampires, Dragons, and Egyptian Kings*. Princeton, NJ: Princeton University Press.

Sellin, Thorsten. 1938. *Culture Conflict and Crime*. New York: Social Science Research Council.

Shaw, Clifford R. 1930. *The Jack Roller*. Chicago: University of Chicago Press.

———. 1931. *The Natural History of a Delinquent Career*. Chicago: University of Chicago Press.

Shaw, Clifford R. and Henry D. McKay. 1931. *Social Factors in Juvenile Delinquency*. Washington, DC: Government Printing Office.

———. 1932. *Juvenile Delinquency in Urban Areas*. Chicago: University of Chicago Press.

Shaw, Clifford, Henry D. McKay, and James F. McDonald. 1938. *Brothers in Crime*. Chicago: University of Chicago Press.

Short, James F., Jr. and Fred L. Strodtbeck, eds. 1965. *Group Process and Gang Delinquency*. Chicago: University of Chicago Press.

Sutherland, Edwin H. 1924. *Criminology*. Philadelphia: J. B. Lippincott.

———. 1937. *The Professional Thief*. Chicago: University of Chicago Press.

Sutherland, Edwin H. and Donald R. Cressey. 1978. *Criminology*. 10th ed. Philadelphia: J. B. Lippincott.

Tittle, Charles R. 1995. *Control Balance*. Boulder, CO: Westview.

Turk, Austin T. 1969. *Criminality and the Legal Order*. Chicago: Rand McNally.

Vold, George B. 1958. *Theoretical Criminology*. New York: Oxford University Press.

PART 1

Accounting for Gender, Race, and Class Differences in Criminality and Crime Control

CHAPTER 1

Differential Association Theory and Female Crime

PEGGY C. GIORDANO
SHARON MOHLER ROCKWELL

Most of the classic theories about why young people turn to criminal activity were formulated with boys in mind. Early theorists essentially believed that "delinquency in general is mostly male delinquency" (Cohen 1955:44). Although the delinquency rate of males exceeds that of females (see, e.g., Steffensmeier 1993), each generation of youth contains a small number of females whose behavior is sufficiently visible and/or serious to warrant official intervention. A key question is whether theories developed to explain male delinquency can be useful in explaining the behavior of this significantly smaller subset of delinquent females.

In this chapter, we focus on an influential social learning perspective, *Sutherland's differential association theory* (Sutherland and Cressey 1970), and assess its utility as an explanatory framework for understanding female crime. We rely on qualitative data derived from in-depth interviews with a sample of serious female delinquents contacted first as adolescents and followed up 13 years later when they had become adults. The interviews provided detailed accounts of the respondents' own perspectives on the factors associated with their initial entry into illegal activity and with the escalation of their criminal careers. The importance of conducting such research is highlighted by a Bureau of Justice Statistics special report indicating that the ranks of female prisoners are growing at a faster rate than the ranks of male prisoners and that the percentage of women in prison is higher than it has been since annual prison statistics were first collected in 1926 (Greenfeld and Minor-Harper 1991).

■ Theoretical Perspectives on Female Criminality

Early explanations for gender differences in crime and for females' involvement stressed constitutional factors. Lombroso (1920), for example, theorized that the basic physiological and psychological makeup of women largely precluded participation in criminal and aggressive behaviors. The few examples of female criminal activity were largely seen as anomalies or perversions in a more general picture of women as passive and interested in domestic concerns (for an excellent review of early work in this area, see Chesney-Lind and Shelden 1998). Although these views now are considered outmoded and even sexist, some of the underlying assumptions of these early works still are present in contemporary treatments of criminal women.

Some researchers have suggested that the low rate of female involvement in crime indicates a *greater level of individual disturbance* (e.g., the presence of psychological disorder) on the part of the small number of women who do evidence antisocial tendencies (see, e.g., Robins 1986; Widom 1984). Theories of male deviance also focused on individualist explanations at one time, but they progressed to a consideration of social and structural influences. For many years, however, individualist explanations had a strong foothold in the female crime literature. For example, Riege (1972) emphasized the loneliness and low self-concept of many delinquent girls, and Konopka (1966) suggested that many of their behaviors should be seen as attempts to fill a relationship void. Although the literature on female crime now includes more attention to social factors, there remains a much larger and more comprehensive body of research on how the "social" affects all phases of males' criminal careers (see, e.g., Kruttschnitt's [1996] recent analysis of the gender and crime literature, which also includes a call for more qualitative research to inform theory development in this area).

This theme has coexisted with a somewhat contradictory notion: even when females engage in delinquency or criminal activity, their involvement is likely to be of a less serious nature than that of males. Females often are portrayed as criminal lightweights who confine themselves to a narrow band of status offenses such as curfew violation and petty larcenies, especially shoplifting. Work in this tradition frequently equates female criminal activity with promiscuous sexual behavior and emphasizes that females often commit delinquent acts at the behest of their romantic partners (for a review of this perspective, see Giordano and Cernkovich 1997).

This portrait remains popular in spite of self-report data from criminal offenders that indicate a good deal of cross-sex similarity in patterns of offending. Investigators generally have found that males and females tend to commit similar offenses; females simply commit them on a less frequent basis. That is, most males do not engage in serious acts of antisocial behavior, and these also are the least frequent behaviors that females report. High-frequency offense categories for both sexes include status offenses such as drinking and disobeying parents (Cernkovich and Giordano 1979; Figueira-McDonough, Barton, and Sarri 1981). In addition, both male delinquency and female delinquency are associated with an earlier age of first intercourse, inconsistent use of birth control, and a greater number of sexual partners (Bowerman 1997).

Nevertheless, the idea of distinct patterns of behavior persists. As a result, different explanations and theories for female and male criminal behavior have developed. For example, feminist scholars point out that many female delinquents have early histories of physical and sexual abuse and suggest that this abuse might be a critical dynamic underlying the onset of their criminal activities. Chesney-Lind and Shelden (1998) suggest that "exploitation of women by men acts as a trigger for behavior by female victims, causing them to run away or begin abusing drugs at an early age" (p. 98).

Ogle, Maier-Katkin, and Bernard (1995) articulate a theory of homicidal behavior by women that also advances this viewpoint. Although women involved in homicides obviously have engaged in very serious criminal acts, these authors contend that such events require a different set of explanations from those that typically are invoked to explain male homicide. Men's socialization makes them more experienced in and comfortable with the expression of anger. Women, on the other hand, do not learn ways in which to express more moderate forms of anger, and so some women might respond to severe stress (including repeated victimization by male partners) with explosions of extreme violence.

Certainly, distinctive aspects of young women's socialization and social experience do affect their behavior, including their criminal behavior. Nevertheless, it is premature to abandon so-called "male-based" theories entirely (see also Smith and Paternoster [1987], who come to a similar conclusion). A comprehensive understanding of female criminality likely will require attention to processes that affect both females and males as well as to those that are clearly "gendered." Thus, the basic tenets of differential association theory, which has been an influential explanation for the onset and continuation of male criminal involvement, also might be useful in understanding the etiology of female crime.

■ An Overview of Differential Association Theory

Differential association theory is credited to Edwin H. Sutherland, who developed a very simple but influential way in which to explain the process through which individuals come to be involved in delinquent and criminal activity (Sutherland 1947). Perhaps it is the spare quality of the ideas he outlined that makes his theory a useful framework for understanding at least some aspects of female offending.

Sutherland believed that people learn criminal behavior through the basic mechanisms that are involved in learning any type of behavior. A most important context for this learning is intimate primary groups, typically families. Through interaction with intimate others, individuals acquire some attitudes that can be conducive to law violations and others that promote conformity.

The principal proposition underlying differential association theory is that "a person becomes delinquent because of an excess of definitions favorable to violation of law over definitions unfavorable to violation of law" (Sutherland 1947:6). This learning involves the acquisition of "(a) techniques of committing the crime, which are sometimes very complicated, sometimes very simple, and (b) the specific direction of motives, drives, rationalizations, and attitudes" (p. 6). In other words, to develop criminal attitudes, a person might be exposed not only to attitudes that make criminal behavior seem possible, tolerable, or even desirable but also to the "mechanics" or "how to" needed to engage in it.

Sutherland (1947) did not mean to suggest that an individual's propensity to act criminally would be the result of a simple calculation of the amount of contact one has with criminals. He emphasized that not all associations have the same degree of impact on the individual: "differential associations may vary in frequency, duration, priority, and intensity" (p. 7). Associations that are recurrent (frequency), last longer (duration), occur early in the life course (priority), and are highly salient for the individual (intensity) are likely to be more influential.

Despite criticisms of this theory, the basic notion that exposure to deviant definitions increases the likelihood of engaging in acts of law violation has received empirical support. A large number of studies have demonstrated that peers exert a significant influence on adolescents and that delinquent attitudes and behaviors of friends are strong predictors of delinquency and drug use (Johnson, Marcos, and Bahr 1987; Warr 1993). Parental deviance also has been shown to be a significant predictor of involvement in delinquency and crime (West 1982), as has sibling deviance (Lauritsen 1993).

However, most of this research has focused on male respondents. When differential association theory is mentioned in regard to female crime, it typically is invoked to address the question of why females do not become involved in delinquency at nearly the rate that their male counterparts do:

> Generally speaking, women are shielded from criminal learning experiences. Even within the same groups as males (like the family), their social position is unequal, and they are frequently taught dissimilar attitudes. More isolated from criminal norms and techniques, they are also more consistently taught law-abiding behavior and are expected to act in accordance with the law. . . . Boys and girls are taught quite different standards and, with this, subtly different attitudes toward law breaking. (Leonard 1982:108)

This type of logic helps to explain disparities in male and female rates of criminal involvement but does not explain the behavior of young women who fail to adopt law-abiding lifestyles. However, our own research has convinced us that differential association theory can indeed be very useful as a framework for understanding female movement into delinquency.

■ A Study of Female Offenders

Most studies of female delinquency draw a survey sample from neighborhood or school populations. However, because serious female criminality is so uncommon, delinquent respondents are very unlikely to be captured with sufficient frequency in such samples to allow for extensive analysis. For example, respondents from the National Youth Survey were classified as serious violent offenders if they exhibited high rates of offending for more than one year of the study. Using these criteria, only two females qualified for inclusion (Huizinga, Morse, and Elliott 1992). Similarly, Stattin, Magnusson, and Reichel (1989), in a follow-up of 1,393 pupils in Sweden, found that only 15 females (as compared to 165 males) had official crime records as juveniles.

Perhaps the most important lesson to be learned from these types of surveys is that gender socialization is very powerful; the average female adolescent is just not very delinquent. Yet, every cohort contains a small subset of females whose behavior is more visibly "antisocial" or disruptive than the behavior of their peers, and we know remarkably little about these young women. To study such women in detail, we decided to depart from traditional approaches by sampling only those individuals who were caught up in the official penal system. The young women we interviewed clearly were at the "high end" in terms of their involvement in criminal behavior.

Specifically, in 1982, we interviewed 127 girls, the total population of Ohio's only state correctional institution for girls, and a comparable sample of 127 boys drawn from three state institutions for males. In 1995, we tracked down and reinterviewed 210 (83 percent) of these respondents (average age 29 years). We interviewed 91 percent of the respondents face to face, whereas the remainder completed a mailed questionnaire. Fully 63 percent of the respondents were white. Of the nonwhite respondents, 84 percent of those sampled were African American. Preliminary analysis of the 1982 and 1995 samples indicated that both waves of respondents have essentially the same profile with respect to race, gender, age, delinquency, family, and social backgrounds.

The unstructured interviews we conducted can be considered a type of life histories. Respondents were asked to describe factors leading up to their 1982 incarcerations in the state institution and events that had occurred since that time. Here we focus on the open-ended interviews conducted with the adult female respondents immediately after they had completed the structured part of their interviews, but our perspective also has been informed by the responses of males to similar questions and by the quantitative results described in more detail in other work (see, e.g., Giordano et al. 1997, 1999).

These interviews and the quantitative results document that members of this cohort of females were indeed serious offenders, a finding that contradicts the idea of females as "criminal lightweights." Prior to their incarcerations at the state level, the adolescent females (and their male counterparts) had numerous police and court contacts, and their self-reported delinquencies typically included involvement in felonies as well as status-type offenses. The follow-up interviews documented that many of the young women continued a pattern of antisocial behavior; fully 72 percent were arrested as adults, and for those arrested, the mean number of arrests was 18. By contrast, although 89 percent of the males were arrested, their average number of arrests was only 12.

□ The Family's Influence on Criminal Definitions

Michele's case seems quite valid as an example of key aspects of differential association theory. Michele was first interviewed in 1982 during one of her three incarcerations at the state institution for girls. As an adult, she had become a prostitute and a crack addict, and she also had served three years in the state adult women's prison for robbery. Michele has three children, is not married, and never has had legitimate or "above the table" employment. In the interview excerpts that follow, the letter Q refers to each question the interviewer asked, and the letter R refers to the answer provided by Michele, the respondent:

Q: Who turned you on to crack?

R: My mom.

Q: Your mom?

Q: Okay, . . . let's go back to your childhood . . . when you were a kid . . . all the way back. . . . There were three of you. . . . Is that right?

R: I'm the oldest.

Q: Okay, . . . you told me that . . . um . . . I think . . . your sister is in prison now. . . . Is that right?

R: No, . . . she just got out of jail . . . doing six months.

Q: Okay, . . . and what about your brother?

R: Guns.

Q: Is he in prison now?

R: Yeah, . . . my baby brother. . . . Yes, . . . my oldest brother is out.

Q: Okay, . . . how old were you . . . what . . . what's the youngest that you remember your parents shooting up?

R: About 11 [years old].

R: [My dad too], . . . whenever he got out of prison he'd come around.

Q: Okay, . . . what kind of things was he going to . . . ah . . . to prison for? Trafficking?

R: Drug trafficking. . . . He had women out on the street. . . . He would buy them clothes and keep them up with drugs. . . . Yeah, . . . that just . . . went on . . . it just . . . everyday.

Q: About how many women do you think your dad was in charge of?

R: Um, . . . about four or five.

Q: [What is] the youngest you remember your mom going in and out of prison?

R: About nine [years old].

Q: Okay, would she be in there for soliciting or drugs or . . .?

R: Just violent stuff . . . fighting . . . cutting people. . . . I went to visit her in prison. . . . I . . . I . . . um . . . I already . . . I knew what Marysville [state adult prison for women] had looked like and everything at a young age . . . 'cause I used to go down there with my grandma. . . . I also knew I was going to end up in prison too. . . . When I was in, I knew I was going to go to prison from Scioto Village [the juvenile institution].

Q: How?

> R: Because all them women down there, they say, . . . "Well, this is it, . . . this is babies' Marysville. . . . After you come here, . . . your next step is Marysville." . . . And then I just figured, you know, . . . I'm just . . . me and my mom are so much alike. . . . She was in Scioto Village, . . . then I went to Scioto Village, . . . and she went to Marysville, . . . and I went to Marysville. . . . We just done did the same thing.

Thus Michele inhabited a social world characterized by open involvement in criminal behavior including drug use and dealing, violence, and prostitution. Although Michele never exhibited the same level of violent tendencies as did her mother, she absorbed many of the features of her parents' lifestyles:

> Some of my mom's dates . . . um . . . waited until I got older and then became my dates . . . just like now. . . . I have one of my mom's dates, . . . Henry. . . . He's about 70-some years old, . . . but he don't do anything . . . he used to years ago with me, . . . but now he just come over and see . . . um . . . do . . . do kids got food . . . or do you need anywhere to go . . . or was you behind your bills or something?

The respondent eventually described in some detail her initial introduction to crack cocaine:

> Q: How did that make you feel to have to go get your mom out of a crack house? Like, how many times do you think you had to do that?
> R: About three times out of the month . . . 'cause she'd only do it when she'd get her check . . . or some extra money . . . or something . . . and um . . . she'd say, . . . "You don't rush me, . . . I'm your mom, . . . I tell you what to do." . . . And I said, "This don't make no sense." . . . I said, "You've been sitting up in here cracking for days" . . . and, um, I would just recall myself sitting out in the living room. She'd be in the bedroom with the door shut, . . . and I'm sitting . . . making sure . . . don't nobody take advantage of her while she's smoking this crack. . . . She comes out there with a stem, . . . and she said, "Here, Michele, hit it," . . . and I said, "No, . . . I told you I ain't going to be smoking that." Then I said to myself, . . . if I hit it, . . . if I hit this, . . . then she . . . she'll leave, . . . I'll get her to leave. . . . So I got ready to hit it, . . . and she said, "You don't even," . . . she said, "You're going to waste the dope." . . . She said, "You don't even know how to do it. . . . You've got to melt that on there." . . . So she melted it on there for me, told me to hold the lighter. . . . I held the lighter . . . and kept holding it down like this. If you hold it down like this, . . . the dope will run, . . . and you don't want it to run . . . 'cause the dope will get oily. . . . You got to keep it held up. . . . So she showed me how to inhale it and everything.

Q: When is the next time that you [used] crack?

R: Well, . . . we don't crack no more in a crack house, . . . we just start doing it at her house. . . . I got my own stems and stuff now.

The preceding example provides a graphic illustration of what can be learned in interaction with others in the context of intimate primary groups. Although Michele came to be involved with some gang members and other streetwise people during her teenage years, Michele's family associations meet all the criteria we associate with even greater levels of influence; her family situation resulted in exposure to "definitions favorable to the violations of law" that were early, frequent, and recurrent, and the sources could not be more important or, as Sutherland termed it, "intense." Aside from learning the specific techniques connected to the enactment of these behaviors (as in the mother's instructions on how to hold the pipe and inhale properly), Michele also internalized a set of attitudes that would facilitate her own eventual involvement in them. It is not likely that Michele's parents actively set out to socialize a daughter to become a prostitute and crack addict. Nevertheless, that they did little to shield Michele from their own actions in itself brought the world of drug use and sales, prostitution, and prison time into the realm of the everyday or the "taken for granted." Michele learned that this behavior was acceptable or at least "tolerable under certain conditions."

Although Michele's case is somewhat dramatic, it is not an isolated example within this sample group. Based on our work with these narrative accounts, we offer the hypothesis that, at least at this "high end" of serious involvement, the deviant behavior of family members seems to be a critical causal factor in understanding the paths taken by these young women. It might be that, in many of these families, the children are literally engulfed in deviant modes of expression; that is, we suggest a type of "total immersion" theory that might account for the onset of their antisocial behavior. The environment in many of these families is so marginal that there would appear to be almost no access to individuals who could provide conforming or prosocial definitions. In such instances, mothers, fathers, grandmothers, siblings, and most adult friends and associates of the parents represent a rather united front of deviance and marginality. This would help to explain why, given the typical family scenario, females do not tend to become delinquent. In the typical case, even if a family member exhibits criminal or antisocial tendencies (e.g., the father), someone else in the family will be available as a relatively conforming source of learning and influence (statistically, this usually would be the mother and/or the grandmother). In such a case, this influence and support, in combination with the press of societal attitudes that typically foster female conformity, might be sufficient to ensure it.

This is not the case for many of our female respondents. For example, Kim also appeared to be heavily influenced by her mother, and as an adult, she admits to repeatedly exposing her own children to her marginal lifestyle. Kim completed the adult follow-up interview in a shelter for battered women, where she lived with her three children. She did not currently have a husband or male partner, but she needed a place to stay because the children had been living in her mother's car previous to their stay in the shelter. She indicated that she had lied to shelter staff about being abused and also withheld the information that she was addicted to crack:

Q: And your mom was a crackhead?

R: Right.

Q: When did she turn crackhead?

R: My mom was smokin' before I was. That's how we started becoming friends.

Q: So the kids have seen you high many times?

R: Many times.

Q: What's that like? How has that influenced your relationship, your ability to . . .?

R: See, I'm an overprotective mother even when I'm not high. So I'm really overprotective when I'm high. That's when they know that I'm high.

Q: But . . . um, how do you see your future shaping up? What kind of life do you think you are likely to have? And what are those tears for?

R: Those tears is for the . . . the strength my son has given me basically and the things I know that he has done without just so I could have . . .

Q: Uh-huh.

R: Just so I could smoke some crack.

Q: Huh.

R: He gave me this hundred-dollar bill his daddy gave him one day.

Q: Wow.

R: And he knew what I was gonna do with it.

□ Indirect Learning

The specific mechanisms through which family deviance eventually comes to influence the child's own behavior likely involve both direct and indirect processes. In some instances, simple observation and repeated exposure to the behavior might be enough to normalize it, increasing the probability that the child eventually will enact the same or a generally compatible behavior. Stacy started using marijuana around seventh grade, but eventually she developed an extensive criminal repertoire that included heavy drug use, robbery, and assaultive behavior. She had been arrested approximately 80 times and served three sentences in the adult women's prison by the date of the follow-up interview:

R: There was always . . . um, drug abuse in my family. . . . Yeah, . . . my father . . . my father was a junkie.

Q: He had a problem?

R: Yeah, he had been to a prison several times. You know, . . . and I had, um, . . . ever since I was a kid, I knew about drugs.

Q: Yeah.

R: You know, I mean . . . it was there.

Q: So it was there.

R: It was there.

Other respondents indicated that their childhoods included repeated exposures to violence, sometimes combined with parents' drug and alcohol use. Both of Monica's parents were extremely violent, and Monica herself was interviewed in the state women's prison, where she was serving time for fatally stabbing a fellow "junkie." This example also is of interest because it indicates that criminal definitions can be learned from individuals who in other ways have claims to respectability:

R: And I knew that, uh, . . . my parents were always engaged in, in, in each other fighting and everything, you know.

Q: Like we are talking 9-1-1?

R: Real serious, serious. Like we're talking real serious pistols, everything. Serious.

Q: Aside from fighting each other.

R: Uh, just out, just out getting high, you know, smoking weed, uh . . .

Q: In front of you?

R: Yeah, in front of, well, in front of . . . my father has always smoked weed in front of me. He was a police officer too. My father was a police officer. Yeah, he was. So it was just that everything was chaotic, you know. If he hurt my mother so bad where he broke her ribs or, uh, jaw or something and the police came, . . . they didn't do anything. They just laughed. . . . [I would like to have been] able to come home from school and not be worried about, when I come home, is my momma gonna be dead? Or is my father gonna be dead? You know, or what has happened this time? You know, I couldn't concentrate in school for fear of that. And when I go home, it's a war. Is the walls gonna be splattered with blood? Or what's gonna happen if I go in there? Is he gonna take us off one by one? I get home first. Sometimes I would stand on the side of the house waiting for somebody else to walk up the driveway because my father was a maniac. And my mother would sometimes snap too and, oh God, three, four times she done told us that she was going to kill us all, pointing my father's gun at us, you know? I mean, what kind of shit is that?

☐ *Direct Transmission Processes*

The preceding examples can be considered illustrations of indirect learning because the respondents do not indicate that the parents communicated directly to the children about the acceptability of criminal definitions. Of course, they might have done so; it is simply that such descriptions are not evident in the narratives these women provided.

In other cases, respondents did point out direct communications within the family context that would appear to foster deviance on the part of the children. This type of direct learning is perhaps most closely in line with Sutherland's original conceptions in that he emphasized that it was through interaction with the source of the criminal definitions that an excess of such definitions accumulates:

R: I'm not a toy, and if you get any ass from me, you gonna pay for it.
Q: Okay.
R: So?
Q: That's how you view sex now?
R: That's how I viewed sex all my life.
Q: That you got to pay for it?
R: All my life.
Q: That it's going to cost you?
R: One way or another, you're gonna pay for it.
Q: Okay.
R: That's the way I was raised. My momma told me you don't lay down and get no wet ass for nothin'.

Even more common within the data are references to parental attitudes that directly promote the use of violence:

Q: How often did you get whoopin's?
R: Every day, just about.
Q: Okay, what kind, what kind of things would cause you to get a whoopin'?

R: Not doing the dishes when mama said do 'em. Uh, getting suspended from school.

Q: What were you gettin' suspended from school for?

R: Fightin'.

Q: Fightin'. Why?

R: I got a whoopin' when I was a kid for not fightin'. I got beat up, and every time I ran home, my mama beat my ass.

Q: For not fightin'?

R: For not fightin'. So I learned how to fight, and I start beatin' everybody's ass that said something to me, and I got suspended from school, and I got my ass whooped.

Q: So you got your ass whooped for not fighting, and then you got your ass whooped for fighting. Is that what you are saying?

R: Exactly.

Q: How old are you when this is going on?

R: I was, uh, between the ages of, let's see, from third grade, I didn't fight. I got my ass beat. When I got to fourth grade, I start fightin' and I started beatin' up people really bad, hurtin' 'em, and mama had to go to court and stuff, and she didn't like that very well. I got into a lot of trouble. I almost, I almost killed this girl. . . . At fourth grade I started fightin' back and, uh, in fifth grade I got suspended from school. That's when I started really getting suspended from school.

Q: Uh-huh.

R: I was hurtin' people. I was doing really, really, really mean things.

Q: Why?

R: Because my mother said she was gonna kick my ass if they got me first, so my best bet was to get them first so they wouldn't get me.

Q: And then your mom would kick your ass anyway.

R: Yup.

Q: So you couldn't win for losing.

Another respondent's grandmother communicated a similar perspective:

R: And I was not a fighter for a . . . a long period of time I use to . . . got chased home from school, . . . and then finally my grandmother said she wasn't going to let me in the house until I learn how to fight my way out of it.

□ The Family's Reactions to Problem Behavior

Another way in which family members provide information about the acceptability of certain behaviors is in the nature and strength of their reactions to misbehavior on the part of the children. In these cases, a lack of moral outrage amounts to tacit acceptance and encouragement of this behavior. In the earlier example, the child was punished only when the consequences of the behavior became a nuisance for her mother (when she was forced to deal with school suspensions, appearances in court, etc.). In other instances, parents and other family members make no effort to deter the youths and might even try to derive some benefits from their illegal activities:

R: Stealing then . . . no . . . I was stealing then.

Q: Stealing from stores.

R: From J. C. Penney's . . . and Sears and all them stores like that . . . Sears . . .

Q: You boosting, . . . are you?

R: Boosting . . . but not for no one . . . but for me . . . like I'd steal my . . . for my babies. . . . I stole their clothes.

Q: What would happen every time you'd get popped for stealing when you got . . . when they would take you home to your mom? . . . What would happen?

R: She wouldn't say anything . . . 'cause they would even put they little bids in when I went to the store. . . . "Get me this and get me that." I'd be, like, I ain't going to steal nothing for nobody but me. . . . If I'm going to the store, it's for me. . . . I'm not . . . trying to steal something for them.

Q: Your mom would tell you to . . . steal stuff?

R: She was, like, . . . uh . . . get her some . . . couple sweaters . . . [laughs] my mother was . . . figured if you going to do it . . . do it . . . I guess.

Q: Okay, . . . so they'd tell you kind of what to steal for them?

R: Um-hmm.

And from another respondent:

R: Like when I got the Reeboks, the Reeboks I got caught with, they wasn't even for me. They was for my Aunt Linda, and I, I would take them and then she would pay me for them so I would have some money.

□ Learning From Other Family Members

Whereas we have emphasized the potentially powerful influence that adult family members can have, there also are many indications of sibling influence in the accounts provided by these women. These contacts also obviously begin at an early age, and they typically are frequent and recurrent, thus heightening the possibilities for influence. In addition, the relationship between siblings is fundamentally more egalitarian than that which exists across generations. This also increases a sense of identification and similarity that can foster the influence process. Although our findings certainly are not definitive in this regard, we note that brothers in particular seemed to be a source for learning criminal definitions. This idea generally is consistent with previous research findings indicating that the mixed-gender group is the most common social context in which girls report committing crimes (Giordano and Cernkovich 1979). Because males in general are more likely to develop delinquent repertoires, and because their interaction styles can tend to amplify risk taking (whereas girls' styles of communication can work to inhibit it), this effect of brothers is somewhat intuitive:

Q: So you kind of knew how the system worked? How did you know that?

R: 'Cause my brothers got sent off before I did.

Q: Then you . . .

R: And they got put on probation and stuff, . . . so I knew I'd have to have a chance on probation, so . . .

Q: Who introduced you to cigarettes?

R: My brother.

Q: Did you ever get in trouble with the law . . . besides truancy as a kid?

R: Yeah, stealing bicycles with my brothers. . . . We'd take them across the bridge [into Kentucky] and sell them. When we'd get done riding them, we just walked until . . . someone . . . ask some . . . everybody if they wanted to buy them.

Another respondent described a similar process:

Q: Okay, when you were younger, . . . did you influence your friends or did your friends influence you? When you were a teenager?

R: Actually, my brother would be the influence on me because he is the one that got me sneaking out.

Q: Yeah, . . . did you . . . did you sneak out by yourself?

R: No, no, I never went out by myself. . . . I was too scared [laughs].

□ Extra-Familial Influences

The level of deviance in these families is considerable; however, influences outside the family also provided these young women with "criminal definitions." Nevertheless, the family effects often still are quite evident in that (1) many of the social contacts these young women eventually forge can be traced back to the families of origin (thus, the families have a role as a conduit to other marginal/deviant actors), (2) the parents' supervision styles (e.g., lax, inconsistent) open up the possibility that the children will have opportunities to associate with these deviant individuals, and/or (3) the state of deviance in their homes sometimes is sufficiently overwhelming that the young women come to believe that their social contacts in the streets are a safer and more attractive (although sometimes delinquency-promoting) alternative:

R: I didn't steal a lot back, back when I first started running away from home, I didn't steal a lot. I got stuff by talkin' to people and askin' for stuff.

Q: Like what?

R: Food, money. I didn't have clothes. When I get money, I go eat. And then these guys taught me how to solicit. They taught me how to sell my body.

Q: What guys?

R: These two guys, they knew my mother.

Q: How old were you when they taught you how to solicit?

R: About 11 or 12 [years]. I had to split the money after I made it. That's what they told me 'cause they taught me how to do it.

A striking feature of these young women's accounts is the frequency with which they recall associating with *significantly older* individuals. There is some indication of this in the existing literature (e.g., Stattin and Magnusson's [1990] finding that dating older males was associated with delinquency and early sexual behavior); however, this phenomenon was not limited to sexual or romantic liaisons:

R: Gina was just a troublemaker. One of the main reasons that I got into trouble as a child . . . [was that] she was an adult that was a bad influence.

Q: Really, . . . how old was Gina when you were a kid?

R: About . . . 20 years.

Q: She's 20 years older than you?

R: About that. I was what, 16, 17, and she was about 37, . . . so yeah.

Q: Wow. What . . . what was your attraction to someone so much older . . . like . . . you know . . . your friends and . . . my friends are?

R: Older people was able to . . . security of life it was. . . . If I wanted a job, . . . I was her live-in babysitter, or if I wanted a part-time job babysitting for any of her friends or something, . . . it was . . . a way to make money.

R: Yeah, . . . it's . . . just . . . it's . . . they sit around and they talk to you and every-thing, . . . talk about life experiences and things, . . . and they just . . . and you just sit there . . . um-hmm . . . um-hmm . . . um-hmm [laughs]. Like, Gina wasn't the very most responsible parent in the world, . . . so when I took, you know, a live-in babysitting job, . . . those kids depended on me for breakfast, lunch, and dinner and anything in between.

Q: So you had to take care of . . . you took care of her kids then . . . when you were a kid. Is that what you're saying?

R: Yeah, she was . . . dealing drugs to a bar called the Uptown bar . . . on Exchange Street. She wanted me to go in. . . . It was Halloween night. She said I can get you in, you know, just for a few minutes, and [here the respondent met more of the group with whom she eventually would develop a pattern of extensive involvement in illegal activity].

The next example focuses on the respondent's peer involvements but provides a dramatic illustration of how these adolescent activities connect back to earlier family events:

R: She didn't . . . Lisa didn't never really get in trouble . . . or nothing like that. . . . If she got in trouble, . . . it was because of some shit that me and Wendy did.

Q: Really?

R: Um-hmm.

Q: What kind of shit would you and Wendy do?

R: When we was kids? Robbery, . . . breaking and entering, . . . felonious assault, . . . stealing cars.

Q: How old were you when you were doing that kind of stuff?

R: From 14 [years old] all the way up til I went to the penitentiary.

Q: Really, . . . how did you get into that kind of stuff? . . . I mean, . . . kids don't generally wake up and go, . . . "Today I'm going to go [steal] a car, break in, or rob somebody."

R: I had nobody tell me what to do. I did what I wanted to do.

Q: Really? Where was your mom?

R: My aunt killed her, killed her back in '78.

Q: Your aunt killed your mom? So who raised you?

R: Me. They was fighting about my aunt's boyfriend, [who] was breaking into my grandmother's house. They were stealing her pills 'cause she had a big thing of medication. My grandmother went and told my mom. . . . My mom come over there all drunk, . . . and her and my aunt got to arguing about my aunt's boyfriend. Then they started to fight, . . . [and] then she stabbed her. Then she died.

Q: In front of you?

R: And my little sister [starting to cry].

Q: How old were you?

R: 12 [years].

□ On the Prosocial Potential of Antisocial Actors

Whereas we have to this point focused on some of the ways in which young women learn criminal definitions, these narratives also point up that even the most marginal or deviant of actors are capable of influencing others in a positive manner. Thus, some of the women found romantic partners who, in spite of significant arrest records, alcohol problems, or difficulties with "anger management," were viewed as very positive influences on the women's own movements toward more conforming and stable lifestyles. In these cases, it is important to recognize the standard against which they often measured what might be considered a positive influence. Thus, compared to prior family circumstances, some of their later relationships were indeed improvements. The following example provides a good illustration of this idea:

> Q: And that was to be . . . to hang out with the 40-year-olds?
> R: Yeah, I was raised by some hookers . . . really . . . you want to know?
> Q: Are you serious, or are you pulling my leg?
> R: I'm damn serious!
> Q: So was I.
> R: Now I'm trying to tell you when I ran away from home, some hookers brought . . . told . . . taught me. . . . They sent me to school, . . . they kept me going to school. But I worked at night to support myself to get to school.
> Q: What'd you do? You worked the streets?
> R: Yeah, . . . but I never been arrested for it.
> Q: Um, how long did you solicit for?
> R: For about five years.
> Q: Five years. So these people that raised you, you said that hookers raised you?
> R: Was hookers.
> Q: They would . . . make you . . . they'd make you work at night?
> R: They didn't make me do nothing. I did it.
> Q: Then?
> R: 'Cause they wanted to . . .
> Q: You got up and . . .
> R: See me go to school.
> Q: Went to school?
> R: 'Cause they knew I wasn't no fool, so they seen to it that I kept my education. Kept going back there, and when I quit school, they made me go back for my GED [general equivalency diploma]. And I appreciate that.

■ Discussion and Conclusion

The theory of differential association sometimes is criticized because Sutherland's conception is vague about why individuals develop the associations that they do. Thus, if we were to focus only on peer contacts, then it would be possible to argue that similarly inclined individuals (already delinquency prone) simply came together for the purpose of acting out their deviant agendas. This viewpoint, espoused in particular by leading control theorists such as Hirschi (1969), tends to deemphasize the interaction processes that are at the heart of differential association theory, that is, the notion that communication with significant others itself has a causal force or impact. Through direct and indirect learning processes, certain acts of law violation come to be seen as tolerable, acceptable, or even desirable behaviors. Our focus on early family context has been useful because it is not possible to argue that the deviance of these young women precedes or fosters the deviant associations (given that such associations occur early in the life course and are largely ascribed).

Control theorists also have suggested that parental deviance cannot be a very important source of criminal learning because parents, even if they are deviant, will tend to "shield this from the children." (Hirschi 1969). This shielding process would then limit the types of observations the child might make or the types of conversations the parent and child will tend to have. In contradiction to this view, our respondents reported repeated exposure to crime, drugs, and violence (*indirect* learning) and often *direct* instruction in life lessons that serve to foster their own involvement in deviance. The *lack of strong sanctions* for the child's misconduct provides further behavioral leeway, sending strong messages about the types of actions that will be tolerated. The family also is important in that, at least initially, the family *structures access to the wider world of social contacts* that can include additional criminal associations; that is, individuals who are deviant tend to have other relatives, friends, and associates who themselves have deviant inclinations. Because many of the parents allow or even force on the children (through their own noxious behavior) a pattern of early autonomy, this provides even more access to such deviant associations and definitions.

Both male and female serious offenders reported exposure to deviant definitions from early family contacts; however, we hypothesize that the type and level of this deviance might be even more important to understanding the behavior of delinquent females. Because the serious female delinquent is a statistical rarity in the population, it might be that a greater push is required to begin some type of deviant career. In many cases, these women appear to have been literally "immersed" in deviant lifestyles—where aunts, cousins, siblings, fathers, and mothers routinely engaged in violence and criminal behavior.

This differential association theory of female crime might be somewhat more comprehensive than those explanations that emphasize a single factor such as sexual abuse. We know that even in the presence of abuse, most females simply do not become delinquent or criminal (Widom 1989). Thus, many of the females we interviewed did describe serious physical and sexual abuse that undoubtedly contributed to their negative trajectories. However, it also is important to consider the broader social milieus in which these events took place. A young woman who experiences abuse in an upper class household and neighborhood rarely will move into these types of behaviors, even if she is severely and negatively affected by these abusive experiences. In those families where abuse also is accompanied by exposure to violence, stealing, drug and alcohol abuse, or prostitution, involvement in such activities becomes a realistic possibility.

■ Policy Implications

Although males are heavily overrepresented in juvenile and prison populations, all jurisdictions within the justice system come into contact with female offenders. Our brief review of the early histories of a sample of such women suggests that it would be a mistake to dismiss their crimes—or their needs. Overviews of correctional facilities and treatment programs for juveniles and adults have documented that females often do not have access to the range of programs available to male offenders and that many staff place excessive emphasis on girls' sexual behaviors (Chesney-Lind and Shelden 1998). A truly comprehensive approach to the problem of female criminality inevitably would include attention to causal processes that appear gender specific (e.g., backgrounds of sexual abuse) and to those that appear to have applicability to both males and females (e.g., family histories that include exposure to criminal definitions and opportunities).

It will be important to allocate additional resources to early intervention strategies that target families at especially high risk. To be effective, such interventions should be intensive and occur early in the life course. This study suggests that programs will need to include attention not only to traditional parenting issues such as monitoring and consistency but also to communication processes that directly and indirectly serve to transmit criminogenic values. In some cases, the traditional goal of maintaining the family unit might need to be abandoned and high-quality foster or group home placements provided.

STUDY QUESTIONS

1. Compare traditional views of the female offender to more recent work including the perspective reflected in this chapter.
2. What are some of the different ways in which family members can transmit "definitions favorable to the violation of law?"
3. Why might one expect maternal deviance to be an especially serious concern?
4. After reading these young women's accounts, how and in what way(s) would you suggest that we as a society intervene to interrupt what seems to be a strong press in some families toward the intergenerational transmission of criminal tendencies?

REFERENCES

Bowerman, Megan M. 1997. "Adult Fertility Outcomes of Deviant and Nondeviant Youth." M.A. thesis, Department of Sociology, Bowling Green State University.

Cernkovich, Stephen A. and Peggy C. Giordano. 1979. "A Comparative Analysis of Male and Female Delinquency." *Sociological Quarterly* 20:131-45.

Chesney-Lind, Meda and Randall G. Shelden. 1998. *Girls, Delinquency, and Juvenile Justice.* 2nd ed. Belmont, CA: West/Wadsworth.

Cohen, Albert K. 1955. *Delinquent Boys: The Culture of the Gang.* New York: Free Press.

Figueira-McDonough, Josefina, William H. Barton, and Rosemary C. Sarri. 1981. "Normal Deviance: Gender Similarities in Adolescent Subcultures." Pp. 17-45 in *Comparing Female and Male Offenders,* edited by M. Q. Warren. Beverly Hills, CA: Sage.

Giordano, Peggy C. and Stephen A. Cernkovich. 1979. "On Complicating the Relationship Between Liberation and Delinquency." *Social Problems* 26:467-81.

———. 1997. "Gender and Antisocial Behavior." Pp. 496-510 in *Handbook of Antisocial Behavior,* edited by David M. Stoff, James Breiling, and Jack D. Maser. New York: John Wiley.

Giordano, Peggy C., Stephen A. Cernkovich, M. D. Pugh, and Jennifer L. Rudolph. 1997. "Gender, Crime, and Desistance: Toward a Theory of Cognitive Transformation." Paper presented at the annual meeting of the American Sociological Association, Toronto.

Giordano, Peggy C., Toni J. Millhollin, Stephen A. Cernkovich, M. D. Pugh, and Jennifer L. Rudolph. 1999. "Delinquency, Identity, and Women's Involvement in Relationship Violence." *Criminology* 37:17-40.

Greenfeld, L. A. and S. Minor-Harper. 1991. "Women in Prison." Special report, Bureau of Justice Statistics, U.S. Department of Justice.

Hirschi, Travis. 1969. *Causes of Delinquency.* Berkeley: University of California Press.

Huizinga, David, Barbara J. Morse, and Delbert S. Elliott. 1992. "The National Youth Survey: An Overview and Description of Recent Findings." National Youth Survey Project Report No. 55, Institute of Behavioral Science, University of Colorado.

Johnson, Richard E., Anastasios C. Marcos, and Stephen J. Bahr. 1987. "The Role of Peers in the Complex Etiology of Adolescent Drug Use." *Criminology* 25:323-40.

Konopka, Gisela. 1966. *The Adolescent Girl in Conflict.* Englewood Cliffs, NJ: Prentice Hall.

Kruttschnitt, Candace. 1996. "Contributions of Quantitative Methods to the Study of Gender and Crime, or Bootstrapping Our Way Into the Theoretical Thicket." *Journal of Quantitative Criminology* 12:135-61.

Lauritsen, Janet L. 1993. "Sibling Resemblance in Juvenile Delinquency: Findings From the National Youth Survey," *Criminology* 31:387.

Leonard, Eileen. 1982. *Women, Crime, and Society: A Critique of Theoretical Criminology.* New York: Longman.

Lombroso, Cesare. 1920. *The Female Offender.* New York: Appleton.

Ogle, Robbin S., Daniel Maier-Katkin, and Thomas J. Bernard. 1995. "A Theory of Homicidal Behavior Among Women." *Criminology* 33:173-93.

Riege, Mary. 1972. "Parental Affection and Juvenile Delinquency in Girls." *British Journal of Criminology* 12:55-73.

Robins, Lee N. 1986. "The Consequences of Conduct Disorder in Girls." Pp. 385-414 in *Development of Antisocial and Prosocial Behavior,* edited by D. Olweus, J. Block, and M. Radkey-Yarrow. San Diego: Academic Press.

Smith, Douglas A. and Raymond Paternoster. 1987. "The Gender Gap in Theories of Deviance: Issues and Evidence." *Journal of Research in Crime and Delinquency* 24:140-72.

Stattin, H. and D. Magnusson. 1990. *Paths Through Life,* vol. 2: *Pubertal Maturation in Female Development.* Hillsdale, NJ: Lawrence Erlbaum.

Stattin, Hakan, David Magnusson, and Howard Reichel. 1989. "Criminal Activity at Different Ages." *British Journal of Criminology* 29:368-85.

Steffensmeier, Darrell J. 1993. "National Trends in Female Arrests 1960-1990: Assessment and Recommendations for Research." *Journal of Quantitative Criminology* 9:411-41.

Sutherland, Edwin H. 1947. *Principles of Criminology.* 4th ed. Philadelphia: J. B. Lippincott.

Sutherland, Edwin H. and Donald R. Cressey. 1970. *Criminology.* 9th ed. Philadelphia: J. B. Lippincott.

Warr, Mark. 1993. "Age, Peers, and Delinquency." *Criminology* 31:17-40.

West, Donald J. 1982. *Delinquency: Its Roots, Careers, and Prospects.* Cambridge, MA: Harvard University Press.

Widom, C. Spatz. 1984. "Sex Roles, Criminality, and Psychopathology." Pp. 183-217 in *Sex Roles and Psychopathology,* edited by C. Spatz Widom. New York: Plenum.

———. 1989. "Child Abuse, Neglect, and Adult Behavior: Research Design and Findings on Criminality, Violence, and Child Abuse." *American Journal of Orthopsychiatry* 59:260-70.

CHAPTER 2

Feminist Theories of Women's Crime
Robbery as a Case Study

JODY MILLER

Feminist scholarship emerges from rich and diverse theoretical traditions. Nowhere is this more apparent than in the field of criminology. Feminist criminologists draw from a number of schools of feminist thought that often begin with very different premises about the nature and root causes of female oppression (for overviews, see Daly and Chesney-Lind 1988; Simpson 1989). Nonetheless, there are a number of central beliefs that guide feminist inquiries. Daly and Chesney-Lind (1988:504) list five aspects of feminist thought that distinguish it from traditional forms of inquiry:

- Gender is not a natural fact but rather a complex social, historical, and cultural product; it is related to, but not simply derived from, biological sex difference and reproductive capacities.

- Gender and gender relations order social life and social institutions in fundamental ways.

- Gender relations and constructs of masculinity and femininity are not symmetrical but rather are based on an organizing principle of men's superiority and social and political-economic dominance over women.

- Systems of knowledge reflect men's views of the natural and social world; the production of knowledge is gendered.

- Women should be at the center of intellectual inquiry, not peripheral, invisible, or appendages to men.

In addition, contemporary feminist scholars strive to be attentive to the inter-locking nature of race, class, and gender oppression, recognizing that women's experiences of gender vary according to their position in racial and class hierarchies (Daly and Stephens 1995; Maher 1997; Schwartz and Milovanovic 1996; Simpson 1991; Simpson and Elis 1995).

Several key issues have guided feminist inquiries of gender and offending.[1] First is the issue of generalizability. For nearly a century, theories developed to explain why people commit crime have actually been theories of why *men* commit crime. Feminist scholars have been keen on the question of whether (or the extent that) these theories can explain *women's* participation in crime. If not, then what alternative explanations can account for women's offending? Second is what is called the "gender ratio" problem: what are the reasons behind men's much greater participation in crime as compared to women? Traditional approaches explained these differences drawing on stereotypical images of women's supposed inferiority (Smart 1976:chaps. 2-3) and viewed gender as an individual trait. By contrast, feminist scholars offer theoretical accounts that draw on the recognition that gender is a key element of social organization (Kruttschnitt 1996:136).

A third issue, which has received less attention, is how gender inequality and stratification within criminal networks shape women's patterns of offending. For example, how do perceptions of women shape the criminal opportunities available to them? Are they excluded from particular types of crime? How do they overcome or resist the blocked opportunities they face in primarily masculine criminal enterprises? These are the issues I explore in this chapter. Using street robbery as a case study, I compare female and male robbers' accounts of their crimes to examine how gender shapes the accomplishment of robbery. First, let me provide more background on each of the feminist themes I have just described.

■ The Issue of Generalizability

As the chapters in this volume indicate, theories about the etiology of crime have been quite diverse. One thing they have routinely shared, however, is a primary orientation toward explaining men's (or boys') crime. Thus, feminist scholars have posed the following questions: "Do theories of men's crime apply to women? Can the logic of such theories be modified to include women?" (Daly and Chesney-Lind 1988:514). Scholars who have attempted to test whether these theories can be generalized to women have focused on things such as the family, social learning, delinquent peer relationships, and (to a lesser extent) strain and deterrence. For the most part, these studies have found mixed results (for an overview, see Smith and Paternoster 1987). As Kruttschnitt (1996) summarizes, "It appears that the factors that influence delinquent development differ for males and females in some contexts but not others" (p. 141).

Feminist scholars have posed two critiques of the generalizability approach. First, racial and economic inequalities often are overlooked in this work. Given that women (and men) live in diverse structural conditions—conditions that are shaped especially by racial inequality—approaches that seek to find general causal patterns in women's and men's offending beg the question of how these factors differentially shape offending across race, class, *and* gender (Simpson 1991). For example, research suggests that urban African American females are somewhat more likely to engage in serious crime than are their female counterparts in other racial groups or settings (Ageton 1983; Hill and Crawford 1990; Laub and McDermott 1985; Mann 1993). Specifically, there is evidence of a link between "underclass" conditions (Wilson 1996) and urban African American women's offending. Hill and Crawford (1990) report that structural indicators appear to be most significant in predicting the criminal involvement of African American women, whereas social-psychological indicators are more predictive for white women. They conclude, "The unique position of black women in the structure of power relations in society has profound effects not shared by their white counterparts" (p. 621; see also Baskin and Sommers 1998; Richie 1996). Thus, theories that attempt to generalize across gender often miss the importance of racial and class inequalities in the causes of crime.

A second critique raised against the generalizability approach is that whereas theorists in this tradition look to find out whether the same processes are at work in explaining women's and men's crime, they cannot account for the gender ratio of offending, that is, men's disproportionate involvement in most crime. Moreover, as I noted earlier, feminist scholars recognize gender as an important feature of the social organization of society and, consequently, of women's and men's experiences. Theories that attempt to be gender neutral are unable to address this pivotal issue (Daly and Chesney-Lind 1988). For example, in much of the generalizability research, it often is taken for granted that variables or constructs (e.g., "family attachment," "supervision") have the same meanings for males and females, but in fact this is an empirical question (Heimer and De Coster 1999).

■ The Gender Ratio Problem

This brings us to the gender ratio problem. Scholars who address this issue raise the following questions: "Why are women less likely than men to be involved in crime? Conversely, why are men more crime prone than women? What explains [these] gender differences?" (Daly and Chesney-Lind 1988: 515). These questions have led scholars to pay attention to gender differences and to develop theories that can account for variations in women's and men's offending (Hagan, Gillis, and Simpson 1985; Heimer and De Coster 1999). Moreover, attention to gender inequality has led feminist theorists to examine the impact of women's victimization as an explanatory factor for their crime (Arnold 1990; Chesney-Lind 1997; Daly 1992; Gilfus 1992; Richie 1996). As such, these works have allowed feminist scholars to move beyond a gender ratio approach to an understanding of "gendered lives" (Daly and Maher 1998).

One such theoretical perspective has been to focus on gender as situated accomplishment (West and Fenstermaker 1995; West and Zimmerman 1987). Here, gender is recognized as "much more than a role or [an] individual characteristic; it is a mechanism whereby situated social action contributes to the reproduction of social structure" (West and Fenstermaker 1995:21). Women and men "do gender," or behave in gendered ways, in response to normative beliefs about femininity and masculinity. The performance of gender is both an indication of and a reproduction of gendered social hierarchies. This approach has been incorporated into feminist accounts of crime as a means of explaining differences in women's and men's offending (Messerschmidt 1993, 1995; Newburn and Stanko 1994; Simpson and Elis 1995). Here, crime is described as "a 'resource' for accomplishing gender—for demonstrating masculinity within a given context or situation" (Simpson and Elis 1995:50).

This approach can help to account for men's greater involvement in particular types of crime (e.g., violence) and also for women's involvement in crime in ways scripted by femininity (e.g., prostitution). In addition, this approach can help to account for differences resulting from racial and class inequalities, with the recognition that constructions of femininity and masculinity vary across these important contexts (Simpson 1991; Simpson and Elis 1995). For example, Simpson (1989) notes that some of women's participation in violent street crime might stem from "the frustration, alienation, and anger that are associated with racial and class oppression" (p. 618). When violence is an extensive part of their lives and communities, urban women might be more likely to view violence as an appropriate or a useful means of dealing with their environment (Simpson 1991).

■ Gender Stratification in Criminal Networks

Regardless of women's position vis-à-vis racial and class inequalities, they also remain in a society that is inextricably shaped by gender inequality. Consequently, feminist scholars recently have focused on how gender stratification within criminal networks mirrors gender stratification elsewhere in society, shaping women's experiences. This work has provided overwhelming evidence that gender inequality is a salient feature of urban street scenes—something with which women involved in these networks must constantly contend (Campbell 1984; Jacobs and Miller 1998; Maher 1997; Maher and Daly 1996; Miller 1986; Miller 1998a; Steffensmeier 1983). Thus, this scholarship is concerned with examining both the nature of gender stratification and women's responses to it.

Steffensmeier (1983) was the first scholar to detail the institutional nature of gender inequality on the streets, examining how homosocial reproduction, gender segregation, and "sex typing" limited women's participation in street networks. Male street offenders often view women as unreliable, untrustworthy, and weak, shunning them as would-be criminal associates (Steffensmeier and Terry 1986). Consequently, women "continue to find themselves with a deficit of 'criminal capital' [Hagan and McCarthy 1997]—the connections, ties, and pull that come with extensive and enduring involvement in street networks" (Jacobs and Miller 1998:554). As a result, they face limited options, restricted participation, and victimization in these settings.

Perhaps the most sophisticated analysis of gender stratification on the streets is Maher's (1997) ethnography of a drug market in Brooklyn, New York. She documents a rigid gender division of labor in the drug economy, shaped as well along racial lines, in which women are "clearly disadvantaged compared to their male counterparts" (p. 54). Describing the three spheres of income generation on the streets—drug business hustles, non-drug hustles, and "sexwork"—Maher details the ways in which women are excluded from more lucrative opportunities and found sexwork to be one of their few viable options for making money.

The current study is housed in this tradition of examining how gender stratification shapes women's involvement in crime. In this chapter, I examine a crime for which the gender ratio problem I described earlier is striking. Robbery is one of the most gender-differentiated serious crimes in the United States; that is, the proportion of men who commit robbery as compared to women is greater than that for nearly every other serious crime. According to the Federal Bureau of Investigation's (1996) Uniform Crime Reports for 1995, women accounted for only 9.3 percent of all robbery arrestees, whereas men accounted for 90.7 percent of those arrested for this crime. As you read my discussion of women's participation in robbery, therefore, it is very important to keep two things in mind. First, women are only a small percentage of street robbers. As such, I am studying a very unusual behavior among women. Second, my discussion of the crime is not meant to suggest that women's participation in robbery is increasing. Instead, I am interested in comparing women's and men's accounts of why they commit street robbery and how gender organizes their commissions of the crime.

■ Gender and Street Robbery

□ The Study

One way in which to find out how gender shapes patterns of offending is to talk to female and male offenders and to compare what they have to say about their crime.[2] As Daly and Chesney-Lind (1988) point out, feminist scholarship often involves interviews because this approach provides "texture [and] social context" (p. 518) that allow us to present more nuanced accounts of women's involvement in crime. Using this method, I draw from in-depth interviews with active male and female robbers. The findings I discuss come from a larger study of urban street robbers in St. Louis, Missouri (Wright and Decker 1997).[3] Respondents were recruited from impoverished urban neighborhoods in the city. St. Louis is typical of a number of midwestern cities devastated by structural changes brought about by deindustrialization. The city is characterized by tremendous economic and racial segregation. Deindustrialization has exacerbated these conditions, also resulting in population loss, the social isolation of many urban dwellers, losses in community resources, and a deepened concentration of urban poverty among African Americans in the city. The neighborhoods from which respondents were drawn are characteristic of what some scholars have called "underclass" conditions (Sampson and Wilson 1995; Wilson 1996). Although I do not discuss these structural conditions further, they are important contexts to keep in mind as I discuss the activities of urban street robbers.

The sample consists of 37 active robbers, a matched sample of 14 women and 23 men who were approximately the same age and who reported committing their first robberies at the same age. Respondents ranged in age from 16 to 46 years, although the majority were in their late teens or early 20s. The vast majority of participants were African American—all of the men and all but 2 of the women. This is one of the greatest limitations of the sample. Whites were a much greater proportion of robbery arrestees in St. Louis than is reflected in the nearly all-black sample. This bias in the data was the result of the snowball sampling techniques used. One individual, an African American ex-offender, was hired and given the charge of locating his former criminal associates to get them to participate in the study. These respondents then referred their friends and associates to participate, and the process continued until the sample was built. Nearly all of these contacts yielded African American robbers. Despite the fact that there were a number of white robbers in St. Louis, "successfully making contact with active black armed robbers proved to be of almost no help . . . in locating white offenders" (Wright and Decker 1997:11).

Data were gathered by using semistructured in-depth interviews. Interviews lasted one to two hours and included a range of questions about the respondents' involvement in robbery. Respondents were asked to describe why they committed robbery, their typical approach when committing robbery, and the details of their most recent offenses. The goal was to gain a thorough understanding of the contexts of these events from the respondents' perspectives. Now, I turn my attention to the two questions that guide my inquiry: situational motives for committing robbery and the accomplishment of the crime.

☐ *Motivations to Commit Robbery*

Because many of the respondents in the sample were young and had begun committing robberies as teenagers, their descriptions of the reasons why they committed the crime resonate with the typical desires of adolescents and young adults. Most of the participants, both female and male, said that they committed robberies to get things such as jewelry and spending money and also because they found the crime exciting. My study cannot address etiological factors, that is, those factors in individuals' lives that led them to commit crime. Instead, my discussion is of motivations that are situational or that emerge in the context of their decisions to commit robbery.

Perhaps what is most striking in their discussions, as I have noted, is that women and men give very similar descriptions of their motives. For example, T-Bone[4] said that he decides to commit robberies when he is "tired of not having money." When the idea comes about, he typically is with friends from the neighborhood and, he explained, "we all bored, broke, mad." Likewise, CMW said that she commits robberies "out of the blue, just something to do. Bored at the time and just want to find some action." She explained, "I be sitting on the porch and we'll get to talking and stuff. See people going around, and they be flashing in they fancy cars, walking down the street with that jewelry on, thinking they all bad, and we just go get 'em." For both males and females, robbery typically was a means of achieving conspicuous consumption.

Asked to explain why they commit robberies instead of other crimes with similar economic rewards, both women and men said that they chose robberies, as Cooper explained, because "it's the easiest." Libbie Jones reported that robbery provides her with the things she wants in one quick and easy step:

> I like robbery. I like robbery 'cause I don't have to buy nothing. You have a herringbone. I'm gonna take your herringbone, and then I have me a herringbone. I don't have to worry about going to the store, getting me some money. If you got some little earrings on, I'm gonna get 'em.

Often they targeted individuals whom they believed were "safe" victims, usually other street-involved individuals who were less likely to go to the police. Most robberies, whether committed by females or males, occurred in the larger contexts of street life, and their victims reflected this. Most also were involved in street contexts, either as adolescents or young adults who hang out on the streets and go to clubs or as individuals involved (as dealers and/or users) in the street-level drug economy (for more on target selection, see Wright and Decker 1997:chap. 3).

In addition to the economic incentives that draw the respondents toward robbery, many also derived an emotional thrill from committing robbery. Little Bills said, "When my first robbery started, my second, the third one, it got more fun.... If I keep on doing it, I think that I will really get addicted to it." Likewise, Buby noted, "You get, like, a rush. It be fun at the time." In particular, when they perceived individuals as "high-catting" or showing off, both female and male robbers viewed these individuals as deserving targets. For example, Treason Taylor described a woman he robbed at a gas station: "Really, I didn't like the way she came out. She was, like, pulling out all her money like she think she hot shit." A few respondents even specifically targeted people they did not like or people who had insulted or hurt them in the past.

For both women and men, then, motivations to commit robbery were primarily economic—to get money, jewelry, and other status-conferring goods—but also included elements of thrill seeking, attempting to overcome boredom, and revenge. Most striking is the continuity across women's and men's accounts of their motives for committing robbery. As the following subsections show, there are clear differences in the accomplishment of robbery by gender. However, these differences apparently are not driven by differences in motivation.

☐ Men's Commission of Street Robbery

The men in my study committed street robberies in a strikingly uniform way. Their descriptions of robberies were variations around one theme: using physical violence and/or a gun placed close to (or touching) the victim in a confrontational manner. This is reflected in Looney's description of being taught how to commit his first robbery at the age of 13 years by his stepbrother:

> We was up at [a fast-food restaurant] one day, and a dude was up there tripping. My stepbrother had gave me a .22 automatic. He told me to walk over behind him and put the gun to his head and tell him to give me all his stuff. That's what I did. I walked up to him and said, "Man, this is a jack, man. Take off all your jewelry and take you money out of your pockets, throw it on the ground, and walk off." So that's what he did. I picked up the money and the jewelry and walked away.

The most common form of robbery described by male respondents was to target other men involved in street life—drug dealers, drug users, gang members, or other men who looked "flashy" because of their clothes, cars, or jewelry. Only seven men (30 percent) said they robbed women as well as men. All of the men in the sample used guns when they robbed, although not everyone used a gun every time. The key was to make sure, as Syco said, that the victims know "that we ain't playing." They conveyed this message by positioning the guns close to the victims' bodies or by physically assaulting the victims. For example, Bob Jones confronted his victims by placing his gun at the backs of their heads, where "they feel it," and saying to them, "Give it up motherfucker. Don't move or I'll blow your brains out!" Explaining the positioning of the gun, he said, "When you feel that steel against your head . . . [it] carries a lot of weight."

Without guns, and sometimes even when they used guns, some men reported using physical violence to ensure the victims' cooperation and the robbers' getaways. Cooper said, "You always got to either hit 'em, slap 'em, or do something to let them know you for real." Likewise, Mike J. said, "You might shake them a little bit. If there is more than one of you, you can really do that kind of stuff like shake them up a little bit to show them you're not messing around." When male robbers did not have guns, they typically used more physical violence to make sure that the victims did not resist. Taz explained,

> If it's a strong-arm [a robbery without a weapon], like, I'll just get up on them and I'll just hit 'em, and [my partner] will grab them or, like, he will hit them and I'll grab 'em, and we keep on hitting them until they fall or something. . . . [Then,] we just go in his pockets, leave him there, we gone.

As I already noted, seven men said that they robbed women as well as men. However, male respondents, including those who did not rob women, said that they believed that robbing women was different from robbing men. They felt that robbing women was less dangerous because women were less likely to resist. Looney explained, "Men gonna act like they the tough guy, . . . but a lady, I just tell them to give it up and they give me they whole purse or whatever they got." Whereas physical violence often was used routinely when men robbed other men, these men said that they rarely used physical violence against women and did so only when the women resisted. Although violence often was deemed necessary to establish a credible threat with male victims, it was not seen as necessary with women victims. Perhaps what is most ironic is that although male robbers were in agreement that women were "easy" victims, as a rule, these men did not target women. Perhaps this was because they did not believe that women would have the kind of money on them that men would (particularly criminally involved men), but it also was because they viewed robbery as a prototypically masculine endeavor, best carried out in male-on-male encounters (see also Katz 1988; Messerschmidt 1993).

In sum, males' robberies were characterized by the routine use of guns, physical contact with the victim, and (in some cases) physical violence. Men's descriptions of their robberies were strikingly similar to each other. By contrast, women's descriptions of their robberies revealed much more varied techniques and provided a telling contrast about the nature of gender on the streets.

☐ Women's Commission of Street Robbery

Women in the sample described three predominant ways in which they committed robberies: targeting female victims in physically confrontational robberies, targeting male victims by appearing sexually available, and participating with males during street robberies of men. It is noteworthy that most women described participating in two or more types of these robberies. Thus, as we will see, they committed robberies differently depending on the circumstances and on who their victims were. In all, 10 women (71 percent) described targeting female victims, usually on the streets but occasionally at dance clubs or in cars. In addition, 7 women (50 percent) described setting up men through promises of sexual favors including 2 women who did so in the context of prostitution. Among the women, 7 (50 percent) described working with male friends, relatives, or boyfriends in street robberies, with 3 (21 percent) reporting this as their exclusive form of robbery.

Robbing Females

The most common form of robbery reported by women in the study was to rob other females in a physically confrontational manner. Of the 14 female respondents, 10 reported committing these types of offenses. Typically, women's robberies of other females occurred on the streets, although a few young women also reported robbing females in the bathrooms or parking lots of clubs, and 1 robbed women in cars. These robberies sometimes were committed alone and other times were committed with another woman or several additional women. But they were not committed with male robbers. In fact, Ne-Ne said that even when she is out with male friends and sees a female target, the men do not get involved: "They'll say, 'Well, you go on and do her.' "

Most robberies of females either involved no weapons or involved knives. Women rarely described using guns to rob other women. Female respondents said that when they chose women victims, it was because they believed that the other women were not likely to be armed and also were not likely to resist or fight back. CMW explained, "See, women, they won't really do nothing. They say, 'Oh, oh, okay, here take this.' A dude, he might try to put up a fight." Likewise, Libbie Jones said, "I wouldn't do no men by myself," but she added that women victims "ain't gonna do nothing because they be so scared." Typically, women felt that it was not necessary to use weapons in these robberies. Quick explained that she sometimes used a knife, "but sometimes I don't need anything. Most of the time it be girls, you know, just snatching they chains or jewelry. You don't need nothing for that."

On occasion, female victims belied the stereotype of them and fought back. When that occurred, several women described stabbing their victims. Janet Outlaw described one such encounter:

> I walked up to her, and I pulled out the knife. I said, "Up that purse." And she looked at me. I said, "Shit, do you think I'm playing? Up that purse." She was like, "Shit, you ain't getting my purse. Do what you got to do." I was like, "Shit, you must be thinking I'm playing." So I took the knife, stabbed her a couple of times on the shoulder, stabbed her on the arm, and snatched the purse. Cut her arm and snatched the purse. She just ran, "Help, help." We were gone.

However, stabbing female victims was a rare occurrence. Instead, women's robberies of other women routinely involved physical confrontation such as hitting, shoving, or beating up the victim. Describing a recent robbery, Nicole Simpson said, "I have bricks in my purse, and I went up to her and hit her in the head and took her money." Kim Brown said that she will "just whop you and take a purse but not really put a gun to anybody's face." Libbie Jones said that she has her victims throw their possessions on the ground, "then you push 'em, kick 'em, or whatever. You pick it up, and you just burn out." Describing why this type of physical force was necessary, Janet Outlaw explained, "It's just a woman-to-woman thing, and we just, like, just don't, just letting them know like it is, we let them know we ain't playing." As will be seen below, this approach is vastly different from women's approaches when they rob men or when they commit robberies with males.

To summarize, notable elements of women's robberies of other women are that they most frequently occurred within street-oriented settings; did not include male accomplices; and typically involved physical force such as hitting, shoving, and kicking rather than the use of weapons. When weapons were used, they were most likely to be knives. In these contexts, women chose to rob other females rather than males because they believed that females were less likely to fight back. They typically did not use weapons such as guns because they believed that female targets were unlikely to be armed.

Robbing Males by Appearing Sexually Available

Women's robberies of men almost always involved guns and rarely involved physical contact. Janet Outlaw, who described using a great deal of physical violence in her robberies of other women (see previous subsection), described her robberies of men in much different terms. She explained, "If we waste time touching men, there is a possibility that they can get the gun off of us. While we wasting time touching them, they could do anything. So we just keep the gun straight on them. No touching, no moving, just straight gun at you." The circumstances of these robberies were different as well. When women robbed men, the key was to pretend to be sexually interested in the male victims, who then would drop their guard, providing safe opportunities for the crimes to occur. Two women, Jayzo and Nicole Simpson, robbed men in the context of prostitution. The other five typically chose victims at clubs or on the streets, flirted and appeared sexually interested, and then suggested that they go to a hotel, where the robberies took place.

Nicole Simpson prostituted to support her drug habit, but sometimes she "just don't be feeling like doing it" and will rob her trick rather than complete the sexual transaction. She chose tricks whom she felt would make safe victims and would be unlikely to resist. Typically, she waited until the man was in a vulnerable position before pulling out her knife. As she explained, "If you are sucking a man's dick and you pull a knife on them, they not gonna too much argue with you." Jayzo's techniques paralleled those of Nicole Simpson, although she used a gun instead of a knife.

Young women who targeted men outside of the context of prostitution played on the men's beliefs about women to accomplish these robberies, including the assumptions that women would not be armed, would not attempt to rob them, and could be taken advantage of sexually. Quick explained, "They don't suspect that a girl gonna try to get 'em. You know what I'm saying? So it's kind of easier 'cause they, like, 'She looks innocent, she ain't gonna do this,' but that's how I get 'em. They put they guard down to a woman." She said that when she sets up men, she parties with them first but makes sure that she does not consume as much as them. "Most of the time when girls get high, they think they can take advantage of us, so they always, 'Let's go to a hotel or my crib or something.' " Janet Outlaw said, "They easy to get. We know what they after—sex." Likewise, CMW said, "They thinking we little freaks . . . whores or something." Men's assumptions that they could take advantage of women led them to place themselves at risk for robbery, on which these women acted.

Except for the two women who robbed tricks when they were prostituting, women typically held their guns at a safe distance from the victims rather than pressing the guns up against them as the male robbers did when they robbed men. Doing so decreased the risk that a victim could resist, grab the gun, and use it on the woman. This was necessary precisely because the women chose male victims who thought that they could take advantage of the women. Janet Outlaw encountered one such man. She picked him up in a nightclub, they went to a hotel together, and then his resistance led her to fire her weapon. She explained,

> We got to smoking a little bud, he got to taking off his little shit, laying it on a little table. He was like, "Shit, what's up, ain't you gonna get undressed?" I was like, "Shit, yeah, hold up," and I went in my purse and I pulled out the gun. He was like, "Damn, what's up with you, gal?" I was like, "Shit, I want your jewelry and all the money you got." He was like, "Shit, bitch, you crazy. I ain't giving you my shit." I said, "Do you think I'm playing, nigger? You don't think I'll shoot your motherfucking ass?" He was like, "Shit, you crazy, fuck that, you ain't gonna shoot me." So then I had fired the thing, but I didn't fire it at him, shot the gun. He was like, "Fuck no." I snatched his shit. He didn't have on no clothes. I snatched the shit and ran out the door. Hopped in my car.

Women often committed these robberies alone, but sometimes they did so in pairs or even had male accomplices follow them to the hotels for backup. In each case, however, the woman always used a weapon and avoided physical contact as much as she could. Thus, the women's robberies of men were strikingly different from their robberies of women.

Street Robberies With Male Robbers

As the previous two subsections illustrated, women commit robberies in very different ways depending on whether their victims are female or male. As a rule, women described that they did not rob females with male accomplices but did sometimes work with male accomplices to set up and rob men. In addition, half of the women in the sample described committing street

robberies of males with male accomplices. The difference between these robberies of men and those I described previously is that, with street robberies,
women did not act sexually available so as to rob men. Instead, in conjunc-
tion with their male partners, they conducted these robberies in much the
same way as the male respondents described robbing men on the streets.
Three women in the sample—Buby, Tish, and Lisa Jones—described working with males on the streets as their only form of robbery. Each of these
women described her participation as secondary. By contrast, other women
who engaged in street robberies with males engaged in other forms of robbery and did not distinguish their roles from roles of their male accomplices
in these robberies.

Lisa Jones and Tish both assisted their boyfriends in the commission of
robberies. Buby went along with her brother and cousins. Lisa Jones said,
"Most of the time, we'll just be driving around and he'll say, 'Let's go to this
neighborhood and rob somebody.' " Usually, she stayed in the car while he
approached the victim, but she was armed and would get out and assist when
necessary. Describing one such incident, she said, "One time, there was two
guys, and one guy was in the car and the other guy was out of the car, and I
seen that one guy getting out of the car, I guess to help his friend. That's
when I got out, and I held the gun and I told him to stay where he was." Tish
and Lisa Jones were the only white respondents in the study, and each
robbed with an African American boyfriend. Both described their boyfriends
as the decision makers in the robberies—deciding when, where, and whom
to rob.

It is striking that all of these young women routinely committed armed
robberies wielding guns on victims yet rejected the view of themselves as
criminals. In fact, during her interview, Lisa Jones was adamant, telling the
interviewer, "I'm not a criminal." Lisa Jones and Tish were the only respondents who downplayed their involvement in armed robbery. It probably is
not coincidental that they were young white women who used their beliefs
about race and gender to minimize the implications of the serious nature of
their crimes.

These respondents were at the far end of the continuum of women's
involvement in robbery, clearly taking subordinate roles in the crime and
defining themselves as less culpable as a result. For the most part, other
women who participated in street robberies with male accomplices described themselves as equal participants. Robberies with male accomplices
typically involved guns and came about when a group of people were driving
around and spotted a potential victim. They committed the crime using the

same techniques as male respondents described, that is, using physical contact and, when necessary, violence. In fact, Ne-Ne said that she preferred committing street robberies with males rather than with females because she viewed her male accomplices as more reliable. She explained,

> I can't be bothered with too many girls. That's why I try to be with dudes or whatever. They gonna be down. If you get out of the car and if you rob a dude or jack somebody and you with some dudes, then you know if they see he tryin' to resist, they gonna give me some help. Whereas a girl, you might get somebody that's scared and might drive off. That's the way it is.

In fact, Ne-Ne was the only woman interviewed to report having committed this type of street robbery of a male victim on her own. Her actions paralleled those of male-on-male robbers described earlier. She explained, "I just turned around the corner, came back down the street. He was out by hisself, and I got out of the car, had the cap pulled down over my face, and I just went to the back and upped him. Put the gun up to his head." Importantly, Ne-Ne told the interviewer that this robbery was successful because the man she robbed did not realize that she was a woman. Describing herself physically, she said, "I'm big, you know." In addition, her dress and manner masked that she was a woman. Being large, wearing a ball cap, and committing the robbery in a masculine style (e.g., putting a gun to his head) allowed her to disguise the fact that she was a woman and thus decrease the victim's likelihood of resisting. She said, "He don't know right now to this day if it was a girl or a dude."

■ Discussion

Perhaps what is most notable about this study is the incongruity between women's and men's motives for committing robbery and the ways in which they go about conducting the crime. Although the comparison of women's and men's motivations revealed gender similarities, when women and men actually committed robbery, the ways in which they went about doing the crime were strikingly different. These differences highlight the clear gender hierarchy that exists on the streets. Although some women are able to carve out a niche for themselves in this setting and even establish partnerships with males, they are participating in a male-dominated environment, and their actions reflect an understanding of this.

To successfully commit robbery, women must take into account the gendered nature of their environment. One way in which they do so is by targeting other females. Both male and female robbers held the view that females were easy to rob because they were less likely than males to be armed and because they were perceived as weak and easily intimidated. Janet Outlaw described women's robbery of other women as "just a woman-to-woman thing." This is supported by Ne-Ne's description that her male friends did not participate with her in robberies of females, and it is supported by men's accounts of robbing women. Whereas women routinely robbed other women, men were less likely to do so, perhaps because these robberies did not result in the demonstration of masculinity (West and Zimmerman 1987).

At the same time as women articulated the belief that other women were easy targets, they also drew on these perceptions of women to rob men. A number of women used men's perceptions of women as weak, sexually available, and easily manipulated to turn the tables and manipulate men into circumstances in which they became vulnerable to robbery by flirting and appearing sexually interested in the men. Unlike women's robberies of other women, these robberies tended not to involve physical contact but did involve the use of guns. Because they recognized men's perceptions of women, the women also recognized that men were more likely to resist being robbed by females, and thus they committed these robberies in ways that minimized their risk of losing control and maximized their ability to show that they were "for real."

West and Zimmerman (1987) note that there are circumstances in which "parties reach an accommodation that allow[s] a woman to engage in presumptively masculine behavior" (p. 139). In this study, it is notable that both women and men recognized the urban street world as a male-dominated one. Nonetheless, a few of the women gained access to male privilege by adopting male attitudes about females, constructing their own identities as more masculine, and following through by behaving in masculine ways. Ne-Ne and Janet Outlaw both come to mind in this regard as women who completed robberies in equal partnerships with men and identified with men's attitudes about other women. Other women, such as Lisa Jones and Tish, accepted not only women's position as secondary but also their own positions as secondary. Whereas Ne-Ne and Janet Outlaw appeared to draw status and identity from their criminality in ways that went beyond their gender identity, Lisa Jones and Tish used their gender identity to construct themselves as noncriminal.

In sum, the women in this sample did not appear to commit robbery differently from men so as to meet different needs or to accomplish different goals. Instead, the differences that emerge reflected practical choices made in the context of a gender-stratified environment in which, on the whole, males are perceived as strong and women are perceived as weak. Motivationally, then, it appears that women's participation in street violence can result from the same structural and cultural underpinnings that shape some of men's participation in this type of crime. Yet, gender remains a salient factor shaping their actions as well as the actions of men.

There are a number of additional questions about gender and robbery that this study cannot address. Although I have noted the striking gender ratio with regard to the commission of robbery, the data I have presented cannot allow me to address the question of why so many more men than women choose to commit robbery. Moreover, as I noted earlier, my discussion of motivation is not the same as discussing the causes of women's and men's crime. Although the women and men in this study gave similar accounts of why they committed robbery, this does not mean that they became criminally involved for the same reasons. However, it does provide an additional layer to our attempts to understand the gendered lives of female offenders by focusing on the ways in which women participate in the urban street world. I opened this chapter by suggesting that gender is a "complex social, historical, and cultural product" and that "gender and gender relations order social life and social institutions in fundamental ways" (Daly and Chesney-Lind 1988:504). Hopefully, seeing how women and men talked about their commission of robbery has helped to bring to life these important insights of feminist theory.

■ Policy Implications

Feminist research, including this study, raises a number of important issues that should be considered in the development of policies for dealing with female offenders. First among these is the recognition that both women and men really do lead gendered lives. That is, in very complex ways, gender has an impact on our experiences at all levels of interactions with others as well as within the social structures of society. The unique features of women's lives need to be taken into account in developing and implementing policies in gender-specific ways. For example, women often are the primary caregivers in their children's lives, and policies for dealing with female offenders should assess the impact of various strategies not just on women but also on their children. Gender inequality and the victimization of women are important causal factors for crime that need to be considered in understanding female offenders. In addition, it is important to recognize that gender inequality constrains the types of opportunities women have available to them. This is especially true in poor communities and even is true when it comes to the commission of crime.

However, as this chapter has highlighted, it is important to strike a balance between recognizing the significance of gender and gender inequality but not to reduce everything to gender. This is important for at least two reasons. First, we have a long history within both our criminal and juvenile justice systems of treating women offenders differently from men offenders, often to the detriment of the women (for an overview, see Chesney-Lind 1997). This often plays itself out through an overemphasis on controlling young women's independence and sexuality (Alder 1998) and through treating women in particularly harsh ways when they do not conform to traditional notions of appropriate femininity (Visher 1983). In fact, Baines and Alder (1996) suggest that notions of girls' "difference," particularly tied to an overemphasis on girls' victimization, negatively affects the treatment that girls receive within juvenile justice.

As important is the second reason for not paying exclusive attention to gender, that is, the need to consider the importance of racial and class inequalities for understanding women's, as well as men's, offending. As this study has documented, many of the motivations both women and men described for why they committed robberies were responses to the relative deprivation they face as marginalized members of an urban underclass community. Paying attention to the broad spectrum of factors that lead to women's offending—both gendered and those they share with their male counterparts—is necessary to create effective solutions for female offenders and society. The important insights of feminist scholarship have led to the recognition of the need to strike this important balance in developing policies to both empower women and create a more equitable society.

STUDY QUESTIONS

1. What are the five aspects of feminist thought that distinguish it from traditional forms of inquiry?
2. What is the issue of generalizability? What two critiques do feminist scholars raise of this approach?

3. What is the gender ratio problem?

4. What does the author mean when she describes gender as "situated accomplishment"? How has this perspective been used to explain crime?

5. What does the author mean when she says that there is "gender stratification" in criminal networks?

6. How do women and men accomplish robbery differently? How does the author explain this difference? Do you agree or disagree with her analysis? Why?

NOTES

1. I limit my discussion in this chapter to feminist work on the question of female offending. However, it is important to note that feminist scholars have focused on several additional important issues in criminology. These include (1) violence against women (e.g., rape, domestic violence, sexual abuse), (2) the impact of gender on women's processing and experiences in the criminal and juvenile justice systems, and (3) how gender shapes women's experiences in law enforcement and criminal justice careers. These topics are beyond the scope of this chapter, but there are a number of sources available for further information. See Belknap (1997), Chesney-Lind and Shelden (1998), Daly and Maher (1998), Dobash and Dobash (1992), Merlo and Pollock (1995), and Price and Sokoloff (1995).

2. This discussion is a condensed version of Miller (1998b).

3. Wright and Decker's (1997) study was funded by the Harry Frank Guggenheim Foundation and the National Institute of Justice (NIJ Grant 94-IJ-CX-0030).

4. The names I use are pseudonyms provided by the respondents to disguise their identities.

REFERENCES

Ageton, Suzanne S. 1983. "The Dynamics of Female Delinquency 1976-1980." *Criminology* 21:555-84.

Alder, Christine. 1998. " 'Passionate and Willful' Girls: Confronting Practices." *Women & Criminal Justice* 9:81-101.

Arnold, Regina. 1990. "Processes of Victimization and Criminalization of Black Women." *Social Justice* 17:153-66.

Baines, M. and Christine Alder. 1996. "Are Girls More Difficult to Work With? Youth Workers' Perspectives in Juvenile Justice and Related Areas." *Crime and Delinquency* 42:467-85.

Baskin, Deborah and Ira Sommers. 1998. *Casualties of Community Disorder: Women's Careers in Violent Crime.* Boulder, CO: Westview.

Belknap, Joanne. 1997. *The Invisible Woman: Gender, Crime, and Justice.* Belmont, CA: Wadsworth.

Campbell, Anne. 1984. *The Girls in the Gang.* London: Basil Blackwell.

Chesney-Lind, Meda. 1997. *The Female Offender: Girls, Women, and Crime.* Thousand Oaks, CA: Sage.

Chesney-Lind, Meda and Randall G. Shelden. 1998. *Girls, Delinquency, and Juvenile Justice.* 2nd ed. Belmont, CA: Wadsworth.

Daly, Kathleen. 1992. "Women's Pathways to Felony Court: Feminist Theories of Lawbreaking and Problems of Representation." *Review of Law and Women's Studies* 2:11-52.

Daly, Kathleen and Meda Chesney-Lind. 1988. "Feminism and Criminology." *Justice Quarterly* 5:497-538.

Daly, Kathleen and Lisa Maher. 1998. *Criminology at the Crossroads: Feminist Readings in Crime and Justice.* Oxford, UK: Oxford University Press.

Daly, Kathleen and Deborah J. Stephens. 1995. "The 'Dark Figure' of Criminology: Towards a Black and Multi-ethnic Feminist Agenda for Theory and Research." Pp. 189-215 in *International Feminist Perspectives in Criminology: Engendering a Discipline,* edited by Nicole Hahn Rafter and Frances Heidensohn. Philadelphia: Open University Press.

Dobash, R. Emerson and Russell P. Dobash. 1992. *Women, Violence, and Social Change.* New York: Routledge.

Federal Bureau of Investigation. 1996. *Crime in the United States 1995.* Washington, DC: Government Printing Office.

Gilfus, Mary E. 1992. "From Victims to Survivors to Offenders: Women's Routes of Entry and Immersion Into Street Crime." *Women and Criminal Justice* 4:63-89.

Hagan, John, A. R. Gillis, and John Simpson. 1985. "The Class Structure of Gender and Delinquency: Toward a Power-Control Theory of Common Delinquent Behavior." *American Journal of Sociology* 90:1151-78.

Hagan, John and Bill McCarthy. 1997. *Mean Streets: Youth Crime and Homelessness.* Cambridge, UK: Cambridge University Press.

Heimer, Karen and Stacy De Coster. 1999. "The Gendering of Violent Delinquency." *Criminology* 37:277-317.

Hill, Gary D. and Elizabeth M. Crawford. 1990. "Women, Race, and Crime." *Criminology* 28:601-23.

Jacobs, Bruce and Jody Miller. 1998. "Crack Dealing, Gender, and Arrest Avoidance." *Social Problems* 45:550-69.

Katz, Jack. 1988. *Seductions of Crime.* New York: Basic Books.

Kruttschnitt, Candace. 1996. "Contributions of Quantitative Methods to the Study of Gender and Crime, or Bootstrapping Our Way Into the Theoretical Thicket." *Journal of Quantitative Criminology* 12:135-61.

Laub, John H. and M. Joan McDermott. 1985. "An Analysis of Serious Crime by Young Black Women." *Criminology* 23:81-98.

Maher, Lisa. 1997. *Sexed Work: Gender, Race, and Resistance in a Brooklyn Drug Economy.* Oxford, UK: Clarendon.

Maher, Lisa and Kathleen Daly. 1996. "Women in the Street-Level Drug Economy: Continuity or Change?" *Criminology* 34:465-92.

Mann, Coramae Richey. 1993. "Sister Against Sister: Female Intrasexual Homicide." Pp. 195-223 in *Female Criminality: The State of the Art,* edited by C. C. Culliver. New York: Garland.

Merlo, Alida V. and Joycelyn M. Pollock. 1995. *Women, Law, and Social Control.* Boston: Allyn & Bacon.

Messerschmidt, James W. 1993. *Masculinities and Crime.* Lanham, MD: Rowman & Littlefield.

———. 1995. "From Patriarchy to Gender: Feminist Theory, Criminology, and the Challenge of Diversity." Pp. 167-88 in *International Feminist Perspectives in Criminology: Engendering a Discipline,* edited by Nicole Hahn Rafter and Frances Heidensohn. Philadelphia: Open University Press.

Miller, Eleanor M. 1986. *Street Woman.* Philadelphia: Temple University Press.

Miller, Jody. 1998a. "Gender and Victimization Risk Among Young Women in Gangs." *Journal of Research in Crime and Delinquency* 35:429-53.

———. 1998b. "Up It Up: Gender and the Accomplishment of Street Robbery." *Criminology* 36:37-66.

Newburn, Tim and Elizabeth A. Stanko, eds. 1994. *Just Boys Doing Business?* New York: Routledge.

Price, Barbara Raffel and Natalie J. Sokoloff. 1995. *The Criminal Justice System and Women: Offenders, Victims, and Workers.* 2nd ed. New York: McGraw-Hill.

Richie, Beth E. 1996. *Compelled to Crime: The Gender Entrapment of Battered Black Women.* New York: Routledge.

Sampson, Robert J. and William Julius Wilson. 1995. "Toward a Theory of Race, Crime, and Urban Inequality." Pp. 37-54 in *Crime and Inequality,* edited by John Hagan and Ruth D. Peterson. Stanford, CA: Stanford University Press.

Schwartz, Martin D. and Dragan Milovanovic. 1996. *Race, Gender, and Class in Criminology: The Intersection.* New York: Garland.

Simpson, Sally. 1989. "Feminist Theory, Crime, and Justice." *Criminology* 27:605-31.

———. 1991. "Caste, Class, and Violent Crime: Explaining Differences in Female Offending." *Criminology* 29:115-35.

Simpson, Sally and Lori Elis. 1995. "Doing Gender: Sorting Out the Caste and Crime Conundrum." *Criminology* 33:47-81.

Smart, Carol. 1976. *Women, Crime, and Criminology: A Feminist Critique.* London: Routledge and Kegan Paul.

Smith, Douglas A. and Raymond Paternoster. 1987. "The Gender Gap in Theories of Deviance: Issues and Evidence." *Journal of Research in Crime and Delinquency* 24:140-72.

Steffensmeier, Darrell J. 1983. "Organizational Properties and Sex Segregation in the Underworld: Building a Sociological Theory of Sex Differences in Crime." *Social Forces* 61:1010-32.

Steffensmeier, Darrell J. and Robert Terry. 1986. "Institutional Sexism in the Underworld: A View From the Inside." *Sociological Inquiry* 56:304-23.

Visher, Christy. 1983. "Gender, Police Arrest Decisions, and Notions of Chivalry." *Criminology* 21:5-28.

West, Candace and Sarah Fenstermaker. 1995. "Doing Difference." *Gender & Society* 9:8-37.

West, Candace and Don H. Zimmerman. 1987. "Doing Gender." *Gender & Society* 1:125-51.

Wilson, William Julius. 1996. *When Work Disappears: The World of the New Urban Poor.* New York: Knopf.

Wright, Richard T. and Scott Decker. 1997. *Armed Robbers in Action: Stickups and Street Culture.* Boston: Northeastern University Press.

CHAPTER 3

Racial Hoaxes
Applied Critical Race Theory

KATHERYN K. RUSSELL

In criminology, as in other disciplines, there is a cluster of theories and perspectives that hold center court. These approaches comprise the core of mainstream criminology. Ideally, these well-known and entrenched analyses would ask, answer, and anticipate all of the important socio-legal questions. The existence of alternative analyses, however, indicates that there are gaps and weaknesses in mainstream approaches. During recent years, critical race theory (CRT) has developed as an alternative approach to traditional legal analysis. CRT provides a framework for assessing whether the law promotes social justice. Its mandate is to identify the overt and covert ways in which race affects the identification, interpretation, and resolution of socio-legal problems.

CRT, the focus of this chapter, is ripe for discussion and analysis. Not only is it a new theoretical approach, it also challenges the dominant view of the appropriate legal remedies for racial discrimination and racism (e.g., civil rights legislation). Furthermore, CRT questions how *race, racism,* and *racial discrimination* should be defined. The novelty of CRT, however, does not end here. The goal of the CRT approach is to meld theory and practice, thereby narrowing the gap between what theory is and how theory operates in the real world.

With the goal of making CRT more accessible, this chapter explores three areas: (1) a historical overview of CRT scholarship beginning with the critical legal studies (CLS) movement; (2) application of CRT to a contemporary sociological fact—racial hoaxes; and (3) a critique of CRT and its policy implications.

■ Critical Race Theory: Background, Theoretical Underpinnings, and a Little History

The story of CRT begins, in part, with the story of the CLS movement. Critical legal scholarship, which emerged during the 1970s, criticized the methods and objectivity of mainstream legal analysis. Critical legal scholars, heirs to the legal realism movement, demonstrated how legal analysis is consistently and predictably used to rationalize inequality (Crenshaw et al. 1995: xviii). For example, CLS questioned the conventional legal wisdom that women occupied a "separate sphere," a rationale used to justify women's exclusion from professional employment (Taub and Schneider 1998). Critical legal scholars concluded that status quo legal orthodoxy often is presented as objective legal reasoning.

Critical legal scholars have applied their methods to a wide array of legal fields including labor law, anti-discrimination law, and gender equality (Kairys 1998). As CLS scholarship developed to include nearly every field of law, the diversity of its membership expanded as well. What began as a critique by white male law professors at Ivy League law schools later expanded to include professors from varied backgrounds, races, and institutions (Russell 1994).

CLS scholarship is organized around several principles including indeterminacy, anti-formalism, and marginality. *Indeterminacy* refers to the belief that the law does not operate in a systematic manner; that is, the law does not ensure predictable outcomes in similar cases. *Anti-formalism* refers to the inability of the law to be either value free or objective; for example, our laws and how they are applied reinforce our value systems, indicating some subjectivity. The principle of *marginality* questions how significant the law is in controlling social behavior; specifically, it asks what other factors, besides the law, affect whether a person will obey or violate the law (Trubek 1984: 1577-79).

For those dissatisfied with traditional legal critiques, CLS came as a welcome change. For others, CLS fell short. Specifically, for academics attempting to make sense of the interplay among race, law, and social structure, the CLS approach ultimately was unsatisfying. During the late 1970s, a number of academics criticized CLS for overlooking the role that race plays in legal reasoning. During this time period, there was a growing dissatisfaction with the civil rights model for racial and social reform. Together, these two factors propelled CRT scholarship. Scholars analyzing the role of law in facilitating racial progress sought to make sense of a racial hierarchy that continues to leave minorities at the bottom. The next subsection outlines and evaluates the elements of CRT.

☐ Components of an Emerging Theoretical Perspective

The first writings that could be labeled critical race theory appeared during the mid-1970s. Derrick Bell wrote several articles addressing the road-blocks embedded in the traditional legal strategies for racial reform. Bell was among the first legal scholars to conclude that new approaches were neces-sary to combat entrenched racism. Contrary to CLS, which primarily explores class and gender issues, CRT scholarship is unblinkingly focused on race. Largely the result of Bell's early writings, a new line of legal analysis and inquiry, later dubbed *critical race theory,* developed (Crenshaw 1988).

What is CRT? First, it takes as given several of the CLS principles. Its explicit goals, however, are found in two constituent parts. First, CRT exam-ines how white supremacy and the subordination of people of color have been created and maintained in the United States. Critical race scholars look at the relationship among the social structure, the rule of law, and equal pro-tection. Second, critical race theorists go beyond documenting how racial privilege and power operate within the law. Their goal is to change and ulti-mately balance out racial relationships. CRT, then, strives to be trans-formative (Crenshaw et al. 1995:xiii). It is this second component that sets CRT apart from traditional social theory.

The twin aims of CRT are undergirded by several assumptions including the following:

- Racism is normal, not aberrant.
- Racial advances for minorities will take place only if they also benefit whites.
- Challenges to the mainstream legal analysis can be made in a variety of writing formats.

The first assumption is based on the determination that although there has been remarkable racial progress, much remains unchanged. Extreme forms of racism and race discrimination have been eliminated (e.g., voting rights legis-lation, school desegregation); however, quieter forms persist (e.g., police abuse against minorities).

Bell's early scholarship addressed the core of the second premise (Bell 1992b). For example, in his historical analysis of race relations, Bell finds that civil rights advances for blacks do not occur in a vacuum. He examines the 19th-century debate at the heart of the Civil War—whether black slaves should be emancipated. A review of historical documents reveals that for Abraham Lincoln, abolishing slavery was a means to an end.[1] This, as well as other historical factors, led Bell to conclude that racial progress is the result of competing interests (Bell 1992b). There are numerous contemporary examples of this principle including the debates surrounding passage of the Civil Rights Act of 1964 and the Voting Rights Act of 1965, affirmative action legislation, Black History Month, and a national holiday in honor of Martin Luther King, Jr.'s birthday.

The third CRT assumption is that developing an alternative legal analysis of social justice requires alternative legal and empirical methods. For example, critical race scholars adopt nontraditional writing styles (e.g., allegory first-person narratives, hypotheticals, anecdotes) as well as standard legal analysis. One of the better known examples of the storytelling approach is "The Space Traders" (Bell 1992a:158-200; see also Bell 1987). In Bell's science fiction-inspired hypothetical, aliens appear on earth to make an offer to the U.S. government. In exchange for the entire black population, the visitors will provide the government with the solutions to all societal ills including a bailout of the federal savings and loans and restoration of the ozone layer. Bell's story presents the twists and turns of the debates over whether the offer should be accepted. He uses this unconventional format to discuss history and race relations and to explore contemporary issues of race.

The Rodrigo Chronicles offers another example of legal storytelling. These stories, written by Richard Delgado, present an ongoing debate between a new and a seasoned minority law professor (Delgado 1995b). Their wide-ranging discussions explore affirmative action, "white crime," race, and civil rights legislation. Delgado's choice of format allows for a lively and probing debate of these issues. Otherwise, Delgado's illuminating critique might have been lost in formalistic legal language.

Patricia Williams's work offers another example of an alternative to traditional legal writing. She often combines personal narratives, biographies, and anecdotes in her legal analyses. For example, in one well-known piece, Williams (1987) explores the effect of subtle racism on the psyche and its potential for inciting violence. To underscore her point, she recounts her experience of being denied entry into a clothing store because of her race. Williams (1991) explains her reaction: "I was enraged. At that moment, I literally wanted to break all the windows in the store and *take* lots of sweaters" (p. 45, emphasis in original). Her writing style allows her to both raise abstract socio-legal questions, such as whether racism causes psychological harm. It also allows her to incorporate her personal experience into her conclusions. In addition, it provides a testimonial anecdote.

Whereas writings by Bell, Delgado, and Williams provide examples of nontraditional scholarship, two points should be noted. First, their work, as well as most critical race scholarship, is written in standard legal form. Second, critical race theorists are not the only scholars to employ narratives, hypotheticals, and other forms of legal writing (Fuller 1949; Morris 1990). Nontraditional writing styles have long been used to provide different ways in which to probe readers to think differently about both new and old legal concepts.

☐ *A Critique of the Critical Race Theory Critique*

Those who are critical of CRT generally raise one of three points: (1) whether CRT is a legitimate theory, (2) whether CRT offers a new and useful understanding of how the law and the world operate regarding race, or (3) whether CRT offers something substantive.

Those who raise the first point observe that, in some ways, CRT is an anathema to traditional definitions of theory. They note that CRT lacks a clear operational definition and methods. Furthermore, there does not appear to be a single canon to which all critical race theorists subscribe. Given this, they ask whether CRT is properly described as a theory. And yes, it is, because CRT does exactly what a good theory should do. It tells us how the world operates (Delgado 1995a). To avoid the pitfall of rigid theoretical structures, some suggest that CRT might be more appropriately labeled critical race *studies*. One researcher aptly summarizes this approach:

> The term *critical race theory* is a misnomer because the phenomenon really serves as a site of contestation and debate rather than as a school of thought with an overarching replicable theoretical formulation. In this regard, it is more precise to say that there is a group of intellectuals in the field of law, critical race theorists, who choose to do a certain type of scholarship—critical race scholarship. (Hackney 1998:141, n. 1, emphasis in original)

Second, some have taken issue with the core of CRT scholarship—its focus on race. These critics note that an "essentialist" approach that emphasizes race overlooks other important variables (e.g., class, gender). Furthermore, those in the second camp ask whether a CRT approach might be better considered a part of other theoretical approaches (e.g., postmodernism, feminist legal theory).

Those who raise the third point question whether there is any substance to CRT. They have criticized its dense prose, labeling it academic mumbo-jumbo (Rosen 1996). A look at some of the early CRT writings lends some support to this criticism. Much of what is now classified as CRT, however, is written in accessible academic prose.

Those who are opposed to CRT also dismiss it as elitist. These detractors argue that the viewpoints of critical race theorists, who are mostly "ivory tower" academics, are as elitist as the legal paradigm they seek to challenge. Some critics appear to question the credulity of some arguments raised by critical race proponents. Others label it racist.[2] Notably, CRT has encountered many of the same criticisms that were leveled against CLS (Russell 1994). With the preceding background, definitions, and criticisms of CRT in mind, the next section demonstrates how CRT can be applied.

■ Applied Critical Race Theory

The CRT approach joins theory and practice. Its practicality and usefulness are regularly tested because it is applied to evaluate contemporary socio-legal problems. Furthermore, this critique can be used to *identify* a social problem. Critical race theorists are uniquely situated not only to analyze existing social problems but also to identify new ones. The next subsection applies CRT methods to evaluate racial hoaxes.

□ Susan Smith and Racial Hoaxes

In the fall of 1994, the nation watched, transfixed, as the tale of Susan Smith unfolded. Smith, who is white, told police that she had been carjacked by a young black man. According to Smith, she was forced out of her vehicle by a man who then drove off with her young sons, buckled securely in the back seat. These claims sparked massive air and ground searches for the boys, the carjacker, and the car. An all-points bulletin was issued based on Smith's description—a black man, between 20 and 30 years old, wearing a skull cap. Smith went on national television and pleaded for the safe return of her boys. In addition, the police department in Union, South Carolina, received assistance from the Federal Bureau of Investigation (FBI). Smith's detailed account placed the town's black community immediately under suspicion.

Nine days after her initial carjacking tale, Smith confessed to murdering her sons. In a fit of depression over a recent breakup with a boyfriend, Smith placed her boys in the back seat of her car, fastened their seat belts, drove to the John D. Long lake, got out of the car, released the emergency brake, and watched the car plunge into the lake. Less than one year later, Smith was convicted of murder and sentenced to life in prison.

Mainstream legal critiques of the Smith case centered on the murder of the two boys. Specifically, once Smith confessed, the focus shifted away from finding the "young black male" whom she had identified as her attacker to determining whether she should receive the death penalty for her crime. This standard approach left very little room to raise or address the issue of Smith's hoax and the law's failure to sanction it. CRT, however, offers a useful method for bridging this legal gap in analysis.

Looking at the same set of facts, a critical race approach would consider several questions including the following:

- What is the appropriate criminal justice system response to Smith's fabricated carjacker?
- How should the law weigh the fact that Smith portrayed her attacker as black?
- What are the sociological impacts of Smith's fabrication on the black community (local and national), the white community, and society in general?
- Are there other cases similar to Smith's?

Contrary to most legal analyses of the Smith case, these questions offer a broad framework within which to consider racial hoaxes. They allow for an analysis that considers both micro- and macro-level effects of racial scapegoating. The next subsections attempt to address these issues by applying CRT to racial hoaxes.

Defining a Racial Hoax

First, what is a racial hoax? A racial hoax is defined as "when someone fabricates a crime and blames it on another person because of his race or when an actual crime has been committed and the perpetrator falsely blames someone because of his race" (Russell 1998:70). As this definition indicates, some hoaxes are used to conceal crimes. Another type of hoax is not created to cover up a crime; instead, it is simply a fictitious report created for any number of reasons. Examples include faking an assault to get attention from a loved one and creating a fictional criminal to hide an embarrassing incident

TABLE 3.1 Overview of Racial Hoaxes, 1987-1996

Race of Offender/Victim	Number of Hoax Cases
White perpetrator/black victim	47
Black perpetrator/white victim	11
White perpetrator/white victim	2
Black perpetrator/black victim	7
Other hoaxes[a]	7

a. The "other" figure represents cases with perpetrators and victims who were neither black nor white.

such as an accidental shooting. The majority of hoax cases fall into the latter category. During the past decade, there have been more than 65 reported racial hoax cases (Russell 1998). As Table 3.1 indicates, the majority of these incidents involve white individuals who falsely accused black individuals of committing crimes.

Racial hoaxes are not a contemporary phenomenon. The 1932 Scottsboro boys case, which involved false allegations that six black boys had raped two white girls, is one of the more notorious examples. In addition, the claim that a white woman had been sexually assaulted by a black man led to the Rosewood massacre in 1923.

Notably, the issue of racial hoaxes has escaped mainstream research attention. Given the CRT premise that the law reinforces and perpetuates the dominant structure, CRT would predict that racial hoaxes would be overlooked. Furthermore, hoaxes reflect one of the theory's underlying assumptions that racism (e.g., racial fingerpointing involved in hoax cases) is the rule rather than the exception.

Hoax Characteristics

Contemporary racial hoax cases have several noteworthy characteristics, including the following:

- Approximately 70 percent involved white perpetrators.
- Hoax perpetrators were charged with filing false police reports in less than half of the cases.

- Hoax perpetrators varied by race, socioeconomic status, geographic region, and age.
- In approximately one-third of the cases, innocent persons were stopped, questioned, and/or arrested.
- Most hoaxes were not created to cover up actual crimes.

As these characteristics indicate, hoaxes cannot be dismissed as a practice engaged in by a fringe group. Hoax perpetrators are white and black, of various ages and incomes, male and female, and hoaxes occur across the nation. An in-depth look at hoax cases reveals several interesting trends. First, many of the hoaxes were fabricated by law enforcement officials. In some instances, hoaxes were used to cover up crimes (e.g., murders); in others, they were used to hide work-related incidents (e.g., scuffles). One incident involved a state trooper who accidently shot herself with her service revolver. Rather than tell the truth and face possible embarrassment, she created a hoax to explain her injury. In another case, two white police officers had a fistfight over who would file a case report. Both men were injured in the fight, which several other officers witnessed. The officers then blamed their fight-related injuries on a fictional black man.

One of the striking features of the reported hoaxes is that 55 percent involved persons who completely fabricated the crimes. In most cases, the perpetrators were not attempting to cover up actual crimes; rather, they used the hoaxes for some other goals. For example, some perpetrators created hoaxes (e.g., sexual assault) to get time off from work, to get attention from spouses, or to avoid getting in trouble for violating curfews.

Black-on-White Hoaxes

As noted, hoaxes involving black perpetrators represent only a fraction of the overall cases. These cases, however, reveal an interesting pattern. Nearly all of them were fabricated as hate crimes; that is, blacks told the police that they were targeted because of their race. For example, some claimed that their homes or cars had been defaced with racial epithets. The Tawana Brawley case is the best-known example of a black-on-white hoax. In this case, a 15-year-old black girl told police that she had been sexually assaulted by a group of white men. Brawley stated that one of the men wore a police badge. She said that she was placed in a garbage bag and smeared with feces. Brawley's claims, later determined to be a hoax, set off a firestorm of racial controversy and years of legal battles.

Social and Economic Costs

The bizarre circumstances of many hoax cases might cause some people to dismiss their seriousness. In reading the details of these incidents, however, one is quickly impressed with their potential for damage. Several types of harm result from racial hoaxes. The first category involves psychological injury, and the second involves economic costs. There are many forms of psychological damage that a racial hoax can produce. For example, each time an interracial hoax is used, it widens the gulf between blacks and whites. Although Smith's carjacking hoax eventually was uncovered, a great deal of damage already had been done. The long-standing suspicion that many blacks have of whites who claim they were victimized by blacks was aroused. Furthermore, Smith's hoax reenergized white fear of black crime. Beyond this, racial hoaxes also *create* stereotypes for young people. For example, consider the impact of the Smith case on children who had never before experienced a hoax case.

Hoaxes also exact a high economic toll. These costs include the wasted police resources used to investigate hoaxes such as interviewing witnesses and potential suspects, enlisting the aid of local media, and (when necessary) enlisting outside assistance (e.g., the FBI). There were estimates that police spent close to $1 million investigating the Smith case. In a few of the reported cases in which hoax perpetrators have been found guilty of filing false reports, they have been required to repay the costs of police investigations of their cases.

The Legal Response

What has been the law's response to racial hoaxes? Silence. Racial hoaxes have attracted very little legal attention; that is, there is no law that specifically punishes someone who engages in a racial hoax. A hoax perpetrator could be charged with filing a false report. This happened in less than one-half of the cases, making deterrence unlikely.

Furthermore, even if false report charges were filed more systematically, this still would not address the racial aspect of hoaxes. For example, even if Smith had been charged with filing a false report under South Carolina law (she was not charged), this would have had little impact. A generic, misdemeanor false report charge is no match for the harm Smith caused to the black community in Union, the larger black community, and black-white race relations in general.

Whether a law specifically designed to punish perpetrators of racial hoaxes would lead to a decrease in the number of hoaxes is an empirical question. A proposed New Jersey law would take us one step closer toward an answer. New Jersey legislators have considered adopting a law that would punish hoax offenders. Specifically, the proposed law would punish anyone who fabricates a hoax and blames it on another person because of his or her race, color, or ethnicity. This legislation, introduced by State Senator Shirley Turner, carries with it a maximum three- to five-year prison term and a maximum fine of $7,500. If passed, this groundbreaking law would represent one of the few attempts to punish hoax offenders. Equally as important, it would provide a starting point for evaluating increased sanctions for hoax perpetrators, thereby making it transformative, one of CRT's core tenets.

Third, because very little is known about hoaxes, no uniform legal response has emerged. There are no national data on their incidence, prevalence, and related sanctions. Some offenders have faced stiff sanctions, including restitution in the amount of police costs of investigation. All told, the "big picture" of racial hoaxes has not yet been drawn. As the overview of reported hoax cases makes clear, a more complete picture is essential in determining the extent of the racial hoax phenomenon.

In addition, racial hoaxes do not exist in a vacuum. They are one form of "race-blaming" crimes. For example, there have been reported incidents of white criminals who have burglarized white homes and demanded that their victims tell the police that the robbers were black (Russell 1998:84). In another odd twist on the racial hoax phenomenon, police uncovered a burglary ring involving a band of white men. The burglars would place mud on their faces so as to appear "black." Cases such as these indicate how widespread and deeply rooted racial scapegoating is. Furthermore, these incidents, like classic racial hoaxes, reproduce a language and climate of interracial mistrust. They also offer strong support for punishing racial hoaxes as part of a larger problem.

■ Discussion and Policy Implications

From a policy perspective, there are both practical and symbolic strengths in applying CRT to socio-legal problems that are not available in applying mainstream analyses. First, CRT analysis is not limited to existing laws or social problems. Traditional models of social and legal theory evaluate *existing* social problems. Consequently, it is easy to see how racial hoaxes have escaped traditional legal analyses. CRT, however, encourages researchers to anticipate social problems (Butler 1995). Furthermore, as the analysis of hoaxes indicates, CRT moves the discussion beyond individual isolated cases.

Second, a CRT approach is, by definition, interdisciplinary. A look at the body of critical race scholarship indicates that it draws from a wide range of disciplines including sociology, criminology, law, anthropology, political science, and economics. This approach encourages cross-fertilization across disciplines, thereby enhancing the link between theory and practice.

Third, CRT offers one of the few theoretical approaches that explicitly addresses race. Furthermore, it does not treat "race" as a synonym for dysfunction. As the discussion of racial hoaxes makes clear, the benefits of CRT are more than practical. Applying CRT sends a clear message that it is important to address racial harms, both overt and subtle.

More remarkable, CRT does not limit its investigation of race to blacks. Critical race scholarship also includes analyses of issues addressing whites, Latinos, American Indians, and Asian Americans. In many instances, CRT analyses address more than one racial group.

There are many reasons to apply a critical race approach to social problems. The strongest reason, however, emerges when we consider what would happen if we did not incorporate CRT into our analyses. The failure to consider the role that race plays in identifying and resolving social issues would make for limited, and ultimately ineffective, legal and empirical responses. As noted, CRT acknowledges the role that race plays in contemporary American society. In sum, CRT offers a series of bridges—those among racial groups, academic disciplines, and theory and practice—to evaluate the intersections of race, law, and social science. CRT is a breath of fresh air.

STUDY QUESTIONS

1. What are some other examples of social phenomena, beyond racial hoaxes, to which CRT could be applied?
2. How does CRT compare to other criminological theories discussed in this textbook? Select one and compare and contrast the relative strengths and weaknesses of CRT.
3. Are there ways in which existing criminological theories might be strengthened to respond to the concerns raised by critical

race theorists? Choose one theory and describe how it might be modified to include a critical race theory component.

NOTES

1. In a letter to a friend, Lincoln wrote, "My paramount object in this struggle is to save the Union and is not either to save or to destroy slavery. If I could save the Union without freeing any slave, I would do it; and if I could save it by freeing all the slaves, I would do it; and if I could save it by freeing some and leaving others alone, I would also do that" (quoted in Bell 1992b:9).
2. "Critical race theory is providing an intellectual foundation for newly flourishing forms of black separateness" (Lewis 1997).

REFERENCES

Bell, Derrick. 1987. *And We Are Not Saved: The Elusive Quest for Racial Justice.* New York: Basic Books.

———. 1992a. *Faces at the Bottom of the Well: The Permanence of Racism.* New York: Basic Books.

———. 1992b. *Race, Racism, and American Law.* Boston: Little, Brown.

Butler, Paul. 1995. "Race-Based Jury Nullification." *Yale Law Journal* 105:677.

Crenshaw, Kimberle. 1988. "Race, Reform, and Retrenchment: Transformation and Legitimation in Anti-discrimination Law." *Harvard Law Review* 101:1331-87.

Crenshaw, Kimberle, Neil Gotanda, Gary Peller, and Kendall Thomas. 1995. *Critical Race Theory: The Key Writings That Formed the Movement.* New York: New Press.

Delgado, Richard. 1995a. *Critical Race Theory: The Cutting Edge.* Philadelphia: Temple University Press.

———. 1995b. *The Rodrigo Chronicles: Conversations About America and Race.* New York: New York University Press.

Fuller, Lon. 1949. "The Speluncean Explorers." *Harvard Law Review* 62:612-45.

Hackney, James R. 1998. "Derrick Bell's Re-sounding: W. E. B. DuBois, Modernism, and Critical Race Scholarship." *Law and Social Inquiry* 23:141-64.

Kairys, David. 1998. *The Politics of Law.* New York: Pantheon.

Lewis, Neil A. 1997. "For Black Scholars Wedded to Prism of Race." *New York Times,* 5 May.

Rosen, Jeffrey. 1996. "Bloods and the Crits: O. J. Simpson, Critical Race Theory, American Law, and the Triumph of Color in America." *New Republic,* 9 December, 27-42.

Russell, Katheryn K. 1994. "A Critical View From the Inside: An Application of Critical Legal Studies to Criminal Law." *Journal of Criminal Law and Criminology* 85:222-40.

———. 1998. *The Color of Crime: Racial Hoaxes, White Fear, Black Protectionism, Police Harassment, and Other Macroaggressions.* New York: New York University Press.

Taub, Nadine and Elizabeth M. Schneider. 1998. "Women's Subordination and the Role of Law." Pp. 151-76 in *The Politics of Law,* edited by David Kairys. New York: Pantheon.

Trubek, David. 1984. "Where the Action Is: Critical Legal Studies and Empiricism." *Stanford Law Review* 36:1575.

Williams, Patricia. 1987. "Spirit-Murdering the Messenger: The Discourse of Fingerpointing as the Law's Response to Racism." *University of Miami Law Review* 42:127.

———. 1991. *Alchemy of Race and Rights.* Cambridge, MA: Harvard University Press.

CHAPTER 4

The War on Crime as Hegemonic Strategy
A Neo-Marxian Theory of the New Punitiveness in U.S. Criminal Justice Policy

KATHERINE BECKETT
THEODORE SASSON

Three strikes and you're out. Chain gangs. Boot camps. The recent adoption of these and other anti-crime programs and policies reveals the increasingly punitive nature of public policy in the United States. Throughout the 1980s and 1990s, both the federal government and the states adopted a variety of such "get tough" measures and encouraged the police and prosecutors to intensify their efforts to apprehend and punish lawbreakers, particularly drug offenders. As a result, the number of prison and jail inmates grew from 500,000 in 1980 to more than 1.8 million in 1998.[1] The United States now has the largest penal system and one of the highest incarceration rates in the world, exceeding average European levels by 5 to 10 times.[2] More people are locked up in the United States for drug offenses (about 400,000) than are incarcerated for any crimes in England, France, Germany, and Japan combined.[3]

Contrary to popular perception, the aggressive practices and punitive policies that led to the expansion of the U.S. prison and jail populations are not the direct result of a worsening or an exceptionally bad crime problem. Although U.S. rates of lethal violence are high and some types of crime have become more worrisome, rates of violent and property crime, as measured in annual surveys administered by the Department of Justice, have been in decline for most of the period in which the government has waged its war on crime.[4] Furthermore, in comparison with other less punitive countries, the United States does not stand out as especially crime-ridden.[5] In short, the adoption of "get tough" crime and drug policies, and the expansion of the penal system that they have caused, is not simply a consequence of rising or unusually high crime rates.

In this chapter, we draw on the theoretical perspective developed by neo-Marxian political theorist Antonio Gramsci to explain the punitive turn in criminal justice policymaking. Gramsci's political sociology rests on the concept of hegemony—the ideological basis for the domination of a ruling class. Following Gramsci, we argue that the adoption of punitive anti-crime and -drug policies is best understood as a core component of a ruling class "hegemonic strategy." In particular, we argue that political representatives of the capitalist class responded to the upheavals of the 1960s and 1970s by attempting to secure hegemony around a vision of government that divests the state of responsibility for social welfare but emphasizes its obligation to provide "security" against foreign and domestic threats. To mobilize support for this form of governance, these political actors argued that welfare worsened poverty and crime, and they portrayed the poor as dangerous and undeserving. Policies that cut welfare payments and caseloads and that lead to the expansion of the penal system reflect the success of this hegemonic strategy.

Our Gramscian argument thus emphasizes the leadership of the capitalist class and its political representatives in generating support for getting tough on crime. We therefore contrast our argument with a Durkheimian perspective that explains growing criminal justice punitiveness in terms of the public's reaction to crime. And in the spirit of criticism that infuses Gramsci's work, we conclude the chapter with critical assessments of both the dramatic expansion of the state penal system and the theory of hegemony used here to explain it.

■ A Neo-Marxian Theory of Hegemony

Before introducing the theoretical contributions of Gramsci, we need to describe the basic elements of the Marxian theory from which Gramsci drew much of his inspiration. In the Marxian perspective, societies are characterized by class conflict rooted in relations of production. In capitalist societies, the central conflict is between capitalists who own the means of production (land, factories, etc.) and workers who must sell their labor for a wage. The logic of capitalist development, with its emphasis on competition and profit maximization, is toward ever greater exploitation of workers by capitalists. Stabilizing the potentially explosive nature of this social arrangement, however, are the major social institutions (the "superstructure") such as schools and the legal system.

Shaped and staffed by the capitalist class and its supporters, these institutions generate ideological support for—and defend by force when necessary—the prevailing relations of production (i.e., capitalism). Marxian theories of education therefore focus on the transmission of class status through schools, arguing that these educational institutions reproduce the unequal social relations that characterize capitalist society.[6] Similarly, Marxian theories of criminal justice focus on the role that penal institutions play in the reproduction of capitalist social relations.[7] And (some) Marxian theories of politics examine the mechanisms by which members of the capitalist class constitute a "ruling class" that, through their political representatives, controls the state.[8]

Gramsci's unique contribution to Marxian thought was to underscore a basic distinction in the means by which capitalist ruling classes secure their social positions. In strong Eastern states, Gramsci argued, governments relied on force and coercion to ensure the compliance of the masses. By contrast, Western elites in advanced capitalist societies lacked a similarly strong state apparatus and therefore relied on cultural mechanisms to secure popular cooperation and consent.[9] According to this formulation, then, (Eastern) societies characterized by strong and coercive states rely predominantly on force to secure the cooperation of the masses, whereas in (Western) countries that lack strong and coercive states, hegemony is secured through cultural and ideological mechanisms. Implicit in this argument is the notion that consent and coercion are mutually exclusive methods of securing the dominant position of the capitalist class.

Much of Gramsci's work examined the ideological mechanisms by which social relations were reproduced in Western capitalist societies such as the United States.[10] Gramsci argued that in these societies, characterized by weak states but highly developed mass media and educational institutions, the ruling classes typically secured their positions by leading in the cultural and political spheres—in "civil society"—rather than by imposing their authority through the brute force of the police or military: "The state, when it wants to initiate an unpopular action or policy, creates in advance a suitable or appropriate public opinion; that is, it organizes and centralizes certain elements of civil society."[11] To the extent that subordinated social groups tolerate the status quo, they do so in part because they accept ruling class definitions of social reality—definitions that invariably depict capitalist society as the most free, democratic, egalitarian, and productive social arrangement.

In the Gramscian view, the ruling class wins popular consent through hegemonic "projects" or "strategies" that seek to generate and solidify popular support for capitalist social relations.[12] For example, Gramsci identified "Fordism" as the leading hegemonic strategy in the United States during the 1930s.[13] Named after the labor management approach adopted by Henry Ford, Fordism emphasized the need for both worker productivity and mass consumption. At his plants, Ford enforced strict rules to ensure that his employees were as productive as possible, but he also paid generously so that his workers could afford to purchase the products they produced. These priorities also were embraced in the Keynesian social and economic policies to be discussed shortly.

Gramsci also deepened the Marxian analysis of the political process by focusing on struggles and rivalries between segments of the ruling class. In capitalist countries, "fractions" of the ruling class, together with their political representatives, vie with one another for control over the state. In the struggles that ensue, the contending blocs sometimes seek to mobilize popular support around rival visions of the roles and purposes of the state. These rival visions necessarily entail defense of private property and the capitalist system (this is what makes them "hegemonic") but envision different ways of accomplishing these goals. The particular ideological inflection or version of hegemony therefore is susceptible to change in ways that reflect the ongoing contest between segments of the ruling class.

Gramsci did not assume that all attempts to secure hegemony would be successful. Rather, he argued that popular common sense, rooted in the lived experience and cultural beliefs of regular people, limits the range of viable hegemonic strategies.[14] The ruling class leads in the sphere of culture and politics but not along any road it chooses. The challenge faced by the ruling class—to craft a form of leadership that secures ruling class interests while simultaneously winning popular consent—is a formidable one. Furthermore, Gramsci argued that hegemonic strategies succeed only partially and provisionally. The popular classes retain some degree of skepticism regarding the legitimacy of prevailing arrangements. And during periods of political or economic crisis, this skepticism can rapidly expand into full-blown opposition:

If the ruling class had lost its consensus, i.e., is no longer "leading" but only "dominant," exercising coercive force alone, this means precisely that the great masses have become detached from their traditional ideologies and no longer believe what they used to believe previously, etc. The crisis consists precisely in the fact that the old is dying and the new cannot be born.[15]

In Gramsci's view, such crises can be resolved only through the elaboration of a new hegemony, either by the forces of political insurgency (in the case of a full-blown revolution) or by a resurgent segment of the ruling class.

■ From Welfare State to Security State

In the United States, ruling elites have been able to reestablish hegemony despite serious challenges to the legitimacy of the existing political and economic system. The Great Depression that began in 1929 caused widespread discontent with U.S. capitalism, but this discontent did not culminate in a revolutionary challenge. Instead, beginning during the 1930s, the dominant segment of the U.S. ruling class shored up the capitalist social order by pursuing Keynesian welfare state and New Deal social policies. The term *Keynesian* (after British economist John Maynard Keynes) refers to economic policies that mitigate the tendency of capitalist economies to swing violently from boom and bust by sustaining worker demand for products across business cycles. Keynesian strategies thus included countercyclical government spending, worker health and safety laws, a minimum wage, and social security.[16] New Deal (and later Great Society) social policies similarly aimed at ameliorating poverty and related social problems through social work and means-tested relief programs such as Aid to Families with Dependent Children (AFDC).[17] (The welfare state's social policy initiatives also included substantial subsidies for the middle class including financing for home ownership and extension of roads and services to new middle class suburbs.) Finally, in the sphere of criminal justice, the welfare state expressed itself through a rhetorical emphasis on the social causes of crime and the need to rehabilitate and reintegrate offenders.[18] In its heyday, then, the welfare state secured the consent of the governed through its emphasis on inclusion and mutual social responsibility as well as scientific planning and risk management.

This hegemonic strategy worked relatively well for several decades. But the late 1960s and early 1970s were a period of tremendous upheaval and political challenge. Civil rights protesters, initially focusing on desegregating the South and enfranchising southern blacks, eventually moved north and challenged national labor, housing, and education practices through increasingly militant tactics.[19] At the same time, the mobilization against the Vietnam War challenged the legitimacy of the state and its political leadership.[20] The youthful counterculture rejected middle class values of sobriety, respect for authority, and patriotism in ways that were disturbing to the more conventionally inclined.[21] The "welfare rights" movement galvanized poor people to demand expanded governmental relief and enroll in poverty relief schemes in unprecedented numbers.[22] And the feminist movement challenged the legitimacy of the traditional family and, later, focused on the expansion of women's reproductive rights, especially the right to choose abortion.[23] Taken as a whole, these protest movements constituted a serious "counter-hegemonic" challenge to prevailing social and economic arrangements.[24] Meanwhile, the robust economic growth that underpinned the extension of citizenship rights and benefits since the 1930s became alarmingly sluggish.[25]

In this crisis-laden context, conservative politicians and intellectuals, representing the fears and interests of economic and social elites, counterattacked.[26] Some, later referred to as "neoliberals," were more accepting of social changes such as alternative lifestyles and families but staunchly opposed the economic reforms sought by the welfare and civil rights movements. Those dubbed "neoconservatives" focused more on social issues and sought to reinstate traditional authority structures such as the patriarchal family. Despite these differences, these political actors were united in their opposition to the expansion—or even the continuation—of Keynesian economic policies and the welfare state, especially those programs aimed at ameliorating poverty.[27] Indeed, the attack on welfare served as a lynchpin that united neoliberals opposed to Keynesianism and the welfare state with neoconservatives concerned about social liberalism and alternative family structures.[28]

Together, these political actors intensified their critique of redistributive social policies and, more generally, the claim that the government is obligated to ameliorate poverty and reduce social inequalities. To discredit the welfare state, they argued that welfare breeds "dependence" and linked welfare spending with a host of social problems including crime, poverty, and illegitimacy. In the words of Nixon administration adviser Daniel Patrick Moynihan,

> Among a large and growing lower class, self-reliance, self-discipline, and industry are waning. . . . Families are more and more matrifocal and atomized;

crime and disorder are sharply on the rise. . . . It is a stirring, if generally unrecognized, demonstration of the power of the welfare machine.[29]

According to this argument, welfare does not ameliorate poverty but rather worsens it by rewarding "parasitism," undermining self-reliance, and weakening the traditional (i.e., patriarchal) family. Furthermore, conservatives argued that by undermining the work ethic, welfare causes rather than alleviates crime. (In fact, the available evidence does not support this claim; greater welfare spending is associated with lower—not higher—levels of crime.[30])

Unlike the elites who secured hegemony during the 1930s through policies aimed at integrating and enhancing the security of the socially marginal, conservatives during the late 1960s sought to discredit those who sought access to mainstream society. For example, conservatives combined criticism of the welfare state with attacks on civil rights challengers, depicting them as criminals rather than as legitimate political opponents.[31] Conservatives also worked to alter popular conceptions of the poor; whereas the rhetoric that gave rise to New Deal and (during the 1960s) Great Society welfare initiatives depicted the poor as "just like us," conservatives during the 1960s painted a picture of the poor as dangerous and undeserving. The conservative emphasis on the dangers of "street crime," widely associated with poverty, was crucial to this attempt to reconfigure the popular image of the poor.

During the 1980s, with lavish support from big business, right-wing politicians and policy "think tanks" (e.g., the Heritage Foundation) refined the conservative critique of the welfare state and developed an alternative model for state-society relations.[32] President Reagan, for example, argued that his liberal predecessors had distorted government's functions. The state, he argued, would be on more legitimate constitutional grounds—and would help the poor more effectively—if it reduced poverty relief and expanded law enforcement:

This is precisely what we're trying to do to the bloated federal government today: remove it from interfering in areas where it doesn't belong, but at the same time strengthen[ing] its ability to perform its constitutional and legitimate functions. In the area of public order and law enforcement, for example, we're reversing a dangerous trend of the last decade. While crime was steadily increasing, the federal commitment in terms of personnel was steadily shrinking.[33]

Conservatives propounded an alternative mode of governance that included, among its core elements, reduced social welfare guarantees and expenditures, weakened state management of business (i.e., deregulation), and increased emphasis on security from threatening others (both foreign and domestic). We describe the mode of governance that resulted from this new hegemonic strategy as the "security state." The security state combines neoliberal economic "reforms," such as weakened provisions for the poor and deregulation, with the social policies favored by conservatives. These social policies are aimed at shoring up traditional authority structures and the capacity of the state to cope with a wide range of social ills through policing and punishment. Thus, the security state is, in our view, a hegemonic project of the ruling class, spearheaded by political conservatives (neoliberals and social conservatives) in response to the various challenges of the late 1960s and early 1970s.

As part of this new hegemonic strategy, the wars on crime and drugs are simultaneously ideological and practical; they are mechanisms for winning the consent of the majority and are ways of governing with important material and institutional consequences. From an ideological standpoint, the rhetoric and policies of the wars on crime and drugs have transformed the symbolic meaning of poverty, thereby legitimating the replacement of the welfare state with the security state. As noted, in debates surrounding New Deal and Great Society anti-poverty initiatives, the poor often were depicted sympathetically as people "in trouble." By contrast, in the context of the wars on crime and drugs, the poor are symbolically transformed into an "underclass" of criminals and addicts—into people who "make trouble."[34] Thus, the moral status of the poor was changed from "deserving" to "undeserving," and as a consequence, the moral foundation of the welfare state was undermined.[35] At the same time, the sense that the poor were dangerous and menacing (rather than sympathetic) legitimated the dramatic expansion of the police, courts, and prisons.

Notably, this transformation of the moral status of the poor was predicated on a change in the identity of the prototypical poor person from white and rural (in the imagery of the Great Depression and the war on poverty) to black and urban (in the iconography of the wars on crime and drugs).[36] Republican politicians targeting white working class constituencies historically loyal to the Democratic party played a key role in this process. Republicans courted these new constituencies through the use of racially charged "code words" or phrases and symbols that "refer indirectly to racial themes but do not directly challenge popular democratic or egalitarian ideals."[37]

Political indictments of "drug kingpins," "hoodlums," and "welfare queens" are leading examples of such coded language and allowed for the indirect expression of racially charged fears and antagonisms. As Nixon adviser John Ehrlichman described the president's campaign strategy in 1968, "We'll go after the racists. That subliminal appeal to the anti-black voter was always present in Nixon's statements and speeches."[38] Twenty years later, Republican presidential candidate George Bush made the mugshot of William Horton, a black man convicted of rape, one of his key campaign symbols.[39]

From a practical standpoint, the transition to security state hegemony has entailed sharp cuts in welfare spending coupled with increased military spending (during the 1980s) and criminal justice spending (during the 1980s and 1990s) (Exhibit 4.1). For example, as a result of federal welfare "reform," the number of families receiving AFDC declined by 44 percent between 1993 and 1998 alone, and the average benefit payment to families entitled to AFDC declined from $376 in 1975 to $220 (1983 dollars) in 1995.[40] By contrast, criminal justice spending has grown considerably. These spending shifts reflect the increased cost of policy innovations aimed at getting tough on crime such as the following:

- *An unprecedented crackdown on drug users and dealers.* The number of annual arrests for drug offenses increased from roughly 500,000 in 1981 to 1.5 million in 1996.[41] Today in the United States, someone is arrested for a drug offense every 20 seconds.[42] The majority of these arrests, between two-thirds and four-fifths of the total number, are for the crime of simple possession.[43]

- *New mandatory minimum sentencing schemes.* The most recent of these are the "three strikes" laws that typically oblige judges to increase penalties for second felony offenses and to sentence "three-time losers" to life in prison.[44] Far more consequential in their overall impact have been mandatory minimum sentencing laws that require lengthy terms of incarceration for individuals caught with even small quantities of drugs.[45]

- *The scaling back of parole eligibility.* New "truth in sentencing" laws, for example, typically require offenders to serve about 85 percent of their court-ordered sentences before becoming eligible for supervision in the community.[46]

- *The revival of the death penalty.* Since 1976, when the U.S. Supreme Court ended the decade-long moratorium on executions, nearly 5,000 prisoners have been sent to death row. Between 1995 and 1998, the United States executed prisoners at an average rate of one per week. As critics point out, it costs more to litigate capital cases and execute people than it would to incarcerate them for life.[47]

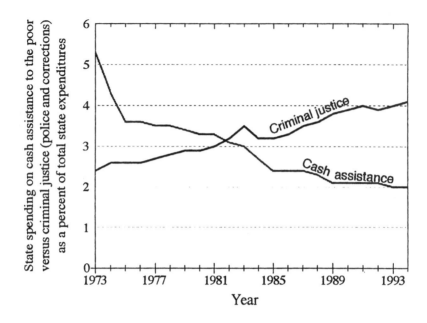

Exhibit 4.1. State Welfare and Criminal Justice Spending
SOURCE: U.S. Department of Commerce, *State Government Finances,* 1973-1994.

■ Gramscian and Durkheimian Explanations Compared

Gramsci recognized that the success of ruling class hegemonic projects depends on the extent to which they resonate with and articulate popular sentiments. As a hegemonic strategy, the security state is a viable alternative to the Keynesian welfare state precisely because it satisfies ruling class interests (in lower taxes and wages, expanded corporate freedom, and reduced responsibility for social welfare) in a way that also resonates with the common sense of large segments of the public. As one analyst argues,

> The dominant morality is neither an alien imposition from above nor an authentic expression of values from below but instead a compromise formation which takes up a position somewhere between these extremes. When ascendant social elites legislate their preferred categories into law and institutional practices, they do not, except in exceptional circumstances, ignore the moral culture of the mass of the people.[48]

For several decades, about 4 in 10 Americans have reported in surveys that they are afraid to walk alone at night in their own neighborhoods.[49] In more recent surveys, nearly 3 in 10 report worrying, at least "somewhat frequently," about getting mugged or having their homes burglarized.[50] Since the mid-1980s, when asked about the nation's most serious problem, Americans often have mentioned drugs or crime.[51] The rhetoric that legitimates the security state thus draws support from, even as it cultivates, these popular fears and concerns. In addition, through its coded reference to the control of minority populations, the security state strategy appeals to reservoirs of "beneath-the-surface" racism that permeates the white population.[52]

This argument is different from neo-Durkheimian explanations of U.S. punitiveness in subtle but important ways. The French sociologist Emile Durkheim argued that, by definition, a crime is an act that offends the "collective conscience"—the shared norms, morals, and values—of the society in question. For Durkheim, the collective conscience emerged naturally; society was characterized by this deep shared understanding rather than by group conflict or attempts to create and enforce a dominant morality.[53] Anger and punishment, in this view, are natural reactions to the violation of these shared norms and are functional in the sense that they reinforce shared morals and enhance group solidarity. Nowadays, many analysts echo Durkheim when they contend that although punitive criminal justice policies might be ineffective and socially destructive, they are democratic in the sense that they reflect the demands of the majority.[54]

What makes our analysis neo-Gramscian is precisely our rejection of this view. Popular common sense on crime is complex and might have been mobilized in a variety of directions, for although a sizable minority of Americans frequently worry about their potential victimization, most report that they do not. For those who do, this fear, in and of itself, does not necessarily lead to support for punitive crime policies. Furthermore, although many Americans express support for enhanced penalties, many also continue to express the belief that crime prevention efforts are preferable to punishment. For example, although most Americans view the courts as "too lenient" and express support for the death penalty, they also prefer that scarce dollars be invested in crime prevention rather than law enforcement.[55] And although Americans believe that prisons should be "no frills" operations, they also firmly support rehabilitation programs for those locked away.[56]

Moreover, members of the public appear to be highly responsive to cues from politicians in evaluating the seriousness of crime as a social problem for the nation as a whole. For example, Americans began naming *drugs* as the nation's most serious problem only during the late 1980s, in direct response to the Reagan and Bush administrations' intensification of the drug war. During the 1990s, Americans began identifying *crime* as the nation's most serious problem only in 1994, in the context of an intense congressional debate over President Clinton's Crime Bill. Although people still might be concerned about crime and drugs even when they do not identify these as the nation's most important problem, these poll results clearly show that Americans become more concerned about crime and drugs in response to political debate and activity. In sum, although members of the public are somewhat worried about crime and inclined toward punitive solutions, politicians have played a crucial role in expressing, channeling, and heightening these inclinations. Thus, it is politicians who are the driving force behind the new criminal justice punitiveness.

■ The Contours of the Security State

The shift from the welfare to the security state is, of course, far from complete. The states and the federal government continue to provide poverty relief, albeit in a more limited and coercive fashion. Businesses continue to be subject to health and safety regulation, although these efforts have been weakened. And opposition to some of the new punitive policies, including mandatory drug sentencing laws, now is quite visible. However, the basic contours of the new security state are largely in place. Democrats and Republicans alike now routinely express support for the limited role of government in poverty relief and for harsh criminal justice practices. Indeed, President Clinton, a Democrat, initiated massive new spending on prisons and police, and he supported welfare "reform" that shunts most federal responsibility for the poor onto the states.[57]

The most direct evidence of the institutionalization of the security state can be found in the nation's rapidly expanding penal apparatus. Between 1980 and 1998, largely as a result of the adoption of the punitive policies already discussed, the number of people incarcerated grew by more than 300 percent, from 500,000 to more than 1.8 million. The proportion of the population imprisoned also has grown rapidly (Exhibit 4.2), and more than 3.8 million people now are on parole or probation. By 1998, nearly 6 million people—nearly 3 percent of the adult population—were under some form of correctional supervision.[58]

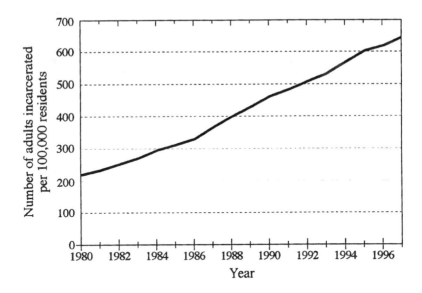

Exhibit 4.2. U.S. Incarceration Rate
SOURCE: Bureau of Justice Statistics, *Correctional Populations in the United States, 1995,* Table 1.5; Kathleen Maguire and Ann L. Pastore, *Sourcebook of Criminal Justice Statistics, 1997* (Washington, DC: U.S. Department of Justice, Bureau of Justice Statistics, 1998).

These developments have disproportionately affected young African Americans and Latinos (Exhibit 4.3). By 1994, 1 of every 3 black males between the ages of 18 and 34 years was under some form of correctional supervision,[59] and the number of Hispanic prisoners had more than quintupled since 1980.[60] In some large cities, the proportions are even more striking. In Baltimore, Maryland, and Washington, D.C., for example, more than half of all African American men between the ages of 18 and 35 years are under the supervision of the justice system. The state of Maryland recently assigned probation officers to Baltimore schools in which as many as 4 in 10 students have served time.

Since 1980, roughly 1,000 new jails and prisons have been constructed; a new prison or jail is built every week.[61] Despite this fact, U.S. prisons and jails continue to be overcrowded. At the end of 1997, state prisons were operating between 15 and 25 percent above their capacities, and federal prisons were operating at 19 percent above their official limits.[62] Resources for prisoner education, vocational training, and recreation have declined significantly.[63]

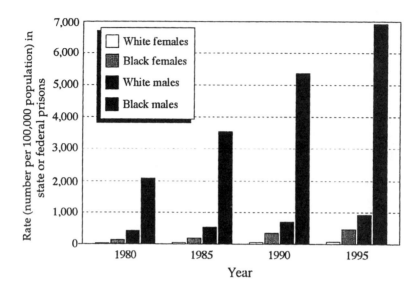

Exhibit 4.3. U.S. Incarceration Rate, by Race and Sex
SOURCE: Bureau of Justice Statistics, *Correctional Populations in the United States, 1990,* Table 1.7; Bureau of Justice Statistics, *Correctional Populations in the United States, 1995,* Table 1.7.

Apprehending, processing, and warehousing so many people is, of course, quite expensive. Over the past two decades, annual expenditures on law enforcement increased from $5 billion to $27 billion.[64] It costs approximately $30,000 to house a prisoner for a year—even with cuts in prison programs—so spending on correctional institutions has grown even more dramatically. By 1993, the annual public cost of such facilities was nearly $32 billion. As shown in Exhibit 4.4, the United States now spends more than $100 billion annually fighting crime.[65]

■ Crime, Punishment, and Democracy

Defenders of the new punitiveness point to dropping crime rates as evidence that this approach is effective. Indeed, the crime rate has declined considerably during recent years, especially among adults. But a closer look at the evidence reveals a more complicated picture. If filling prisons and jails

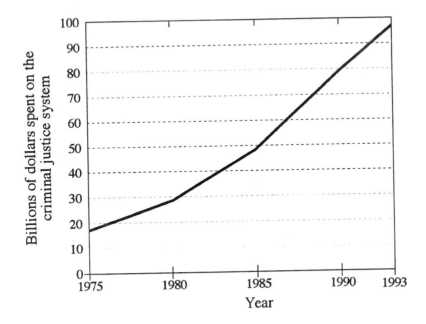

Exhibit 4.4. U.S. Criminal Justice Expenditures
SOURCE: Bureau of Justice Statistics, *Sourcebook of Criminal Justice Statistics, 1980*, Table 1.3; Bureau of Justice Statistics, *Sourcebook of Criminal Justice Statistics, 1996*, Table 1.2.

reduces crime, then crime rates should have dropped consistently since the late 1970s. But this did not occur. Similarly, although the average prison sentence per violent crime tripled between 1975 and 1989, there was no discernible impact on the overall rate of criminal violence during this period.[66]

Indeed, the historical evidence shows no correlation between patterns in incarceration and crime; throughout the 20th century, crime rates were largely unaffected by the size of the prison population.[67] The argument that *prison works* also is inconsistent with contemporary cross-sectional evidence. Between 1992 and 1997, for example, New York experienced one of the sharpest drops in serious crime in the country but one of the smallest increases in prison population (just 13.4 percent) and no increase in its jail population.[68] Similarly, Canada's rate of violent crime has been dropping since 1991, but its rate of incarceration has increased only slightly.[69] More generally, countries that punish more severely tend to have higher rather might have had some impact on levels of crime, the correlation between declining crime rates and penal expansion during the 1990s is largely spurious.

If the dramatic growth in correctional and prison populations does not explain the recent declines in serious crime, then what does? Epidemiological research sponsored by the National Institutes of Health finds that declines in homicide by city are correlated with changes in the drug market, especially the decline of the market for crack cocaine. This development, in turn, is likely a consequence of the natural course of the drug epidemic rather than law enforcement interventions.[71] These research findings are consistent with the emerging consensus that the crack trade was responsible for a great deal of homicides in major U.S. cities during the late 1980s and early 1990s.[72] Researchers seeking to explain the recent drop in serious crime also have cited declining opportunities in the illicit labor market, demographic changes, and an improved economy.[73]

In fact, rather than reducing the volume of serious crime in society, there is good reason to believe that growing criminal justice punitiveness is itself an increasingly important source of serious crime. In his book, *Search and Destroy: African American Males in the Criminal Justice System,* Jerome Miller uses the term *social iatrogenesis* to describe the impact of the new "get tough" policies. The term *iatrogenesis* refers to a "cure" that is actually responsible for the underlying illness. Miller uses the term to describe "a 'treatment' that maims those it touches and exacerbates the very pathologies that lie at the root of crime. It suggests that the criminal justice system itself has been a major contributor to breakdown in the inner cities."[74]

Consider, for example, the war on drugs. Like alcohol prohibition during the 1930s, the contemporary prohibition on marijuana, cocaine, and other drugs is directly responsible for the black market and for the violence it has spawned.[75] Crackdowns on drug dealers also tend to drive up prices and profits and hence make the risk taking associated with the trade more rational. Similarly, massive drug arrests in effect create new "job openings" for dealers while setting the stage for violent battles over ever shifting "turf." Finally, prohibition has facilitated the formation of violent drug cartels— especially in Colombia, Peru, and Mexico—that have seriously destabilized those states. In short, drug prohibition has proved to be a boon for daring criminals and has done little to stem the tide of drug use and abuse.[76]

More generally, the "get tough" approaches to crime and drugs fuel the material, social, and cultural ills that give rise to crime and drug dependency.

First, the cost of the new criminal justice policies has resulted in cuts in education and social welfare programs. In individual states, the trade-offs sometimes are quite stark. In California, for example, between 1980 and 1995, the proportion of state spending devoted to prisons increased from 2.0 to 9.9 percent while the proportion devoted to higher education dropped from 12.6 to 9.5 percent.[77] (Nationwide, more African American men now are behind bars than are enrolled in colleges and universities.[78]) And in 1993, more money was spent nationwide at the federal, state, and local levels on the war on drugs alone ($31 billion) than on the nation's premier "welfare" program, AFDC ($25 billion).[79]

Second, massive criminal justice interventions foster joblessness and family disruption. Most prisoners have unimpressive work histories. Having served time and earned the label *ex-con,* former prisoners typically find it more difficult than ever to secure stable employment.[80] Jobless and incarcerated men are among the least likely to get married and support children.[81] Female-headed households also are disrupted by incarceration. For example, three-fourths of the 54,000 women incarcerated for drug law violations have children.[82] Nationally, nearly 2 million children have parents or close relatives in jail or prison, and many experts argue that these kids are at increased risk of future incarceration.[83] The expansion of prisons and jails thus exacerbates rather than ameliorates joblessness, family breakdown, and crime.

Finally, massive criminal justice intervention increases the political and social isolation of poor people and minorities. In 14 states, ex-felons are denied the right to vote. That translates into the disenfranchisement of 13 percent of African American men.[84] In Florida, 31 percent of black men are barred from voting because of criminal records.[85] Meanwhile, in some big cities, imprisonment has become virtually a formal "rite of passage" for young minority men, signaling their transition into a new way of life. Sadly, what prison best prepares its visitors for is survival in a violent predatory world, that is, for survival on the inside. Beyond the prison walls, the skills and beliefs cultivated within prisons frequently lead ex-cons back into lives of crime, addiction, and trouble. Less directly, the fact that so many young people, especially minorities, are targeted and controlled by criminal justice institutions confirms the ideological association among criminality, danger, and urban youths that helped to justify the expansion of prisons and jails in the first place. In sum, "get tough" policies are not merely ineffective strategies for crime reduction. To the extent that these practices contribute to crime, social inequality, and family and community breakdown; foster aggression and personal difficulties among ex-cons; and stigmatize minority youths, they are increasingly significant causes of the very problems they purport to correct.

■ Conclusion

In this chapter, we have used Gramsci's theory of hegemony to explain the shift from the welfare state to the security state. According to this argument, conservative politicians, representing the concerns and interests of neo-liberal economic elites, united in opposition to the social movements of the 1960s and 1970s and to the expansion of the welfare state. By politicizing crime and drug use and demanding new policies that "get tough," these political actors discredited their political opponents, Great Society welfare initiatives, and poor people in general. Conservative politicians thereby paved the way for sharp cuts in government spending for poverty relief and massive expansion of the state's penal (and military) apparatus.

Our emphasis on the leadership of politicians in the shift from the welfare state to the security state differentiates our Gramscian approach from Durkheimian accounts that highlight popular reactions to crime. At the same time, our account challenges one aspect of Gramsci's approach: his tendency to treat coercion and ideology as diametrically opposed mechanisms used by the ruling classes to secure their dominance. According to the analysis developed in this chapter, politicians used the rhetoric of the wars on crime and drugs to legitimate the dramatic expansion of the state's coercive capacity. Thus, ideological processes helped to justify the growth of the formal social control apparatus. The growth of prisons, jails, and other penal institutions, in turn, has meant the stigmatization of more and more minority youths. This stigmatization has reinforced the image of the poor as dangerous and undeserving, an image that has been crucial in legitimating the shift from the welfare state to the security state. As one analyst put it, "As people are prosecuted and sentenced as criminals, the law produces convictions and punishments. These punishments reinforce the rhetoric of dangerousness with a truth of incarcerated bodies."[86] To the extent that our interpretation is accurate, the Gramscian assumption of incompatibility between ideological and coercive means of domination should be set aside in favor of a perspective that recognizes the possibility of their complementarity.

Finally, we conclude this chapter by underscoring our view that the punitive turn in criminal justice is neither an unavoidable response to the realities of crime and poverty nor an inexorable historical development rooted in deep social structures. Rather, the wars on crime and drugs are best viewed as political maneuvers by conservative politicians and the economic elites they represent to defend prevailing social practices and arrangements against various counter-hegemonic threats. As such, these "wars" are one piece of a general turn toward a more polarized, insecure, and repressive society, but they are policies that can and ought to be opposed. Indeed, the very "political" nature of our theoretical explanation for criminal justice punitiveness implies the possibility of alternative policies, but only the mobilization of adequate political muscle to counter the new security state hegemony can make these alternatives a reality. Growing demands from activists and public officials for a reconsideration of mandatory minimum drug sentences, marijuana prohibition, and the death penalty, together with renewed public discussion of persistent child poverty and racial inequality in the wake of rapid overall economic growth, provide us with reasons for optimism about the future. As Gramsci reminded us, hegemonic projects succeed only provisionally—for a period of time—before foundering on their own contradictions and creating space for opposition and change.

STUDY QUESTIONS

1. How did Gramsci draw on and extend Marx's theoretical framework?

2. What are hegemonic projects or strategies? What shapes their success or failure?

3. What hegemonic strategy prevailed in the aftermath of the Great Depression? What led to the collapse of this mode of governance during the 1960s and 1970s?

4. What is the security state? How does it differ from the Keynesian welfare state that preceded it? How do the wars on crime and drugs relate to the security state?

5. How does the authors' Gramscian perspective differ from neo-Durkheimian accounts of the war on crime?

6. How do the authors support their argument that the war on crime is not responsible for recent declines in the crime rate and might actually cause crime?

NOTES

1. Bureau of Justice Statistics, *Prison and Jail Inmates at Midyear 1998* (Washington, DC: Bureau of Justice Statistics, 1999).

2. Timothy Egan, "The War on Drugs Retreats, Still Taking Prisoners," *The New York Times*, 28 February 1999, A1; Bruce Western and Katherine Beckett, "How Unregulated Is the U.S. Labor Market? The Penal System as Labor Market Institution," *American Journal of Sociology* 104, no. 4 (1999): 1030-60.

3. Egan, "The War on Drugs Retreats."

4. Estimates of the crime rate based on the number of crimes known to the police suggest that rates of violent crime fluctuated throughout the 1980s and declined during the 1990s. Property crime, according to these data, declined throughout both decades. See Katherine Beckett and Theodore Sasson, *The Politics of Injustice: Crime and Punishment in America* (Thousand Oaks, CA: Pine Forge, 2000); Scott Boggess and John Bound, "Did Criminal Activity Increase during the 1980s? Comparisons across Data Sources," *Social Science Quarterly* 78 (1997): 725-36.

5. The exception to this generalization is homicide; the United States does have a significantly higher rate of homicide than do other industrialized nations. However, because only a tiny percentage of those sentenced to prison were convicted of murder or manslaughter, this cannot account for the exceptionally high rate of incarceration in the United States. See Beckett and Sasson, *The Politics of Injustice*; Boggess and Bound, "Did Criminal Activity Increase during the 1980s?"; Franklin Zimring and George Hawkins, *Crime Is Not the Problem* (New York: Oxford University Press, 1997).

6. Samuel Bowles and Herbert Gintis, *Schooling in Capitalist America* (New York: Basic Books, 1977).

7. Georg Rusche and Otto Kirchheimer, *Punishment and Social Structure* (New York: Columbia University Press, 1939); Jeffrey Reiman, *The Rich Get Richer and the Poor Get Prison* (New York: Macmillan, 1990).

8. See, for example, Ralph Miliband, *The State in Capitalist Society* (New York: Basic Books, 1969). Those now identified as "structuralist" Marxists might object to this formulation, arguing that the structural requirements of capitalism, rather than a ruling class, shape state policy. For a thorough overview of Marxian theories of the state, see Robert Alford and Roger Friedland, *Powers of Theory: Capitalism, the State, and Democracy* (New York: Cambridge University Press, 1985).

9. Perry Anderson, "The Antinomies of Antonio Gramsci," *New Left Review* 100 (1976-77): 5-80.

10. Carl Boggs, *The Two Revolutions* (Boston: South End Press, 1984); Joseph Femia, *Gramsci's Political Thought* (Oxford, UK: Clarendon, 1981).

11. Femia, *Gramsci's Political Thought*, 27.

12. See, for example, Stuart Hall, Chas Critcher, Tony Jefferson, John Clarke, and Brian Roberts, *Policing the Crisis: Mugging, the State and Law and Order* (New York: Holmes and Meier, 1978); Bob Jessop, *State Theory: Putting Capitalist States in Their Place* (University

Park: Pennsylvania State University Press, 1990); Michael Omi and Howard Winant, *Racial Formations in the United States* (New York: Routledge and Kegan Paul, 1986).

13. Boggs, *The Two Revolutions,* 180-85.

14. Ibid.

15. Ibid., 165.

16. Alan Wolfe, *The Limits of Legitimacy: Political Contradictions of Contemporary Capitalism* (New York: Free Press, 1977); G. William Domhoff, *The Power Elite and the State: How Policy Is Made in America* (New York: Aldine de Gruyter, 1990); Anthony Giddens, *Beyond Left and Right: The Future of Radical Politics* (Stanford, CA: Stanford University Press, 1994).

17. Frances Fox Piven and Richard Cloward, *Breaking the Social Compact* (New York: New Press, 1997); Michael Katz, *Improving Poor People: The Welfare State, the 'Underclass,' and Urban Schools as History* (Princeton, NJ: Princeton University Press, 1997).

18. Jonathan Simon, *Poor Discipline* (Chicago: University of Chicago Press, 1993); David Garland, *Punishment and Modern Society: A Study in Social Theory* (Chicago: University of Chicago Press, 1990).

19. James Ralph, *Northern Protest: Martin Luther King, Jr., Chicago, and the Civil Rights Movement* (Cambridge, MA: Harvard University Press, 1993).

20. James Miller, *Democracy in the Streets: From Port Huron to the Siege of Chicago* (Cambridge, MA: Harvard University Press, 1994).

21. Winnie Breines, *Community and Organization in the New Left, 1962-1968* (New York: Praeger, 1982); Barbara Ehrenreich, *Fear of Falling: The Inner Life of the Middle Class* (New York: Pantheon Books, 1989).

22. Katz, *Improving Poor People,* 26.

23. Suzanne Staggenborg, *Gender, Family, and Social Movements* (Thousand Oaks, CA: Pine Forge, 1997).

24. Dario Melossi, "Gazette of Morality and Social Whip: Punishment, Hegemony, and the Case of the USA, 1970-1992," *Social and Legal Studies* 2 (1993): 259-79.

25. Ibid.

26. For a discussion of the relationship between the capitalist class and conservative politicians, see G. William Domhoff, *Who Rules America? Power and Politics in the Year 2000* (Palo Alto, CA: Mayfield, 1998).

27. Pat O'Malley, "Volatile and Contradictory Punishment," *Theoretical Criminology* 3, no. 2 (May 1999): 175-96.

28. Barbara Ehrenreich, "The New Right Attack on Social Welfare," in *The Mean Season: The Attack on the Welfare State,* edited by Fred Block, Richard A. Cloward, Barbara Ehrenreich, and Frances Fox Piven, chap. 4 (New York: Pantheon Books, 1987).

29. Quoted in Katherine Beckett, *Making Crime Pay* (New York: Oxford University Press, 1997).

30. Cities with higher welfare payments have, on average, lower rates of burglary and homicide. See Lance Hannon and James Defronzo, "The Truly Disadvantaged, Public Assistance, and Crime," *Social Problems* 45 (August 1998): 383-92.

31. Beckett, *Making Crime Pay;* Dan Carter, *The Politics of Rage* (New York: Simon & Schuster, 1995).

32. On big business support for conservative politicians and think tanks during the 1980s, see Thomas Ferguson and Joel Roger, *Right Turn: The Decline of the Democrats and the Future of American Politics* (New York: Hill & Wang, 1987); Domhoff, *The Power Elite and the State.*

33. Beckett, *Making Crime Pay.*

34. The distinction between people "in trouble" and people who "make trouble" is Gusfield's. See Joseph Gusfield, "Moral Passage: The Symbolic Process in Public Designations of Deviance," *Social Problems* 15 (1967): 175-88.

35. Herbert Gans, *The War against the Poor* (New York: Basic Books, 1995); Michael B. Katz, *The Undeserving Poor: From the War on Poverty to the War on Welfare* (New York: Pantheon Books, 1989).

36. Ibid.

37. Michael Omi and Howard Winant, *Racial Formation in the United States* (New York: Routledge and Kegan Paul, 1986).

38. Cited in Beckett, *Making Crime Pay*.

39. David Anderson, *Crime and the Politics of Hysteria* (New York: Times Books, 1995).

40. Katherine Beckett and Bruce Western, "The Institutional Sources of Incarceration: Deviance Regulation and the Transformation of State Policy," unpublished manuscript, Indiana University.

41. Beckett and Sasson, *The Politics of Injustice*.

42. Egan, "The War on Drugs Retreats."

43. Kathleen Maguire and Ann L. Pastore, eds., *Sourcebook of Criminal Justice Statistics 1998* [online], Tables 4.1 and 4.29. (Available: http://www.albany.edu/sourcebook/)

44. These laws vary from state to state. In California, the third crime need not be a felony but rather one among many enumerated "serious offenses." See John Clark, James Austin, and D. Alan Henry, "Three Strikes and You're Out: A Review of State Legislation," occasional paper, National Institute of Justice, U.S. Department of Justice, September 1997.

45. For a discussion of mandatory sentencing laws, see Michael Tonry, *Sentencing Matters* (New York: Oxford University Press, 1996).

46. In the 1994 Crime Bill, the U.S. Congress mandated that states applying for $10.5 billion in federal assistance for new prison construction have "truth-in-sentencing" laws on their books.

47. Robert M. Bohm, "The Economic Costs of Capital Punishment," in *America's Experiment with Capital Punishment: Reflections on the Past, Present, and Future of the Ultimate Penal Sanction,* edited by James R. Acker, Robert M. Bohm, and Charles S. Lanier, 437-58 (Durham, NC: Carolina Academic Press, 1998).

48. Garland, *Punishment and Modern Society,* 53.

49. Beckett and Sasson, *The Politics of Injustice*.

50. Timothy Flanagan and Dennis Longmire, eds., *Americans View Crime and Justice* (Thousand Oaks, CA: Sage, 1996).

51. Beckett and Sasson, *The Politics of Injustice,* chap. 7.

52. Steven Cohn and William Halteman, "Punitive Attitudes toward Criminals: Racial Consensus or Racial Conflict?" *Social Problems* 38 (1991): 287-96; see also Sasson and Beckett, *The Politics of Injustice,* chap. 7.

53. Garland, *Punishment and Modern Society*.

54. For an especially subtle Durkheimian analysis, see David Garland, "The Culture of High Crime Societies: Some Preconditions of Recent 'Law and Order' Policies," *British Journal of Criminology* 40 (2000).

55. Somewhat surprisingly, when asked to choose between spending money on prisons and police, on the one hand, or spending money on education and job training, on the other, two-thirds of those polled chose the latter. See Francis T. Cullen, Sandra Evans Skovron, Joseph E. Scott, and Velmer S. Burton, Jr., "Public Support for Correctional Treatment," *Criminal Justice and Behavior* 17, no. 1 (1990): 2-18. Similarly, a 1997 poll found that 82 percent of those surveyed favored investing in crime prevention rather than punishment and that 57 percent would be willing to transfer money from the prison budget to

community youth violence prevention projects. See Susan Estrich, *Getting Away with Murder: How Politics Is Destroying the Criminal Justice System* (Cambridge, MA: Harvard University Press, 1998), 89, 135.

56. Theodore Sasson, *Crime Talk: How Citizens Construct a Social Problem* (New York, Aldine de Gruyter, 1995).

57. For an account of the Clinton administration's 1994 Crime Bill, see Lord Windlesham, *Politics, Punishment, and Populism* (New York: Oxford University Press, 1998).

58. Bureau of Justice Statistics, *Probation and Parole Populations, 1997;* Fox Butterfield, "Inmates Serving More Time, Justice Department Reports," *The New York Times,* 11 January 1999, A10.

59. Steven Donziger, ed., *The Real War on Crime* (New York: Harper Perennial, 1996); Windlesham, *Politics, Punishment, and Populism;* Elliott Currie, *Crime and Punishment in America* (New York: Henry Holt, 1998).

60. Currie, *Crime and Punishment in America,* 14.

61. Egan, "The War in Drugs Retreats"; Eric Schlosser, "The Prison Industrial Complex," *Atlantic Monthly,* December 1998, 51-77.

62. Bureau of Justice Statistics, *Prison Statistics, 1997* (Washington, DC: Bureau of Justice Statistics, 1998).

63. Currie, *Crime and Punishment in America;* John Irwin and James Austin, *It's about Time* (Belmont, CA: Wadsworth, 1997).

64. Donziger, *The Real War on Crime.*

65. Kathleen Maguire and Ann L. Pastore, eds., *Sourcebook of Criminal Justice Statistics, 1997* (Washington, DC: U.S. Department of Justice, Bureau of Justice Statistics, 1998), Table 1.1; Donziger, *The Real War on Crime.*

66. Albert Reiss, Jr., and Jeffrey Ross, eds., *Understanding and Preventing Violence* (Washington, DC: National Academy Press, 1993). Comparable findings have been reported by government-sponsored panels of social scientists in both Canada and Great Britain; for details, see Tonry, *Sentencing Matters,* 137.

67. Michael Tonry, *Malign Neglect* (New York: Oxford University Press, 1995); Currie, *Crime and Punishment in America;* Franklin Zimring and George Hawkins, *The Scale of Imprisonment* (Chicago: University of Chicago Press, 1995).

68. Marc Mauer, *Americans behind Bars: U.S. and International Use of Incarceration, 1995* (Washington, DC: Sentencing Project, 1997). On New York's prison and jail populations, see Bureau of Justice Statistics, *Prisoners in 1997* (Washington, DC: U.S. Department of Justice, 1998), Table 4; Bureau of Justice Statistics, *Correctional Populations in the United States, 1995* (Washington, DC: U.S. Department of Justice, 1997), Table 2.8.

69. Schlosser, "The Prison-Industrial Complex."

70. Currie, *Crime and Punishment in America.*

71. Andrew Lang Golub and Bruce Johnson, *Crack's Decline: Some Surprises across U.S. Cities* Washington, DC: U.S. Department of Justice, National Institute of Justice, July 1997).

72. See discussion in Sasson and Beckett, *The Politics of Injustice,* chap. 3.

73. Alfred Blumstein and Richard Rosenfeld, "Assessing the Recent Ups and Downs in U.S. Homicide Rates," *National Institute of Justice Journal* 237 (October 1998): 9-11; Jeffrey Fagan, Franklin Zimring, and June Kim, "Declining Homicide in New York City: A Tale of Two Trends," *National Institute of Justice Journal* 237 (October 1998): 12-13.

74. Jerome Miller, *Search and Destroy: African American Males in the Criminal Justice System* (New York: Cambridge University Press, 1996), 9.

75. Beckett and Sasson, *The Politics of Injustice,* chap. 3.

76. On the war on drugs, see Mike Gray, *Drug Crazy* (New York: Random House, 1998); Eva Bertram, Morris Blachman, Kenneth Sharpe and Peter Andreas, *Drug War Politics*

(Berkeley: University of California Press, 1996); Elliott Currie, *Reckoning: Drugs, the Cities, and the American Future* (New York: Hill & Wang, 1993); Dan Baum, *Smoke and Mirrors: The War on Drugs and the Politics of Failure* (Boston: Little, Brown, 1996).

77. Fox Butterfield, "New Prisons Cast Shadow over Higher Education," *The New York Times,* 12 April 1995, A21.
78. Vivian Stern, *A Sin against the Future* (Boston: Northeastern University Press, 1998), 51.
79. Beckett and Sasson, *The Politics of Injustice.*
80. Western and Beckett, "How Unregulated Is the U.S. Labor Market?"
81. Elliott Currie, *Confronting Crime: An American Challenge* (New York: Pantheon Books, 1995).
82. Egan, "The War in Drugs Retreats."
83. Fox Butterfield, "As Inmate Population Grows, so Does a Focus on Children," *The New York Times,* 7 April 1999, A1, A18.
84. Jonathan Kaufman, "Prison Life Is All around for a Girl Growing Up in Downtown Baltimore," *The Wall Street Journal,* 27 October 1998, A1.
85. "Voting Rights for Felons?" *The New York Post,* 27 February 1999.
86. Sally Engle Merry, "The Criminalization of Everyday Life," in *Everyday Practices and Trouble Cases,* edited by Austin Sarat, Marianne Constable, David Engel, Valerie Hans, and Susan Lawrence, 14-39 (Chicago: Northwestern University Press, 1998), 36.

Traditional Criminological Theory Updated

CHAPTER 5

The Systemic Theory of Neighborhood Crime Rates

ROBERT J. BURSIK, JR.

■ The American public consistently has been exposed to messages suggesting that the main cause of crime is an inability for some people to "just say no" when criminal opportunities present themselves. This belief fosters the idea that crime and delinquency prevention activities should focus almost exclusively on those social-psychological attributes that put an individual at risk. Such impressions are strongly reinforced by the extensive involvement of law enforcement agencies in popular school-based programs such as the Drug Abuse Resistance Education (DARE), which in part attempts to enhance the self-esteem that is assumed to be necessary for students to resist pressures to use illegal substances (Ringwalt et al. 1994). However, although such factors certainly are critical considerations, the fact that they are *social*-psychological means that they are not developed and maintained in isolation from others. Moreover, even if one grants the existence of a "core personality" that emerges during early childhood and remains relatively persistent throughout the life course, the manner in which such a personality manifests itself is not consistent across all social situations. For example, although people tend to have images of themselves as being particular "types" of individuals, many students will act very differently at an end-of-semester party than they did in a statistics class that they were required to take. Therefore, it should not be surprising that most criminologists assume that it is impossible to fully understand the dynamics of illegal behavior without an appreciation of the group contexts within which those processes unfold.

The important role that the neighborhood plays as one of these contexts often is taken for granted, for even the most naïve observer of urban conditions recognizes that those parts of the city that are characterized by extreme poverty also are those that tend to have the highest rates of crime. However, this apparently straightforward relationship actually represents quite a complicated process. As a result, social programs that try to reduce crime simply by easing or eliminating poverty are doomed to a limited degree of success at best. The goal of this chapter is to provide the reader with a sense of the complex manner by which certain neighborhood features make criminal behavior more or less likely and an appreciation for the difficulties entailed in its successful control at that level.

■ Types of Neighborhoods Versus Types of Residents

Neighborhoods, of course, are found in urban areas throughout the world, and delinquency is an almost universal phenomenon. However, the development of neighborhood-based theories of delinquent behavior has been a particularly American enterprise (Bursik, forthcoming). One reason for this focus is that public opinion in the United States traditionally has associated crime with the activities of particular ethnic and racial groups who, in turn, often have been identified with particular sections of the city. For example, a study commissioned by the Order Sons of Italy in America (Lichter and Amundson 1996) found that fewer than half of the Italian Americans portrayed on prime-time television during 1994 and 1995 were positive characters, and these characters largely were associated in some manner with organized crime. From this perspective, neighborhood differences in crime and delinquency rates merely reflect differences in the criminogenic tendencies of the populations who reside in those areas.

This explanation was called into serious question by the pioneering work of Clifford Shaw, Henry McKay, and their colleagues (Shaw and McKay 1931, 1942; Shaw et al. 1929; see also Bursik and Grasmick 1993b:25-26), who argued that Chicago's local communities tended to maintain their statuses as high-, medium-, or low-delinquency areas over a 30-year period despite dramatic changes in their racial and ethnic compositions. This conclusion was severely criticized by Jonassen (1949), who claimed that their "rather improbable" findings (p. 614), especially pertaining to differences between blacks and whites, were the result of a poor statistical and methodological research design. Shaw and McKay (1949) defended their position by noting that "it is impossible to reproduce in white communities the circumstances under which Negro children live, . . . [most notably] the effects of segregation and the barriers to upward mobility" (p. 617). That is, because the racial composition of urban neighborhoods is so strongly correlated with many other characteristics of those areas, they felt that it was extremely difficult to separate the effects of community characteristics on delinquency from the effects of the racial status of the individuals who live there. More generally, it traditionally has been very difficult to determine the degree to which local crime rates reflect characteristics of urban neighborhoods per se (i.e., group effect) as opposed to reflecting the characteristics of the individuals who live there (i.e., compositional effect) (Sampson 1989).

Recent advances in statistical modeling have enabled criminologists to overcome many of these methodological difficulties, and research that has used these new tools indicates that *neighborhood differences in crime rates cannot be accounted for solely on the basis of the types of people who live in those areas.* For example, Sampson, Raudenbush, and Earls (1997) show that crime tends to be highest in neighborhoods that lack the relational network structures that foster informal social control. Similar findings are presented by Bellair (1997). Such evidence confirms the basic assumptions of the most important and influential theory of neighborhoods ever to have been proposed within criminology—the social disorganization model of Shaw and McKay.

■ The Social Disorganization Theory of Crime

Shaw and McKay's discovery of two basic patterns in the geographic distribution of crime and delinquency served as the foundation for their formulation of the social disorganization theory. The first already was noted in the preceding section (i.e., the relative levels of crime and delinquency rates in Chicago's neighborhoods were not affected by changes in the racial and ethnic compositions of those areas). In addition, their research showed that these rates tended to be lowest in communities of high economic status and highest in areas with widespread economic deprivation. On the basis of this evidence, Shaw and McKay concluded that the dynamics that gave rise to the economic differentiation of local urban communities also were related to the associated distribution of crime and delinquency.

It might appear as if Shaw and McKay were suggesting that the basic cause of crime is poverty. However, their focus on the processes that shape the economic character of neighborhoods led to the development of a theory that, in fact, is far more subtle. To appreciate the complexity of their argument, it is necessary to place their work within the context of other urban research that was being conducted in Chicago at the same time by Robert Park and Ernest Burgess (Burgess 1925; Park and Burgess 1924).

The early 20th century was a period of rapid population change in Chicago as people moved into the city to take advantage of the jobs provided by the stockyards, steel mills, railroads, and other local industries. In addition to the waves of white ethnic immigrants that were arriving from Europe, many African Americans from the South were relocating to Chicago in pursuit of not only work but also the greater degree of racial tolerance that they had been led to believe existed in this thriving northern city. The extreme diversity of lifestyles, languages, and cultural traditions that were found in Chicago at this time fascinated Park and Burgess, and it led to their research into urban life in general and neighborhood development in particular.

On the basis of a wide-ranging series of neighborhood case studies conducted mostly by their students, Park and Burgess developed a model of human ecology that assumed that competition over the control of scarce but desirable space was the fundamental form of social interaction and that this competition determined the parts of the city in which different populations could reside. Because newly arrived immigrant groups with few financial assets could afford only inexpensive housing, they tended to move into the older run-down sections of the city that surrounded the central business district. Because the supply of cheap housing was relatively limited, different immigrant groups initially settled in the same residential areas, leading to a high degree of racial and ethnic heterogeneity in the poorest sections of town. However, as these groups became assimilated into the occupational structure of Chicago and had greater economic resources at their disposal, they moved progressively outward into increasingly expensive neighborhoods where more attractive housing was available. This relocation process was assumed to be most rapid in the poorest sections of the city because residents would abandon their dilapidated surroundings as soon as they could afford to move.

Drawing from the work of Thomas and Znaniecki (1920), Shaw and McKay extended the model of Park and Burgess by proposing that rapid population change and heterogeneity were likely to result in *social disorganization,* which referred to the declining influence of existing social values and rules of behavior (e.g., those pertaining to criminal activity) on individual members of the community. The declining influence of rules, or social disorganization, was considered by Shaw and McKay to be the primary cause of high rates of crime and delinquency. The economic deprivation of a neighborhood was predicted to be related to crime *only to the extent* that it increased the likelihood that a community was characterized by relatively high levels of residential instability and population heterogeneity. These two factors, in turn, were the principal causes of social disorganization (Bursik, forthcoming; Bursik and Grasmick 1993b).

Although the social disorganization framework was a central component of American criminology for many years, a number of important shortcomings led to its demise (Bursik 1988; Bursik and Grasmick 1993b). Two are of particular importance for the purposes of this chapter. First, although the theory proposes that economic deprivation has only an indirect causal role in this process, many studies have shown that poverty has an effect on crime over and above that which is mediated by instability and heterogeneity (Bursik 1998; Bursik and Grasmick 1993a; Elliott et al. 1996).

Second, the concept of social disorganization itself was not well developed in Shaw and McKay's work, and they sometimes did not clearly differentiate between the presumed outcome of disorganization (i.e., crime) and disorganization itself. This problem was further compounded by the fact that they were unable to incorporate any direct measures of this concept into their model and therefore could only make educated guesses about its effects. This led a number of criminologists to mistakenly (but understandably) equate social disorganization with the phenomenon it was intended to explain (Lander 1954). As a result, the theory of social disorganization increasingly came to be viewed as an exercise in circular reasoning.

The growing disenchantment with the social disorganization model accelerated during the 1960s as additional criticisms were made of its reliance on official records and its assumption that all groups in the American society shared the same set of values (Bursik 1988). At the same time, criminology began to focus increasingly on social-psychological issues rather than the group dynamics emphasized by Shaw and McKay. By 1970, despite the occasional appearance of neighborhood-based research in the literature, most criminologists considered the social disorganization model to be historically interesting but theoretically irrelevant.

■ A Systemic Approach to Social Disorganization

Although studies of neighborhoods were not a high criminological priority during the late 1960s and 1970s, a great deal of exciting urban research was being conducted in other fields in the social and behavioral sciences that necessitated dramatic revisions of many traditional theories such as the human ecology model of Park and Burgess. Because there were very few departments of criminology or criminal justice at that time, most people who wanted to formally study crime did so within the context of a much broader disciplinary curriculum such as economics, political science, psychology, social work, or (especially) sociology. As a result, they took courses in a wide variety of substantive areas including those in which contemporary neighborhood research was being conducted. Thus, it is no surprise that many criminologists who received their degrees during the late 1970s and early 1980s had strong interests in the relationship between local community dynamics and crime. Neighborhood studies began to appear in the criminological literature with increasing frequency as these new graduates became professionally active, and by 1986 the area had reestablished itself to the point where an entire volume of the prestigious Crime and Justice series was devoted to the topic (Reiss and Tonry 1986).

One of the noteworthy aspects of this resurgence has been the reformulation of Shaw and McKay's social disorganization theory in terms of a systemic model of human ecology (Berry and Kasarda 1977:56; see also Sampson 1988; Sampson and Groves 1989; Taylor 1997). The hallmark of the systemic social disorganization model is its focus on the degree to which a neighborhood can employ the *interactional networks* that tie together community residents to effectively regulate the nature of the activities that occur within its boundaries. Bursik and Grasmick (1993a, 1993b), for example, define disorganization as the inability to use these networks to exercise the types of social control that are necessary to achieve the goal of living in an area relatively free from the threat of crime. Sampson et al.'s (1997) closely related concept of "collective efficacy" broadens the focus to include the goals of effective supervision of children and the maintenance of public order.

Relational networks are central to the systemic approach because they represent the primary structural mechanism through which informal sanctions can be imposed on persons and by which effective supervision can be achieved. For example, assume that a resident is upset that some of her neighbors spend each evening getting drunk on the front porch of their apartment house. She can let them know of her disapproval only if she either confronts them about this issue personally or has a mutual acquaintance do so on her behalf. The effectiveness of her complaint will depend on the strength of her interpersonal ties with those people. That is, if this is the first time that she or the intermediary ever has interacted with the neighbors, then they might not be likely to take her disapproval very seriously.

However, the drinkers will be much more sensitive to her opinion if there has been prior interaction between the drinkers and her in which at least minimal bonds of attachment have been developed (Hirschi 1969). Likewise, Greenberg, Rohe, and Williams (1985) show that urban residents are not likely to intercede in criminal events that involve strangers and are reluctant to assume responsibility for the welfare of property of people whom they barely know.

Criminologists have focused on three different dimensions of these networks. The *structural* dimension refers to the number of people who are bound together through formal or informal ties (size), the percentage of all possible network ties that actually exist (density), and the degree to which the networks link together the various groups residing in the area (breadth). Such an orientation formalizes many of the propositions that were implicit to Shaw and McKay's framework but that were left relatively undeveloped. For example, the development of large and dense networks is difficult when people are moving into and out of a neighborhood at a rapid rate. Likewise, network ties are not likely to have much breadth in racially/ethnically heterogeneous neighborhoods if mutual distrust among such groups exists.

Networks also vary along a *functional* dimension. Drawing from the work of Hunter (1985), Bursik and Grasmick (1993b) emphasize three particular types of networks (Bursik and Grasmick 1995; Rose and Clear 1998; Taylor 1997). *Private* networks integrate residents into the intimate primary groups of a neighborhood such as families and friendship groups. *Parochial* networks represent relationships that do not have the same degree of intimacy as at the private level such as those among acquaintances and fellow members of local clubs or organizations. The most important departure of the systemic approach from the traditional orientation of Shaw and McKay is found in its emphasis on *public* networks through which the neighborhood can solicit political, economic, and social resources that are controlled by persons or agencies located outside of the local community. Unfortunately, this is the component of the systemic model that has been studied the least. One exception is Bursik's (1989) analysis of public housing construction in Chicago, which shows that these facilities were built in areas that could not mobilize sufficient political support to locate them elsewhere. The construction increased the residential instability of the affected areas, thereby leading to a subsequent rise in their delinquency rates. Such findings suggest that the failure to examine how social control is facilitated by public network linkages has led to a seriously incomplete understanding of the neighborhood dynamics related to crime and delinquency.

Finally, whereas systemic models assume that the existence of neighborhood-based relational networks is a necessary condition for the exercise of social control, it is not a sufficient one. Anderson (1993) shows that inner-city parents with very strong bonds of attachment to and conventional aspirations for their children do not always socialize them fully in accordance with standard middle class expectations of behavior for fear that they might be victimized when outside of the home. Therefore, there is significant variation in the *content* of the interchanges among network members. The systemic approach assumes that relational networks will serve as an effective source of social control only when the linkages are used, at least in part, to transmit group norms and expectations pertaining to appropriate behavior for neighborhood residents and to impose a wide variety of informal negative sanctions if those expectations are violated. This is called the transference of *social capital* (Bursik 1999; Sampson 1997; Taylor 1997).

In sum, the contemporary systemic social disorganization theory of neighborhood crime rates makes the following predictions:

1. The levels of residential instability and population heterogeneity will be highest in economically deprived neighborhoods.

2. Private and parochial networks will be smaller, be less dense, and have less breadth in neighborhoods with high levels of residential instability and population heterogeneity.

3. Public networks will be smaller, be less dense, and have less breadth in economically deprived neighborhoods.

4. Crime rates are a function of the ability of private, parochial, and public networks to transfer the types of social capital that are necessary for the effective control of crime.

5. The total effects of economic deprivation, residential instability, and population heterogeneity on crime are mediated by these intervening systemic factors.

■ Policy Implications

Shaw was an extraordinarily unique criminologist, for in addition to his extensive empirical studies of crime and delinquency, he also was a committed social activist who believed that his findings concerning the social disorganization model could be used to develop effective delinquency prevention projects. The result was the Chicago Area Project, one of the most widely discussed and controversial programs since its initial organization in 1932 (Bursik and Grasmick 1993b; Schlossman et al. 1984).

The central philosophy of the Chicago Area Project was that for delinquency prevention activities to be effective, they first must become the activities of the adults who constitute the natural social world of the juveniles. Such activities would be designed to achieve three primary goals: bringing community adults into meaningful contact with local youths; exposing local residents to new scientific perspectives on child rearing, child welfare, and delinquency; and opening up channels of communication between local residents and institutional representatives who might provide useful resources to the neighborhood (Finestone 1976:127-28). Thus, the private, parochial, and public forms of control not only were recognized but also were intrinsic to the operation of the program. Thus, it was the first fully systemic crime prevention program to have been developed in the United States.

The basic assumptions of the systemic social disorganization model in general, and the Chicago Area Project in particular, continue to be reflected in the efforts of many contemporary programs to involve a wide range of residents and local institutions in crime prevention activities. For example, one of the goals of the federal SafeFutures project (Morley and Rassman 1997) is the strengthening of networks within the community and the efficient coordination and delivery of social and health services to local community residents. This is far from being an isolated example of modern prevention programs that have been strongly influenced by the framework described in this chapter. As such, the systemic model of social disorganization continues to have an important effect on the daily lives of many urban residents.

■ Unresolved Issues

The fullest test to date of the systemic social disorganization theory is the study of Chicago conducted by Sampson and his colleagues (1997). As predicted, the degree of social organization in an area (or, in their terms, collective efficacy) was determined by the levels of economic disadvantage, residential instability, and population heterogeneity; in turn, it had a very strong effect on the violent crime rate found in these neighborhoods. Nevertheless, economic disadvantage and residential stability also had effects on crime that were unrelated to the level of organization, which contradicts the fifth prediction listed earlier.

Although the findings of Sampson et al. generally are consistent with the systemic social disorganization model, they also indicate that some problematic conceptual issues have not yet been satisfactorily resolved. These include, in particular, the following.

First, although we have suggested that the theoretically unexpected effect of poverty on crime might represent the lack of strong public networks, it also might be the case that a purely systemic model cannot account for this pattern. Anderson (1990), for example, suggests that underclass African American communities are characterized by "oppositional cultures" that reject many traditional middle class values including those pertaining to the "rightness or wrongness" of certain illegal activities such as dealing drugs. Given the extreme and persistent social isolation of such communities, conventional values might come to be seen by a wide range of the residents of such communities as being irrelevant to their daily lives (Sampson and Wilson 1995).

The existence of oppositional cultures would call the entire systemic framework into question because it invalidates the central assumption that all residents share the goal of crime control. However, Matza and Sykes (1961) argue that the entrepreneurial culture of the United States that encourages risk taking and the search for adventure and excitement also might promote the types of illegal behavior discussed by Anderson (1990), thereby enabling people to rationalize involvement in behaviors that they actually believe are wrong. For example, Campbell and Muncer (1989) note that even gangs embody many mainstream values, although they become manifest in "distorted" forms.

The social dynamics that lead to such normative flexibility have been explored most fully in the "institutional anomie" theory developed by Messner and Rosenfeld (1994). They argue that economic institutions in the United States are considered to be the most important and that others, such as those pertaining to education, are valued only insofar as they lead to eventual financial rewards. As a result, people will use illegal activities to achieve the "American Dream" if they cannot do so by conventional means. Thus, much illegal activity actually reaffirms the dominant cultural system. In fact, as Kooistra's (1989) fascinating study of the "criminal as hero" documents, many successful uses of nonlegitimate avenues to economic gain have become admired parts of American folklore that are passed from generation to generation.

Given the economic orientation of the Messner and Rosenfeld (1994) argument, the relevance of the institutional anomie theory seems to be restricted to property offenses and armed robbery (Short 1997), and it might appear as if a different theory would be needed to account for violent offenses such as homicide, aggravated assault, and rape. However, arguments similar in spirit to those of Messner and Rosenfeld have been made that differ only in the core American values assumed to be reflected in criminal activity. In particular, the work of Horowitz (1983) indicates that when people do not have histories of conventional personal accomplishments or social roles that establish their claims to deference, respect, and honor, the only recourse is to be able to back those claims physically (p. 81). As a result, violent crimes might be committed in an attempt to realize this aspect of the conventional value system.

If future research is not able to confirm the expectation that a more extensive consideration of the public networks can account for the theoretically unexpected relationship between poverty and crime, then the biggest challenge facing the systemic model is the integration of the dynamics associated with the neighborhood distributions of such normative rationalizations into the model in a manner that is logically consistent with the other basic assumptions.

Second, it has become increasingly apparent that the dynamics underlying the systemic model are far more complicated than originally assumed. Some striking illustrations of this complexity have been presented in research that compares the effectiveness of social control that is exercised by private and parochial networks. Hirschi's (1969) formulation of control theory argues that constraints on illegal behavior are strongest when there are relatively high levels of attachment to others. Therefore, given the intensely personal interactions that characterize private networks, one would assume that the forms of social control that are transmitted within such relationships would have much stronger effects on behavior than would those transmitted within the more impersonal and transitory parochial networks. However, Bursik (1999) shows that the residents of Oklahoma City, Oklahoma, are as concerned about sanctions imposed by other parochial network members as they are when those sanctions come from persons in their private networks. Likewise, Bellair's (1997) research suggests that social control is most effective when it occurs among people who interact with each other at least once a year rather than on a daily basis. These findings indicate that the social capital transmitted in nonintimate relationships might be just as effective in the control of crime as that which is derived from primary groups. Although the findings of Bursik (1999) and Bellair (1997) cannot be considered definitive until they are replicated with other data sets, they represent some exciting avenues for future work.

An equally intriguing theoretical complication involves the relationships among economic deprivation, residential mobility, population heterogeneity, and crime. Warner and Pierce (1993) show that in Seattle, Washington, racial heterogeneity is associated with high crime rates in neighborhoods with little poverty but with lower crime rates in impoverished areas. In addition, they present evidence that the effects of stability and homogeneity on the level of the informal social control depends on the socioeconomic status of the neighborhood; that is, control is relatively weak in homogeneous stable neighborhoods if they also are economically deprived. An equally complicated situation can be found in Sampson et al.'s (1997) analysis of data from Chicago. Although residential mobility has the expected negative association with collective efficacy and the overall rate of violence, it is positively related to the homicide rate.

Whereas such findings are surprising from a systemic viewpoint, they are consistent with Wilson's (1987) observations about the concentration of problems found in extremely poor, socially isolated underclass neighborhoods. In particular, residential stability can be achieved in two very different ways. The image that has dominated systemic social disorganization theory is that stable communities arise when residents of desirable areas develop long-term stakes in those neighborhoods including the formation of strong systemic networks. However, many members of the economic underclass have been stranded in undesirable high-crime areas, abandoned by former neighbors who were financially able to relocate into better communities. As opposed to the first type of stable community, the low level of population turnover in such neighborhoods does not reflect freely made residential choices. Thus, there are few incentives to invest time and energy into the development of social ties. The fact that such contemporary urban dynamics have not yet been more fully integrated into the systemic model is an important shortcoming of the systemic approach. However, some important initial steps have been made by Sampson and Wilson (1995).

Third, one of the most basic assumptions of the theories of human ecology that have informed social disorganization theory is that local populations continually adapt to changes in their social environment. From this perspective, crime rates are not just an outcome of the complicated processes described heretofore. Rather, crime rates in themselves might be an important source of change in the compositional and systemic characteristics of local urban communities.

There have been several explorations of this issue at the theoretical level. Skogan (1986) argues that the fear expressed by residents of high-crime communities can lead to a social-psychological withdrawal from the life of the neighborhood. This, of course, would weaken the systemic basis of social control, thereby leading to further increases in illegal behavior. A somewhat more complex set of dynamics has been proposed by Rose and Clear (1998), who observe that the incarceration of many individuals from a single neighborhood can significantly disrupt the private and parochial network structures of that community, thereby increasing the crime rate. Although very different processes are emphasized by Skogan (1986) and Rose and Clear (1998), there is no question that a full understanding of the neighborhood dynamics associated with criminal behavior is impossible without a consideration of such reciprocal effects.

Unfortunately, although Liska and his colleagues (Liska and Bellair 1995; Liska, Logan, and Bellair 1998; Liska and Warner 1991) show that high rates of robbery depress the amount of social interaction in a city and that violent crime has an effect on the population size and racial composition of urban and suburban areas, few studies have statistically examined this issue at the neighborhood level. To make matters worse, the findings from this handful of studies have been inconsistent. For example, although Bursik (1986), Morenoff and Sampson (1997), and Schuerman and Kobrin (1986) show that crime rates affect the demographic character of neighborhoods in Chicago and Los Angeles, this apparently is not the case in Racine, Wisconsin (Shannon 1982). Therefore, until such research has been conducted in a broader and more representative set of cities, no firm conclusions can be drawn about the degree to which these mutual relationships represent a general pattern.

■ Summary

There is no question that the social disorganization model of Shaw and McKay is the most famous and influential theory of neighborhoods and crime that ever has been developed. This chapter has presented an introduction to that framework and has examined the reasons for its contemporary reformulation as a systemic framework that focuses on the structure, function, and content of the relational networks that represent the mechanisms by which the social capital associated with social control is circulated among the residents. Given its relatively recent appearance as a criminological theory, it is obvious that a great deal of additional work will be required before the systemic approach fully and satisfactorily captures the rich and complex nature of the local community dynamics associated with criminal behavior. Nevertheless, this chapter has attempted to show that it provides an excellent starting point for that understanding.

STUDY QUESTIONS

1. The social disorganization model often is referred to as a type of control theory. What features of the framework would lead to such a characterization?

2. Researchers have successfully used the social disorganization model to study neighborhood variation in relatively serious forms of crime. Do you think it would provide an equally successful explanation of community differences in the rates of minor crimes such as gambling and the occasional use of marijuana? Why or why not?

3. Think of the various private and parochial networks to which you belong. What types of sanctions have been imposed on members who have violated expectations considering appropriate forms of behavior? Based on your experience, what factors affect the likelihood that these sanctions have the desired effect?

REFERENCES

Anderson, Elijah. 1990. *Streetwise: Race, Class, and Change in an Urban Community*. Chicago: University of Chicago Press.

———. 1993. "Violence and the Inner-City Poor." *Atlantic*, May, 81-94.

Bellair, Paul E. 1997. "Social Interaction and Community Crime: Examining the Impact of Neighbor Networks." *Criminology* 35:677-704.

Berry, Brian J. L. and John D. Kasarda. 1977. *Contemporary Urban Ecology*. New York: Macmillan.

Burgess, Ernest W. 1925. "The Growth of the City." Pp. 47-63 in *The City*, edited by Robert E. Park, Ernest W. Burgess, and Roderick D. McKenzie. Chicago: University of Chicago Press.

Bursik, Robert J., Jr. 1986. "Delinquency Rates as Sources of Ecological Change." Pp. 63-74 in *The Social Ecology of Crime*, edited by James M. Byrne and Robert J. Sampson. New York: Springer-Verlag.

———. 1988. "Social Disorganization and Theories of Crime and Delinquency: Problems and Prospects." *Criminology* 26:519-51.

———. 1989. "Political Decision-Making and Ecological Models of Delinquency: Conflict and Consensus." Pp. 105-17 in *Theoretical Integration in the Study of Deviance and Crime*, edited by Steven F. Messner, Marvin D. Krohn, and Allen E. Liska. Albany: State University of New York Press.

———. 1998. "The Public Dimension of Systemic Control: Neighborhood Crime Rates and the Municipal Political Structure." Paper presented at the meeting of the American Sociological Association, San Francisco.

———. 1999. "The Informal Control of Crime Through Neighborhood Networks." *Sociological Focus* 32:85-97.

———. Forthcoming. "Community." In *Handbook of Law and Social Science: Youth and Justice*, edited by Susan O. White. New York: Plenum.

Bursik, Robert J., Jr. and Harold G. Grasmick. 1993a. "Economic Deprivation and Neighborhood Crime Rates, 1960-1980." *Law and Society Review* 27:263-83.

———. 1993b. *Neighborhoods and Crime: The Dimensions of Effective Community Control*. Lexington, MA: Lexington Books.

———. 1995. "Neighborhood-Based Networks and the Control of Crime and Delinquency." Pp. 107-30 in *Crime and Public Policy: Putting Theory to Work*, edited by Hugh D. Barlow. Boulder, CO: Westview.

Campbell, Anne and Steven Muncer. 1989. "Them and Us: A Comparison of the Cultural Context of American Gangs and British Subcultures." *Deviant Behavior* 10:271-88.

Elliott, Delbert S., William Julius Wilson, David Huizinga, Robert J. Sampson, Amanda Elliott, and Bruce Rankin. 1996. "The Effects of Neighborhood Disadvantage on Adolescent Development." *Journal of Research in Crime and Delinquency* 33:389-426.

Finestone, Harold. 1976. *Victims of Change: Juvenile Delinquents in American Society*. Westport, CT: Greenwood.

Greenberg, Stephanie W., William M. Rohe, and Jay R. Williams. 1985. *Informal Citizen Action and Crime Prevention at the Neighborhood Level*. Washington, DC: National Institute of Justice.

Hirschi, Travis. 1969. *Causes of Delinquency*. Berkeley: University of California Press.

Horowitz, Ruth. 1983. *Honor and the American Dream*. New Brunswick, NJ: Rutgers University Press.

Hunter, Albert J. 1985. "Private, Parochial, and Public Social Orders: The Problem of Crime and Incivility in Urban Communities." Pp. 230-42 in *The Challenge of Social Control: Citizenship and Institution Building in Modern Society*, edited by Gerald D. Suttles and Mayer N. Zald. Norwood, NJ: Ablex.

Jonassen, Christen T. 1949. "A Re-evaluation and Critique of the Logic and Some Methods of Shaw and McKay." *American Sociological Review* 14:608-14.

Kooistra, Paul. 1989. *Criminals and Heroes: Structure, Power, and Identity*. Bowling Green, OH: Popular Press.

Lander, Bernard. 1954. *Toward an Understanding of Juvenile Delinquency*. New York: Columbia University Press.

Lichter, S. Robert and Daniel R. Amundson. 1996. *Portrayal of Italian American Characters in Prime-Time Television*. Washington, DC: Center for Social Justice.

Liska, Allen E. and Paul E. Bellair. 1995. "Violent Crime Rates and Racial Composition: Convergence Over Time." *American Journal of Sociology* 101:578-610.

Liska, Allen E., John R. Logan, and Paul E. Bellair. 1998. "Race and Violent Crime in the Suburbs." *American Sociological Review* 63:27-38.

Liska, Allen E. and Barbara D. Warner. 1991. "Functions of Crime: A Paradoxical Process." *American Journal of Sociology* 96:1441-63.

Matza, David and Gresham Sykes. 1961. "Juvenile Delinquency and Subterranean Values." *American Sociological Review* 28:712-20.

Messner, Steven F. and Richard Rosenfeld. 1994. *Crime and the American Dream*. Belmont, CA: Wadsworth.

Morenoff, Jeffrey D. and Robert J. Sampson. 1997. "Violent Crime and the Spatial Dynamics of Neighborhood Transition: Chicago, 1970-1990." *Social Forces* 76:31-64.

Morley, Elaine and Shelli B. Rassman. 1997. *Helping at-Risk Youth: Lessons From Community-Based Initiatives*. Washington, DC: Office of Juvenile Justice and Delinquency Prevention.

Park, Robert E. and Ernest W. Burgess. 1924. *Introduction to the Science of Sociology*. Chicago: University of Chicago Press.

Reiss, Albert J., Jr. and Michael Tonry, eds. 1986. *Communities and Crime*. Chicago: University of Chicago Press.

Ringwalt, Christopher C., Jody M. Greene, Susan T. Ennett, Ronaldo Iachan, Richard R. Clayton, and Carl F. Leukefeld. 1994. *Past and Future Directions of the D.A.R.E. Program: An Evaluation Review*. Washington, DC: U.S. Department of Justice, National Institute of Justice.

Rose, Dina R. and Todd R. Clear. 1998. "Incarceration, Social Capital, and Crime: Implications for Social Disorganization Theory." *Criminology* 36:441-80.

Sampson, Robert J. 1988. "Local Friendship Ties and Community Attachment in Mass Society: A Multilevel Systemic Model." *American Sociological Review* 53:766-79.

——. 1989. "The Promises and Pitfalls of Macro-Level Research." *The Criminologist* 14:1-5.

——. 1997. "The Embeddedness of Child and Adolescent Development: A Community-Level Perspective on Urban Violence." Pp. 31-77 in *Violence and Childhood in the Inner City*, edited by Joan McCord. Cambridge, UK: Cambridge University Press.

Sampson, Robert J. and W. Byron Groves. 1989. "Community Structure and Crime: Testing Social Disorganization Theory." *American Journal of Sociology* 94:774-802.

Sampson, Robert J., Stephen W. Raudenbush, and Felton Earls. 1997. "Neighborhoods and Violent Crime: A Multilevel Study of Collective Efficacy." *Science* 277:918-24.

Sampson, Robert J. and William Julius Wilson. 1995. "Toward a Theory of Race, Crime, and Urban Inequality." Pp. 37-54 in *Crime and Inequality*, edited by John Hagan and Ruth D. Peterson. Stanford, CA: Stanford University Press.

Schlossman, Steven, Gail Zellman, Richard Skavelson, Michael Sedlak, and Jan Cobb. 1984. *Delinquency Prevention in South Chicago: A Fifty Year Assessment of the Chicago Area Project*. Santa Monica, CA: RAND.

Schuerman, Leo A. and Solomon Kobrin. 1986. "Community Careers in Crime." Pp. 67-100 in *Communities and Crime*, edited by Albert J. Reiss, Jr., and Michael Tonry. Chicago: University of Chicago Press.

Shannon, Lyle W. 1982. "The Relationship of Juvenile Delinquency and Adult Crime to the Changing Ecological Structure of the City." Executive report submitted to the National Institute of Justice.

Shaw, Clifford R. and Henry D. McKay. 1931. *Social Factors in Juvenile Delinquency*. National Commission on Law Observation and Enforcement, No. 13, Report On the Causes of Crime, vol. 2. Washington, DC: Government Printing Office.

———. 1942. *Juvenile Delinquency and Urban Areas*. Chicago: University of Chicago Press.

———. 1949. "Rejoinder." *American Sociological Review* 14:614-17.

Shaw, Clifford R., Frederick M. Zorbaugh, Henry D. McKay, and Leonard S. Cottrell. 1929. *Delinquency Areas*. Chicago: University of Chicago Press.

Short, James F., Jr. 1997. *Poverty, Ethnicity, and Violent Crime*. Boulder, CO: Westview.

Skogan, Wesley G. 1986. "Fear of Crime and Neighborhood Change." Pp. 203-9 in *Communities and Crime*, edited by Albert J. Reiss, Jr., and Michael Tonry. Chicago: University of Chicago Press.

Taylor, Ralph B. 1997. "Social Order and Disorder of Street Blocks and Neighborhoods: Ecology, Microecology, and the Systemic Model of Social Disorganization." *Journal of Research in Crime and Delinquency* 34:113-55.

Thomas, William I. and Florian Znaniecki. 1920. *The Polish Peasant in Europe and America*. Vol. 4. Boston: Gorham Press.

Warner, Barbara D. and Glenn L. Pierce. 1993. "Reexamining Social Disorganization Theory Using Calls to the Police as a Measure of Crime." *Criminology* 31:493-517.

Wilson, William Julius. 1987. *The Truly Disadvantaged: The Inner City, the Underclass, and Public Policy*. Chicago: University of Chicago Press.

CHAPTER 6

Strain Theory and School Crime

ROBERT AGNEW

There already was much concern about school crime when two students at Columbine High School in Littleton, Colorado, shot 13 others to death and then killed themselves in April 1999. This incident prompted massive concern about school crime, with people across the country, including politicians and criminologists, asking the following questions:

1. How common is crime and violence in our schools? The incident at Columbine was preceded by several other well-publicized school incidents involving multiple deaths. Such incidents have led many to seriously question the safety of our schools.
2. How can we explain the crime in our schools? That is, why do some students kill, injure, and steal at school? Related to this, why do some schools have higher crime rates than do other schools?
3. What can we do to make our schools safer?

This chapter addresses each of these questions.

I begin by briefly reviewing the evidence on the extent of crime, including violence, in our nation's schools. Some of this evidence will surprise you. I then use strain theory to explain why some *students* are more likely to engage in school crime than are other students and why some *schools* have higher rates of crime than do other schools. In particular, I focus on the ways in which *school-related factors* can contribute to school crime. Whereas strain theory is just one of several theories capable of explaining school crime, I believe that it has some important and unique insights to offer. Finally, I draw on strain theory to suggest strategies for reducing school crime.

■ How Common Is School Crime?

Perhaps the best way in which to estimate the extent of school crime is with data from the National Crime Victimization Survey (NCVS). This survey involves interviews with people in 55,000 representative households throughout the United States. Each person age 12 years or over in these households is asked whether he or she has been the victim of various violent and property crimes, and each person is asked a number of questions about each victimization including the location of the victimization. Because we are dealing with a representative sample of people, we can use their responses to estimate the extent of crime, including school crime, in the United States as a whole. The NCVS provides a more accurate estimate of the extent of crime than do police reports because most crimes are not reported to the police. The NCVS includes both crimes that are and are not reported to the police, although it probably still underestimates the true extent of crime (Wells and Rankin 1995). Data from the 1996 NCVS indicate the following about the extent of school crime (Kaufman et al. 1998; also see Anderson 1998; Elliott, Hamburg, and Williams 1998).

There were about 1.3 million violent crimes committed against students ages 12 through 18 years at school or on the way to or from school. That works out to about 5 incidents of violence per 100 students. The large share of these crimes were minor in nature; that is, they involved fistfights or other minor altercations in which no one was physically hurt or there were only minor injuries. About 255,000 of these crimes were serious in nature— rapes/sexual assaults, robberies, or serious assaults. That works out to about 1 incident of serious violence per 100 students. There were about 2.1 million thefts at school. That works out to about 8 thefts per 100 students.

Is school more or less safe than the environment outside of school? It depends on the type of crime we are discussing. Students are about as likely to experience a violent crime away from school as they are at school. But they are about three times as likely to experience a *serious* violent crime away from school as they are at school. So, students are much more vulnerable to serious violence outside of school (violence peaks during the few hours after the school day ends). Students, however, are somewhat more likely to experience thefts at school than away from school.

What about the chances of being killed at school? A total of 76 students were murdered or committed suicide at school during the combined 1992-1993 and 1993-1994 school years. Another 29 individuals, including teachers and staff, also suffered violent deaths at school during this period. During the 1992 and 1993 calendar years, 7,294 juveniles ages 5 through 19 years were murdered and 4,353 committed suicide away from school. So, students are much more likely to be killed or commit suicide away from school than at school. Only about 1 percent of all violent deaths to school-age children occur at school. For school-age children, the chance of being the victim of a violent death at school is about 1 in 1 million.

How about trends in school crime? Are schools becoming less safe? Data from several sources suggest that the answer is no. Generally, rates of violence and theft at school have been stable or declining during recent years. This also is true of violent *deaths* at school. I should note, however, that there has been a very recent increase in the number of "multiple-death" incidents at schools. There was an average of one multiple-death incident per year at schools from August 1992 to July 1995, but that increased to an average of five incidents per year from August 1995 to June 1998 (this increase in multiple-death incidents occurred even though the *overall* rate of violent deaths at school decreased). These incidents receive a great deal of publicity, and they partly account for the widespread impression that schools are unsafe and school violence is increasing.

Overall, the data indicate that serious violence is not as common at school as many people might believe, that it is not increasing, and that it is much more common away from school. At the same time, a large number of serious violent incidents do occur at school, and less serious crime is common at schools. Furthermore, certain schools, particularly schools in poor urban areas, suffer from high rates of both minor crime and serious violence. For example, some data indicate that poor schools in urban areas have rates of serious violence up to 15 times higher on average than less poor schools in suburban, small town, and rural areas (Kaufman et al. 1998:61).

It is, of course, important to understand why some students are more likely than others to engage in school crime and why some schools have much higher rates of crime than do others. Such crime not only has a devastating effect on many of its victims, but it interferes with the fundamental mission of schools. It is difficult for learning to occur when one's safety is in doubt.

■ How Can We Explain School Crime?

Politicians and others have blamed school crime on several factors including the effects of mass media violence, an increase in gangs, the absence of school prayer, the availability of guns, lax security in the schools, the "breakdown" of the family, and a failure to impose severe punishments on juvenile offenders. Many of these explanations reflect the two dominant theories of crime: differential association/social learning theory and control theory. Differential association/social learning theory says that we learn to engage in crime from others including family, friends, gang members, and the media. These others might model criminal behavior (which we then imitate), reinforce or reward our criminal behavior, and teach us beliefs conducive to crime (e.g., we should respond with violence if someone treats us with disrespect). Control theories argue that we are more likely to engage in crime when we are low in social control. Social control can be external or internal. When external control is low, we have little fear of sanction from others including family, friends, teachers, and police. We feel that these others will not catch us committing crimes or that, if they do catch us, we have little fear of the punishments they will impose. When internal social control is low, we can engage in crime with little guilt because we do not believe that crime is wrong.

I do not deny the relevance of these and other theories. In fact, I encourage the reader to apply the other theories in this book to the explanation of school crime. My focus, however, is on strain theory. Strain theory makes a rather simple argument: when other people treat us badly, we might get upset and respond with crime. I elaborate on this simple idea and then apply it to the explanation of school crime.

□ A Brief Overview of Strain Theory

Strain theory first describes the two major ways in which people can treat us badly, that is, treat us in ways we do not like.

First, people can prevent us from achieving our goals. Strain theory argues that juveniles can pursue a variety of goals. These goals include money and the things that money can buy such as nice clothes and a good car. They include status and respect; most people want to be positively regarded and treated in a respectful manner by others. They include autonomy, as many juveniles have a strong desire for autonomy from adults; they do not like to be told what to do and instead want the freedom to make their own decisions. Juveniles, however, often are prevented from achieving these goals through legitimate channels. For example, their parents do not give them the money to buy the clothes they want or finance their social activities. Certain people do not treat them with the respect they feel they deserve, and their parents and teachers try to control things such as how they dress, how late they stay out, and with whom they associate.

Second, people can take things that we value or present us with negative or noxious stimuli. For example, people can take our possessions, or our romantic partners can break up with us. So, we lose something that we value. Or, people can verbally insult us or physically attack us.

Strain theory then argues that this bad treatment makes us *feel* bad; that is, it makes us feel angry, frustrated, depressed, anxious, and the like. These bad feelings create pressure for corrective action; we want to do something so that we will not feel so bad. This is especially true if we are angry or frustrated. These emotions energize us for action, create a desire for revenge, and lower our inhibitions. There are several possible ways in which to respond to the strain and negative emotions we feel, certain of which involve crime. We might engage in crime to end the bad treatment we are experiencing. For example, we might steal to get the money we want, or we might attack people to stop them from harassing us. We might engage in crime to seek revenge against the people who are mistreating us, and we might engage in a crime such as illicit drug use to make us feel better.

Whether we engage in crime is said to depend on a number of factors. Individuals are more likely to respond to strain with crime if they have poor problem-solving skills. For example, individuals who lack the verbal skills to negotiate with others are more likely to respond to harassment with crime. Individuals are more likely to respond to strain with crime if they have few conventional social supports. For example, individuals who cannot turn to their parents for assistance when they face problems are more likely to resort to crime. Individuals are more likely to respond with crime when they are in situations where the costs of crime are low and the rewards are high. For example, individuals are more likely to steal when there are no police or teachers around and valuable objects are within easy reach. Individuals also are more likely to respond with crime when they have dispositions for crime. For example, some individuals have traits that are conducive to crime such as impulsivity and irritability. Some individuals are low in social control; they do not fear sanctions from others, and they do not believe that crime is wrong. Furthermore, some individuals have been taught to engage in crime in certain situations. (For fuller descriptions of strain theory, see Agnew 1992, 1997, forthcoming.)

□ *Using Strain Theory to Explain Why Some Individuals
Are More Likely to Engage in School Crime*

At the most basic level, some individuals are more likely to engage in crime, both within school and outside of school, because they experience more strain and are more likely to respond to strain with crime. Studies suggest that individuals are more likely to engage in crime when they experience the following types of strain: dissatisfaction with the amount of money they have, child abuse or neglect, criminal victimization, physical punishment by parents, negative relations with parents, negative relations with peers, neighborhood problems, homelessness, and a wide range of stressful life events such as the divorce/separation of parents, parental unemployment, and changing schools (Agnew 1997, forthcoming). There has been less research on those factors that influence whether one responds to strain with crime, and the few studies in this area have produced mixed results (Agnew, forthcoming). Nevertheless, strain theory would predict that crime is especially likely among strained individuals who are low in problem-solving skills and conventional social support, are in situations where the costs of crime are low and the rewards are high, and have dispositions for crime.

Much of the strain that individuals experience originates outside of school. The family, for example, is a major source of strain. But a good deal of strain occurs at school, and such strain is the focus of this chapter. We might classify school strain into four categories: negative peer relations, negative teacher relations, low grades, and a general dissatisfaction with school. Data suggest that individuals who experience these types of strain are more likely to engage in crime including school crime (Agnew 1985, 1997, forthcoming; Agnew and Brezina 1997; Cernkovich and Giordano 1992; Hawkins and Lishner 1987; Jenkins 1997; Maguin and Loeber 1996; Welsh, Greene, and Jenkins 1999).

Negative Peer Relations

Schools, in particular middle schools and high schools, usually bring together large numbers of students. These students did not choose to associate with one another, they have different interests and personalities, and they do not have much experience coping with difficult situations. Nevertheless, they are concentrated in the same small space for several hours a day, and they often are placed in situations where they compete against one another for things such as good grades and status in the adolescent world. It is not surprising that many of them get into conflicts with one another. In particular, they sometimes treat one another in disliked ways. One common problem in schools, for example, is "bullying," which occurs when a person "is exposed, repeatedly and over time, to negative actions on the part of one or more other persons" (Olweus 1991:413). Negative actions are defined as those intentional actions that inflict or attempt to inflict injury or discomfort on another person.

Negative peer relations such as bullying are a major type of strain. In fact, when students are asked about the things that upset or anger them, they frequently talk about interpersonal problems with peers. Surprisingly, criminologists have not devoted much attention to the impact of such problems on crime. But the few studies that have been done in this area suggest that such problems increase the likelihood of crime (Agnew and Brezina 1997). In this connection, I should note that many of the students who have committed mass murder at school were in part motivated by the fact that they had been bullied by others or had experienced other interpersonal problems with peers. The large majority of students, of course, do not react to peer problems in such an extreme manner. Nowadays, it is difficult to explain, and especially difficult to predict, why a few students go to such extremes. Nevertheless, negative peer relations is one source of school crime.

Lockwood (1997) has done some fascinating research on the connection between peer problems and crime including school crime. He interviewed 110 middle and high school students from schools with high rates of violence. These students discussed 250 violent incidents in which they had been involved. About half of these incidents occurred at school, followed by public areas and homes. Most of these incidents (58 percent) involved acquaintances, followed by friends (16 percent) and family members (15 percent). Only 11 percent involved strangers. So, the most common setting for a violent crime was an encounter with an "acquaintance" at school. These violent incidents almost always began when one of the students did something that the other student did not like. One of the most common things was "unprovoked offensive touching" such as pushing, grabbing, hitting, or throwing something at someone. Other disliked behaviors included interfering with someone else's possessions, refusing to do something when requested, saying something bad about someone else, verbally teasing someone, and deliberately insulting someone. These actions threaten one's status and autonomy, involve the loss of valued things, and/or involve the presence of negative stimuli. They usually lead to an argument, the argument sometimes escalates with insults being exchanged, and violence sometimes is the result.

The violence is performed to end the disliked behavior, seek revenge, and/or save face.

Negative Teacher Relations and Poor Grades

Data also suggest that poor relations with teachers increases the likelihood of crime. Teachers might present students with negative stimuli. One study, for example, found that crime was more likely among students who reported that their teachers often lost their tempers, made negative comments, and talked down to students (Agnew 1985). Related to this, students might become upset when they receive poor grades from teachers. Not all students care about their grades, but some do, and limited data suggest that the receipt of poor grades is an important source of strain and crime in certain cases.

School Dissatisfaction

Finally, many students experience a more general type of strain at school. They find school boring and a "waste of time," partly because they have trouble understanding what is going on in class and keeping up with schoolwork. They do not feel that school is relevant to their future lives. They have little involvement in school activities, and they would rather be elsewhere. In short, they dislike school. Data suggest that such students also are more likely to engage in crime.

I should note that the association between crime and factors such as poor grades and dissatisfaction with school does not prove that strain theory is correct. These factors might be related to crime for reasons that have to do with social control theory or other theories. Individuals who have poor grades and dislike school, for example, are lower in social control. They have less to lose by engaging in crime and so are less deterred by the threat of punishment. Nevertheless, some data suggest that these factors affect crime at least partly by increasing the anger of students (Agnew 1985).

☐ Using Strain Theory to Explain Why Some Schools Have Higher Crime Rates

Some schools have much higher crime rates than do other schools. A few researchers have tried to determine why this is the case. They usually find that school differences in crime are largely a function of differences between the students who attend the schools and the communities in which the schools are located. School crime usually is higher in schools that have higher percentages of students who are less able, poor, male, and members of minority groups. School crime usually is higher in schools that are located in urban communities with high rates of crime, poverty, unemployment, and female-headed households. To a large extent, then, school crime is a function of forces that are external to the school. However, when we take account of student and community characteristics, we find that school characteristics do have a small to modest association with rates of school crime (Catalano and Hawkins 1996; Elliott et al. 1998; Gottfredson and Gottfredson 1985; Hawkins and Lishner 1987; Hellman and Beaton 1986; Lawrence 1998; Weishew and Peng 1993; Welsh et al. 1999).

Although not all studies agree with one another, the evidence suggests that school crime tends to be lower in the following types of schools:

- Small schools with good resources
- Schools with good discipline where there are clear rules for behavior and these rules are consistently enforced in a fair manner (there is some evidence, however, that overly punitive discipline contributes to higher rates of school crime; certain studies, for example, suggest that delinquency rates are higher in schools that use physical punishment and that make frequent use of punishment)
- Schools that provide opportunities for students to succeed, including students who do not plan to attend college, and that praise student accomplishments
- Schools that have high expectations for students and that make rigorous but not unrealistic work demands on them
- Schools where teachers have positive attitudes toward students, show concern for students, and create a pleasant physical space for students to work
- Schools with good cooperation between the administration and teachers, with the administration keeping teachers informed of disciplinary problems and supporting/assisting teachers in their disciplinary efforts

The association between these factors and school crime can be *partly* explained in terms of strain theory. Schools with the preceding characteristics create less strain among students. On the one hand, schools with these characteristics are firm; rules are clearly stated and consistently enforced. One likely consequence of this firmness is that students are less likely to mistreat one another; such mistreatment is not tolerated. So, a major source of school strain is reduced. At the same time, these schools show much concern for students. Whereas there are firm rules for behavior, such rules are not overly strict or punitive, and they are fairly enforced. This also reduces strain because students resent punishments that are overly harsh or unfairly applied. These schools provide more opportunities for student success and involvement, which reduces poor grades and dissatisfaction with school. Teachers in these schools try to create good relationships with students and positive working relationships with them. For example, they frequently praise student accomplishments as they attempt to assist students in need. Not only does this reduce strain, but teachers are more likely to help students cope with the strain they do experience.

☐ *Summary*

So, students who are high in strain are more likely to engage in crime including school crime. I focused on four types of strain: negative peer relations, negative teacher relations, low grades, and dissatisfaction with school. Also, it might be the case that strained students are more likely to engage in crime when they have low problem-solving skills and low social support, encounter situations in which the costs of crime are low and the rewards are high, and have dispositions for crime. Again, there are other reasons why students engage in school crime, but these are the primary reasons derived from strain theory. Schools are more likely to have high rates of crimes when they do not possess the characteristics listed in the previous subsection. Whereas these characteristics likely are related to school crime for a variety of reasons, their association with school crime can be partly explained in terms of strain theory.

■ What Can We Do to Reduce School Crime?

Many recommendations have been made in this area. Some derive from social control theory. People argue that we should increase the likelihood that school crime will be detected and punished. For example, we should place metal detectors and armed guards in schools. We should encourage students to report threats and suspicious activity to school authorities. And we should severely punish students who do engage in crime. Other recommendations derive from social learning theory. For example, we should regulate media violence more closely and do more to get gangs out of the schools. Still other recommendations focus on those factors that facilitate school crime or increase the severity of such crime. For example, we should increase the controls on guns and reduce drug use among juveniles. Excellent overviews of the various strategies for reducing school crime, especially the strategies that can be implemented by schools, can be found in Agnew (1995); Anderson (1998); Arnette and Walsleben (1998); Brewer et al. (1995); Catalano et al. (1998); Elliott et al. (1998); Gottfredson (1998); Walker, Colvin, and Ramsey (1995); and Weissbourd (1996).

My focus is on those strategies suggested by strain theory, especially strategies that can be employed by schools. Basically, strain theory would suggest two fundamental strategies for reducing school crime. First, we should reduce the amount of strain that students experience. There are several things we can do in this area including things that reduce the amount of strain experienced at school. It is unlikely, however, that we can eliminate all strain. No matter how hard we try, for example, it is likely that students still will mistreat one another at times. So, a second strategy is to reduce the likelihood that students respond to strain with crime. There are several things we can do in this area.

In what follows, I present brief descriptions of some of the programs we might employ to reduce school crime. I should note that most of these programs were not developed with strain theory in mind, but they nevertheless are compatible with strain theory. Evaluations of these programs indicate that they hold much promise for reducing crime.

□ Reducing School Strain

One of the major reasons why students experience school strain is because they lack adequate preparation for school. As a result, they do poorly in school, often get into conflicts with teachers and others, and develop a general dislike for school. Certain *preschool programs,* however, can better prepare students for school. These programs attempt to foster the social and intellectual development of children and better involve parents in the educational process. The most effective of these programs begin early in life, last two years or more, have low student-to-teacher ratios, and employ carefully designed curricula. Such programs have been found to increase school performance, increase attachment to school, and reduce crime.

Other programs reduce school strain by *changing the classroom environment.* For example, several innovative teaching techniques attempt to increase the opportunities for students to succeed. In the process, they create better relations between teachers and students and among students. One technique, for example, involves the formation of cooperative learning groups in which students help one another master class materials. Another technique, known as interactive teaching, provides students with specific objectives they must master, provides frequent feedback, provides help when necessary, employs objective grading, and bases grades on mastery of material and improvement over past performance rather than comparisons with other students. Not only does this technique increase opportunities for success, but the grading methods increase perceptions of fairness and decrease competition with other students.

Still other programs reduce strain by *changing the school environment*. Most notable in this area are programs that try to change school disciplinary practices. Such programs can reduce the extent to which students mistreat one another and improve relations between students and school staff. Drawing from several studies, the elements of proper discipline include the following:

- Establish clear rules that prohibit various forms of student misbehavior. There might be some advantage in involving students in the rule-making process because the rules are likely to be seen as more fair.
- Remind students of these rules regularly. Again, there might be some advantage in having students help to publicize the rules.
- Closely monitor student activities both inside and outside the classroom. Teachers, for example, should monitor student activities in the cafeteria, halls, rest rooms, and school grounds. Also, teachers and others should be taught to recognize the early warning signs of trouble so that they might intervene before a situation escalates (Lockwood 1997).
- Consistently sanction rule violators in a nonhostile and nonphysical way.
- Support and protect the victims of student violence.

Evidence suggests that such strategies can significantly reduce the extent to which students mistreat one another. These steps, for example, resulted in a dramatic reduction in bullying behavior in one study (Olweus 1991).

Some schools have attempted to change the school environment in ways that extend well beyond disciplinary procedures. For example, some schools have formed teams that include students, teachers, administrators, parents, and others. These teams evaluate the schools and then develop and implement school improvements. Many of these improvements have the effect of reducing school strain. For example, efforts might be made to increase the involvement and success experiences of students at high risk for crime. Such efforts might involve the creation of special academic programs such as career exploration programs and programs that teach job- seeking skills. They might involve efforts to better involve such students in extracurricular activities. They might involve special counseling and tutoring programs as well. The teams also launch school pride campaigns, which might include pep rallies and school cleanup programs. The teams might create "schools within schools" to address the problems associated with large schools.

☐ Reducing the Likelihood That Students Will Respond to Strain With Crime

Again, it is not possible to completely eliminate the strain that people experience, but we can reduce the likelihood that people respond to strain with crime. Several programs are relevant here.

Some of the more successful delinquency prevention programs teach juveniles a range of social and problem-solving skills that enable juveniles to respond to strain without engaging in crime. Certain of these skills are rather specific, for example, how to respond to problems such as teasing by peers and criticism from teachers. Other skills are more general such as how to negotiate with others, how to be assertive rather than aggressive, and how to control one's anger, At the most general level, these programs teach juveniles to think before they act. Rather than acting impulsively or letting their anger get the best of them, these programs teach juveniles to pause before they act, analyze the problems they confront, develop solutions, and select the most appropriate solutions. Data suggest that students who complete such programs are less likely to engage in crime.

Other programs try to increase the social support available to students. Some programs try to foster closer ties between students and their parents. Others try to foster closer ties between students and teachers. Still others provide juveniles with adult mentors who offer advice and assistance in solving problems and who model appropriate behavior. Finally, some schools train students and others in conflict mediation so that they might better respond to difficult situations before violence erupts. Although not all of these programs are effective, many of the better implemented programs have been able to reduce levels of crime.

Finally, some programs try to reduce juveniles' predispositions to delinquency. For example, they might attempt to alter those traits that are conducive to delinquency such as impulsivity and irritability. They might attempt to increase juveniles' levels of social control. They might attempt to reduce the presence of gangs in school and foster beliefs that condemn delinquency. Fuller descriptions of these programs and other programs can be found in the sources cited previously.

■ Conclusion

Much data suggest that one of the major causes of school crime is the strain that students experience including the strain experienced at school. Strain theory focuses on several important sources of school crime that have not received much attention in the media, and it highlights the importance of several strategies for controlling school crime that have been neglected in the media and by many politicians.

STUDY QUESTIONS

1. List some of the things that have upset or angered you during the past month. To what extent do they fall into the major types of strain described by strain theory?

2. Why is crime sometimes an appealing response to strain? What are some of the noncriminal ways in which to respond to strain?

3. Describe the characteristics of a student who is likely to respond to strain with crime.

4. Pick any two of the other theories described in this book. How do such theories differ from strain theory? How would these theories explain school crime?

5. What changes would you make in your high school to reduce school crime? To what extent are these changes compatible with strain theory? To what extent do they reflect other theories of crime?

6. Many people want to control school crime through the use of "get tough" strategies such as installing metal detectors, placing police in schools, searching lockers, encouraging students to report on one another, and severely punishing students who

misbehave. Do you think that a strain theorist would favor or oppose such strategies?

REFERENCES

Agnew, Robert. 1985. "A Revised Strain Theory of Delinquency." *Social Forces* 64:151-67.

———. 1992. "Foundation for a General Strain Theory of Crime and Delinquency." *Criminology* 30:47-87.

———. 1995. "Controlling Delinquency: Recommendations From General Strain Theory." Pp. 43-70 in *Crime and Public Policy*, edited by Hugh D. Barlow. Boulder, CO: Westview.

———. 1997. "Stability and Change in Crime Over the Life Course: A Strain Theory Explanation." Pp. 101-32 in *Advances in Criminological Theory*, vol. 7: *Developmental Theories of Crime and Delinquency*, edited by Terence P. Thornberry. New Brunswick, NJ: Transaction Publishers.

———. Forthcoming. "An Overview of General Strain Theory." In *Essays in Criminological Theories*, edited by Ray Paternoster. Los Angeles: Roxbury.

Agnew, Robert and Timothy Brezina. 1997. "Relational Problems With Peers, Gender, and Delinquency." *Youth & Society* 29:84-111.

Anderson, David C. 1998. "Curriculum, Culture, and Community: The Challenge of School Violence." Pp. 317-63 in *Crime and Justice: A Review of Research*, vol. 24, edited by Michael Tonry and Mark H. Moore. Chicago: University of Chicago Press.

Arnette, June L. and Marjorie C. Walsleben. 1998. *Combating Fear and Restoring Safety in Schools*. Washington, DC: U.S. Department of Justice, Office of Juvenile Justice and Delinquency Prevention.

Brewer, Devon D., J. David Hawkins, Richard F. Catalano, and Holly J. Neckerman. 1995. "Preventing Serious, Violent, and Chronic Juvenile Offending: A Review of Evaluations of Selected Strategies in Childhood, Adolescence, and the Community." Pp. 61-141 in *A Sourcebook of Serious, Violent, and Chronic Juvenile Offenders*, edited by James C. Howell, Barry Krisberg, J. David Hawkins, and John J. Wilson. Thousand Oaks, CA: Sage.

Catalano, Richard F., Michael W. Arthur, J. David Hawkins, Lisa Berglund, and Jeffrey J. Olson. 1998. "Comprehensive Community- and School-Based Interventions to Prevent Antisocial Behavior." Pp. 248-83 in *Serious and Violent Juvenile Offenders*, edited by Rolf Loeber and David P. Farrington. Thousand Oaks, CA: Sage.

Catalano, Richard F. and J. David Hawkins. 1996. "The Social Development Model: A Theory of Antisocial Behavior." Pp. 149-97 in *Delinquency and Crime*, edited by J. David Hawkins. Cambridge, UK: Cambridge University Press.

Cernkovich, Stephen A. and Peggy C. Giordano. 1992. "School Bonding, Race, and Delinquency." *Criminology* 30:261-91.

Elliott, Delbert S., Beatrix A. Hamburg, and Kirk R. Williams. 1998. *Violence in American Schools*. Cambridge, UK: Cambridge University Press.

Gottfredson, Denise C. 1998. "School-Based Crime Prevention." In *Preventing Crime: What Works, What Doesn't, What's Promising*, edited by Lawrence W. Sherman. Washington, DC: U.S. Department of Justice.

Gottfredson, Gary D. and Denise C. Gottfredson. 1985. *Victimization in Schools*. New York: Plenum.

Hawkins, J. David and Denise Lishner. 1987. "Schooling and Delinquency." Pp. 179-221 in *Handbook on Crime and Delinquency Prevention*, edited by Elmer H. Johnson. Westport, CT: Greenwood.

Hellman, Daryl A. and Susan Beaton. 1986. "The Pattern of Violence in Urban Public Schools: The Influence of School and Community." *Journal of Research in Crime and Delinquency* 23:102-27.

Jenkins, Patricia H. 1997. "School Delinquency and the School Social Bond." *Journal of Research in Crime and Delinquency* 34:337-67.

Kaufman, Phillip, Xianglei Chen, Susan P. Choy, Kathryn A. Chandler, and Michael R. Rand. 1998. *Indicators of School Crime and Safety, 1998.* Washington, DC: U.S. Department of Education and U.S. Department of Justice.

Lawrence, Richard. 1998. *School Crime and Juvenile Justice.* New York: Oxford University Press.

Lockwood, Daniel. 1997. *Violence Among Middle School and High School Students: An Analysis and Implications for Prevention.* Washington, DC: U.S. Department of Justice, National Institute of Justice.

Maguin, Eugene and Rolf Loeber. 1996. "Academic Performance and Delinquency." Pp. 145-264 in *Crime and Justice: A Review of Research,* vol. 20, edited by Michael Tonry. Chicago: University of Chicago Press.

Olweus, Dan. 1991. "Bully/Victim Problems Among Schoolchildren: Basic Facts and Effects of a School-Based Intervention Program." Pp. 411-48 in *The Development and Treatment of Childhood Aggression,* edited by Debra J. Pepler and Kenneth H. Rubin. Hillsdale, NJ: Lawrence Erlbaum.

Walker, Hill M., Geoff Colvin, and Elizabeth Ramsey. 1995. *Antisocial Behavior in School: Strategies and Best Practices.* Pacific Grove, CA: Brooks/Cole.

Weishew, Nancy L. and Samuel S. Peng. 1993. "Variables Predicting Students' Problem Behaviors." *Journal of Educational Research* 87:5-17.

Weissbourd, Richard. 1996. *The Vulnerable Child.* Reading, MA: Addison-Wesley.

Wells, Edward L. and Joseph H. Rankin. 1995. "Juvenile Victimization: Convergent Validation of Alternative Measurements." *Journal of Research in Crime and Delinquency* 32:287-307.

Welsh, Wayne N., Jack R. Greene, and Patricia H. Jenkins. 1999. "School Disorder: The Influence of Individual, Institutional, and Community Factors." *Criminology* 37:73-116.

The Dramatization of Evil

Reacting to Juvenile Delinquency During the 1990s

RUTH TRIPLETT

In 1985, a lengthy period of stability in juvenile arrest rates came to an end (Cook and Laub 1998). At that time, the United States witnessed an increase in the overall juvenile arrest rate. Close examination of the increase in juvenile arrest rates revealed, however, that the juvenile arrest rate for property crime had remained stable. What was driving the increase in the overall juvenile arrest rate was dramatic increases in arrests for violent offenses, in particular, homicide. Arrest data indicate that between 1985 and 1994, arrests for homicide among juveniles increased by 140 percent. The increase in the juvenile arrest rate for homicide was particularly striking because the homicide arrest rate for those over 25 years of age had actually declined (Blumstein 1995).

Our reaction to juvenile offending during the 1980s and early 1990s was as dramatic as the increase in violent offenses. During that period, we witnessed sweeping changes in the laws governing violent juvenile offenders. The changes included U.S. Supreme Court rulings that declined to set a limit on the age below which a death sentence would be "cruel and unusual" punishment, increasing methods for transfer of juveniles to adult court, and lowering the age at which a juvenile can be transferred. Overall, these changes indicate a strong "get tough" stance on juvenile delinquency with a resulting increase in the severity of sentences. For example, one study found that average sentences for juveniles in California went from 14.8 months in 1985 to 23.7 months in 1989 (Freedberg 1989). Others report that there has been a dramatic increase in the numbers of youths confined in juvenile facilities as well as in adult jails and prisons (Schwartz 1989).

Our reaction to juvenile delinquency, however, has not been limited to violent crimes and the juveniles who commit them. Figures show that of those youths incarcerated, 27 percent are violent offenders, with most of the remainder incarcerated for property and drug offenses (Office of Juvenile Justice and Delinquency Prevention 1989). Furthermore, although there is variation across jurisdictions, there also is evidence of increasing criminalization of status offenses and institutionalization of status offenders after a long period of attempts at decriminalization and deinstitutionalization.

Although the juvenile arrest rate for violent crimes has been declining since 1994, fears about violent juvenile offending and about juvenile delinquency in general remain high. These fears are fed by a concern for an impending crime wave that several noted criminologists have predicted. Given this, it is more important now than ever that we develop a greater understanding of not just the causes of juvenile delinquency but also our attempts to control it. One theoretical perspective that can help us to do this is labeling theory. This theory aids in our understanding in the following ways:

- giving us a framework for characterizing our reaction to juvenile delinquency in terms of labeling;
- predicting what the effect of labeling will be; and
- encouraging us to think about how we can respond to juvenile delinquency in a way that avoids the negative effects of labels.

The chapter begins by examining the work of labeling theorists. It then turns to an exploration of the nation's response to youth crime during the 1980s and 1990s through a framework provided by labeling theory. The final half of the chapter explains how labeling could affect the level of juvenile offending in America and how we can react to juvenile delinquency in a way that responds to crime without labeling offenders.

■ Labeling Theory From the 1930s to the 1990s

The individual usually identified as the first labeling theorist is Frank Tannenbaum. Labeling theorists of the 1950s and 1960s built on Tannenbaum's (1938) ideas to develop a perspective that had a tremendous impact on the way in which criminologists thought about crime and criminals. Central to the work of these labeling theorists are ideas that remain important to labeling theory during the 1990s. The ideas they expressed find their most recent expression in theories such as that proposed by Bruce Link and his colleagues (Link 1987; Link and Cullen 1983; Link et al. 1987, 1989). Their modified labeling theory provides an excellent framework for understanding the possible effect of our present attempts at controlling delinquency.

□ Tannenbaum and the Early Labeling Theorists: The Dramatization of Evil

Tannenbaum (1938) began his analysis of juvenile delinquency with a discussion of how people in general, and criminologists in particular, view youths who break the law. Both groups tend to view these youths as evil, abnormal, or somehow different from those who do not commit crimes. In fact, the predominant criminological thought today is based on just this assumption of differentiation. Tannenbaum argued that this view of juvenile delinquents as different affects both the way in which society reacts to the youths that it defines as delinquent and how youths who are defined as delinquent respond to society's reaction.

According to Tannenbaum (1938), the process of defining a youth as delinquent begins with a conflict between the youth and the community over the definition of a situation. For example, a youth might define activities such as spray-painting the side of a building, stealing CDs from a music store, and loitering in public areas as play, fun, or adventure. In other words, to the youth, these are normal childhood activities. The community, however, is more likely to define these same behaviors as delinquent or evil. The process through which the community defines normal childhood activities as evil is one form of what Tannenbaum called the dramatization of evil.

Over time, this conflict between the youth and the community over the definition of the youth's activities hardens the community's attitude toward the youth. Now it is not merely the act that is defined as evil but the youth as well. Once community members begin to define the youth as evil, changes begin in the way that they interact with the youth. Parents begin to exclude the youth from activities with their children, and the youth begins to feel isolated from others. These changes in the way that people respond to the youth make him or her conscious of the fact that the community views the youth as different or evil. Slowly, the youth comes to define himself or herself as evil as well. It is this process of "defining, identifying, segregating, describing, emphasizing, making conscious and self-conscious" that Tannenbaum (1938:20) referred to as tagging. According to Tannenbaum, it is the changes in the youth caused by the dramatization of evil and tagging that lead the youth to further delinquent acts.

Although Tannenbaum laid the groundwork for labeling in 1938, the labeling perspective did not become popular in criminology until the 1960s. Edwin Lemert and Howard Becker are two of the central theorists who expanded Tannenbaum's ideas on the role of social reactions in creating delinquency. Lemert (1951) is most known for the distinction he made between primary and secondary deviance:

- *Primary deviance:* Initial acts of deviance or criminality committed by an individual are those that Lemert called primary deviance. Lemert believed that almost everyone commits acts of primary deviance. The reasons why an individual might commit an act of primary deviance include peer pressure, lack of social control, and psychological defects. Lemert, however, was not trying to explain the causes of primary deviance, for he believed that it was temporary and less serious than the second type of deviance.

- *Secondary deviance:* This is deviance that occurs "when a person begins to employ his deviant behavior or role based upon it as a means of defense, attack, or adjustment to the overt and covert problems created by the consequent societal reaction to him" (Schur 1951:76). A good example of secondary deviance is the deviance that occurs after an offender adopts a criminal identity. According to Lemert, the movement from primary deviance to secondary deviance occurs as a result of a sequence of interactions that begins with an act of primary deviance. This act causes a social reaction. Further acts of deviance then occur, resulting in stronger reactions. If this cycle continues, then an individual might embrace a deviant role, thus leading to secondary deviance.

A large part of Becker's (1963) contribution to labeling theory comes from his discussion of the development of deviant careers. He believed that deviant or criminal careers emerge from passage through three phases:

1. An act of initial rule-breaking, whether intentional or not, occurs.
2. "Being caught and publicly labeled deviant," which has important consequences for an individual's public identity, social interaction, and self-identity. Becker argued that the label *criminal* or *juvenile delinquent* is so stigmatizing in our society that it becomes a master status, overriding any other role or position an individual might hold. Once it is known that a person is a criminal, that

status becomes more important to people than the fact that the person also is a mother or a father, a teacher or a farmer, fun or boring. In short, a master status as *criminal* becomes the defining characteristic of an individual so labeled regardless of any other characteristics the person might have. Once an individual's social identity has changed, social interaction changes as people begin to react to the label. The labeled individual is excluded from interaction with conventional others and from involvement in conventional activities and opportunities. As a result, the labeled individual gets "caught up in" the criminal role, a process referred to as role engulfment. These changes in social identity and social interaction lead to a change in the individual's self-image.

3. The labeled person moves into a deviant group. Becker argued that movement into a deviant group, such as a gang, further affects the individual's social identity, social interaction, and self-image. Movement into a deviant group also provides the individual with rationalizations, motives, and attitudes that support deviant behavior.

□ *Supporting Evidence*

Labeling theory became popular during the 1960s with the publication of Becker's (1963) book, *Outsiders*. It soon received both wide support and wide criticism. Support for labeling theory came from those who valued the theory for turning attention to the way in which attempts at social control can lead to more crime. Support for the theory led to support for movements toward the deinstitutionalization of juvenile offenders, the decriminalization of status offenses, and the diversion of juvenile offenders from the juvenile justice system.

Critics, however, offered a number of important concerns regarding labeling (Ball 1983; Wellford 1975). Central to their criticisms was the idea that not everyone who is labeled goes on to commit more crimes. In fact, critics argued that punishment often reduces the likelihood that a juvenile will re-offend. They also argued that labeling theory ignores the response of the individual to the label. In addition, some critics were concerned about how we were to respond to crime if every response led to labels and more crime. These individuals found the call of some labeling theorists for radical nonintervention (see, e.g., Schur 1973) as unsatisfactory.

In the face of these concerns, support for labeling theory declined as we moved into the late 1970s. However, by the late 1980s, a number of criminologists once again began discussing the effect of labeling individuals. These newer versions tempered the original statements by the labeling theorists of the 1960s, addressing some of the criticism just mentioned. A good example of this recent work is that of Link and his colleagues.

☐ Link: Social Conceptions of Crime

In a series of articles during the late 1980s, Link and his colleagues outlined what they called a modified labeling theory (Link 1987; Link and Cullen 1983; Link et al. 1987, 1989). Although focused on the mentally ill, it has particular relevance for those who are interested in the effects of our present attempts to control juvenile delinquency.

Link and his colleagues began their argument by suggesting that, as part of socialization into American society, people come to internalize particular societal conceptions of the mentally ill—who the mentally ill are, what it is to be mentally ill, and how the mentally ill will be treated in our society. We all know jokes about the mentally ill and have seen how they are portrayed in movies and on television. Some of us might have seen the negative ways in which people react to those who are labeled mentally ill. Overall, our socialization teaches us that those who are labeled mentally ill will be devalued (they will suffer a loss of status) and discriminated against (people will distance themselves from them).

Knowledge of how our society treats the mentally ill leads those who need psychiatric treatment to expect that they will be devalued and discriminated against or rejected. This expectation of rejection leads such labeled persons to one of three possible responses:

- *Secrecy:* Those who are seeking treatment hide that fact from their friends, family, and co-workers to avoid the rejection they expect if people know about the treatment.
- *Withdrawal:* Individuals withdraw from their friends, family, and others who they expect will reject them.
- *Education:* Individuals disclose their problems and actively try to change the attitudes of those around them.

Link and his colleagues argued that each of these responses has different negative consequences for the individual's social ties, earning power, and self-esteem. Of the three responses, withdrawal is expected to be the most harmful because it leads the individual to break ties with family and friends. The reduction in these ties can open the individual up to decreases in earning power and to lower self-esteem. It is the reduction in ties to others, earning power, and self-esteem that Link argued leaves the individual vulnerable to a new mental disorder or a repeated episode of an existing disorder.

Link's model might have something important to tell us about juvenile delinquents as well as the mentally ill. It is quite possible that our society has developed a particular societal conception of juvenile delinquents that involves devaluation and discrimination. Research already has shown that adult offenders are viewed more negatively than the mentally ill and that adult offenders are discriminated against in terms of employment. Research on the public's perception of juvenile offenders is lacking, but there is reason to believe that, even though the stigma might be less for juveniles labeled delinquent than for adults labeled criminal, it still is present. To the extent that those labeled juvenile delinquent know of this societal conception, they might react to their expectations of devaluation and discrimination in ways that increase their chances of re-offending.

■ Responding to Juvenile Delinquency During the 1990s

From the work of the labeling theorists, we can develop a framework for examining our reaction as a nation to juvenile delinquency and the possible effect of our reaction for the labeled individual. We can use Tannenbaum's (1938) discussion of the dramatization of evil to categorize some of the recent changes in the handling of juvenile delinquents that have swept the nation. From his work can be drawn three types of the dramatization of evil: the act as evil, the child as evil, and the generalization of evil.

□ The Act as Evil

When Tannenbaum (1938) referred to dramatizing the act as evil, he was referring to a community's definition of "normal childhood activities" as evil. In this chapter, the phrase is used to refer to reactions to an offense that increase the punishment of the offense and thus its perceived seriousness. Using this definition of dramatizing the act as evil, we can identify two examples of how recent changes in our reaction to juvenile delinquents define the act as evil:

1. The inclusion of status offenses in sentencing guidelines (the purpose of which is to sanction offenders)

The most powerful example today of defining the act as evil is the response of some states to status offenses such as truancy and running away. Many children at some point skip school or decide to leave home to express their anger at their parents. From the perspective of labeling theorists, these acts can be viewed and responded to as acts of rebellion against authority that are a normal part of growing up. In fact, that this belief is the normality of much status offending was a big part of the movement begun during the 1970s for the decriminalization of status offenders, removing status offenders from secure facilities (see, e.g., Schwartz 1989). States that take this stance toward status offenders include Delaware, Alaska, and Maine (Maxson and Klein 1997). These states have made changes in legislation that remove status offenses from the jurisdiction of the juvenile court. The belief underlying this and similar policies is that decriminalization normalizes the behavior and thus avoids the negative consequences of labels.

Others, however, look at the same behavior in a very different light. They see running away and failure to attend school as a result of a lack of supervision and discipline and as indicators of a non-normal lack of respect for authority. The response of this group is to keep the status offenses as offenses so that the offenders can be dealt with by the juvenile justice system. Michigan and Idaho are examples of states that have taken this position on status offenses (Maxson and Klein 1997). In both of these states, status offenses are kept under the jurisdiction of the juvenile court. Two of the ideas behind this are that the court will have the authority to see that status offenders get the supervision and discipline they need and that the court will be allowed to use punishment as a method of deterring offenders from committing future offenses.

Beyond the idea that states that keep status offenses under the jurisdiction of the juvenile court illustrates their dramatizing the evil of status offenses is the punishments that status offenses merit. By keeping status offenses under the jurisdiction of the juvenile court, sentences for status offenses are included in the sentencing structures for property and violent crimes. For example, Texas now has a progressive sanctions model for dealing with juvenile offenders in which offenses are categorized by level of seriousness and progressively serious sanctions are associated with each level. In Texas, the levels go from one to seven, with status offenses such as truancy and running away from home placed at the first level (Dawson 1996). Another good example of this is seen in states such as Michigan and Idaho, where status offenders are subject to many placements usually reserved for those who have committed criminal offenses. These include placing status offenders in detention facilities and secure facilities as well as using probation or restitution programs (Maxson and Klein 1997).

2. The recriminalization of violent offenses that occurs when these offenses are automatically waived to adult court

Whereas defining as evil acts that might well be defined as normal behavior for adolescents still is relevant as an example of the dramatization of youths' activities, today there is a second meaning to dramatizing the evil of juvenile behavior that comes from our response to violent juvenile crime. As with our treatment of status offenses, we are recriminalizing violent offenses based on a deterrence argument. To understand what is meant by the recriminalization of violent juvenile offenses, remember that one of the purposes behind the creation of the juvenile justice system was the *decriminalization* of the misbehavior of youths, even serious criminal acts.

Recriminalization of violent juvenile offenses is occurring through recent changes in many states in the transfer of juveniles to adult court. One example of the changes that legislatures are making in transfer comes from New York (Singer 1996). The New York state legislature passed a juvenile offender law that lowered the eligible ages for transfer to the adult court to 13 years for murder and 14 years for other violent offenses (Singer 1996). Other changes in methods of transfer go beyond lowering the age at which a juvenile who commits a particular crime might be transferred. They mandate that certain offenses, when committed by individuals over 13 or 14 years of age, be excluded from the jurisdiction of the juvenile court.

It might well be argued that violent offenses are "evil." The point, however, is that the recent changes have increased the evilness with which we view these offenses. As with the change in our view of status offenses, we must ask ourselves what the dramatization of the act as evil does. Will it help us to achieve the goals we are trying to achieve?

□ Child as Evil

For labeling theorists, more harmful than dramatizing the evil of acts is the second type of dramatization of evil—dramatizing the child as evil. Tannenbaum (1938) used this type of the dramatization of evil to refer to the situation in which the community's response goes beyond defining the act as evil to defining the person who has committed the act as evil. The difference between dramatizing the evil of the act and the evil of the child is the difference between telling a child who breaks the law that he or she did something bad and telling the child that he or she is bad. We can look at two good examples of how current practices dramatize the nature of the child as evil. One example comes from our treatment and discussion of violent juvenile offenders, whereas the other deals with status offenders.

1. The violent juvenile offender as a "super-predator"

An excellent indication of our tendency today to define the juvenile who commits an offense as evil is shown in the terminology used to describe violent juvenile offenders. There is no better example of this than the phrases *super-predators* (Bennett, DiIulio, and Walters 1996) and *stone-cold predators* (DiIulio 1996) recently used by a few criminologists to characterize a particular type of juvenile offender. These phrases also were recently used in federal legislation for the treatment of juvenile offenders. The phrase stone-cold refers to an offender who has no remorse, no guilt, and no conscience, whereas the word predator suggests someone who preys on the weak. The image of the juvenile delinquent underlying these phrases is of an animal stalking its prey, but for pleasure rather than survival.

Our tendency to define the child as evil, however, goes beyond mere phrases to theories that explain why youths of today are, in the words of some, more vicious than those of the past. DiIulio, who we just saw popularized the phrase super-predators with his co-authors Bennett and Walters, puts forth a theory that exemplifies this thinking (see Cook and Laub 1998). In a book titled *Body Count* (Bennett et al. 1996), the authors argue that the underlying cause of the rise in violent crime and its concentration among inner-city African American males is the moral poverty that comes about when children grow up without people to properly socialize them. Although caused by inadequate socialization, the cause of crime for these children is something intrinsic to them—their lack of moral feeling (Cook and Laub 1998). What is depicted in this theory, and in those like it, is that these youths are evil and that they are different from those of us who do not commit crimes.

As important as the imagery behind the language in the writings of criminologists and politicians might be, more important still is how defining the child as evil has shown itself in revisions of practices in state juvenile justice systems around the country. Three changes in particular illustrate how we are dramatizing evil by defining the child as evil. The first is the move to determinant and mandatory sentencing in the juvenile court. The traditional sentence in the juvenile court is indeterminant to allow the court to fit the sentence to the individual needs of the child it is trying to help. The move to determinant sentencing signals a move to a punishment orientation that excludes any understanding of why the offense was committed beyond the establishment of men's *rea* or evil intent. The idea is that anyone who intentionally commits an act that causes harm must be bad. The second change that illustrates the dramatization of the child as evil is the change occurring in the transfer of youths to adult court. Just as the recriminalization of offenses by automatically waiving them to adult court illustrates defining the act as evil, the waiver of juveniles to adult court illustrates a criminalization of the child.

A third and final illustration of how our attempt to control juvenile delinquency is taking us toward a dramatization of the child as evil is the U.S. Supreme Court's decisions during the late 1980s on the death penalty for juveniles. In 1988, the court ruled in *Thompson v. Oklahoma* that the death penalty for an individual under 16 years of age at the time of the crime is unconstitutional. A year later, however, in the cases *Stanford v. Kentucky* and *Wilkins v. Missouri,* the court ruled that it is constitutional to give the death penalty to a juvenile who is 16 or 17 years of age at the time of the crime. The court's reasoning was that there is no consensus in our society that it is cruel and unusual punishment to give the death penalty to an individual who is 16 or 17 at the time of the crime. The court's ruling, and America's stance toward the death penalty for juveniles, is the most compelling indication of how we define the child as evil. Although the stated reason for giving a juvenile the death penalty might be deterrence or retribution, there certainly is no other sentence that most clearly says that society has given up on the individual and that society sees nothing worth redeeming.

2. Status offenders and the possibility of serious offending

The example that we are dramatizing the evilness of children who commit violent offenses might not be problematic for those who believe that those who commit evil acts must themselves be evil. We have, however, begun to go beyond dramatizing the evil of violent offenders. The best example of this today is some of the reasoning behind practices that keep status offenders under the jurisdiction of the juvenile court. As we discussed previously, two of the reasons for keeping status offenders under the jurisdiction of the juvenile court are to give the status offenders the supervision and discipline they are lacking and to deter them from committing future status offenses. There is, however, another idea behind this practice. It is the idea that many status offenders, if ignored by the juvenile justice system, would go on to commit more serious offenses. The potential for evil in status offenders would be fulfilled without the intervention of the court.

Recent changes in the way that we react to juvenile delinquents, both those who are violent offenders and those who commit status offenses, have moved us toward a greater dramatization of the child as evil. It is this tendency, to define the person who commits offenses as different or evil, that labeling theorists saw as central to the development of a deviant identity. More than defining the act as evil, labeling a juvenile as evil stigmatizes the juvenile in such a way that the label is all people see and removal of the label is difficult.

☐ Generalization of Evil

Our final type of the dramatization of evil was not discussed by Tannenbaum (1938). However, it is relevant to understanding the reaction of our society today to juvenile delinquents. This third type is the generalization of evil. This refers to the idea that our reaction to violent juvenile offenders has generalized to all juvenile offenders and, to some extent, to all juveniles, especially all inner-city African American males. This theme runs through both the language and the imagery used to describe delinquent youths and the practices that are dramatizing the act and the child as evil.

In terms of the language, a good example of how discussions of violent juvenile delinquents quickly come to be about all juvenile offenders is found again in Bennett et al.'s (1996) *Body Count.* In one place, Bennett et al. write, "We face a simple stark choice. We can continue on our present course, which means *another generation of children* who will grow up having received virtually no love or sound moral instruction. They will be meaner and angrier and more violent than the current generation of super-predators" (p. 206, emphases added). To whom does the "generation of children" refer? The children of the super-predators? The children growing up in inner cities? All youths? Although in the context of the book the authors might well be referring to a specific group of youths, the problem with phrases such as "super-predators" and "another generation of children" is that their "catchiness" means that they will be used out of context.

It is not merely the language we use to describe juvenile delinquents that exemplifies the generalization of evil. It also is seen in our practices. With some exceptions, such as the transfer of juveniles to adult court and the death penalty, all of the recent changes in reactions to juvenile crime discussed earlier encompass nonviolent youthful offenders. We see a particularly clear example of this again in the progressive sanction model that Texas now uses (discussed earlier). In our efforts to deal with violent crime, every youth who has committed an offense—from running away from home to larceny theft, from vandalism to drug abuse—is included in the solution.

Another example shows how our actions are generalizing the "evil" of juvenile offending to all juveniles—the increasing role of the police in schools. At one time, the role of the police in schools was fairly limited. The police came into the schools to instruct, such as in Drug Abuse Resistance Education (DARE), or to join with the school in activities for youths, such as in some police athletic league programs. Today, however, a growing number of schools have police officers in the schools whose role is one of law enforcement. A good example of this is the growing number of school districts in Texas that have their own police departments. At first thought, this might make parents feel better about the safety of their children. At second thought, however, parents realize the message that this is sending—that the school is an incredibly dangerous place and that the youths in the school cannot be handled except by state control.

■ The Effect of the Dramatization of Evil

If we are indeed responding to juvenile delinquency in a way that dramatizes the evil of the act and the child, then what is the result likely to be? Labeling theorists provide us with a way in which to predict the effects that attempts to control juvenile delinquency discussed heretofore might have.

For Tannenbaum (1938), Lemert (1951), and Becker (1963), the effect is to isolate and segregate the juvenile delinquent from the rest of society. As we identify the juvenile delinquent as different, in this case evil, we push the juvenile away from conventional society. For the labeling theorists, this isolation from conventional society establishes in the juvenile the idea that he or she is different and is delinquent. The developing conception of himself or herself as delinquent leads to involvement with delinquent others who support the delinquent in his or her activities and beliefs. The result of all this is more delinquent behavior, not less.

For Link and his colleagues (Link 1987; Link and Cullen 1983; Link et al. 1987, 1989), the effect is much broader. Their theory shows us how the societal conceptions of juvenile delinquents that we create can lead to expectations in the individual about how he or she will be treated. This expectation itself can cause the labeled individual to act in ways that increase the chance of re-offending. Even more than this, however, Link's discussion of societal conceptions warns us of the harmful effects that can result when we create an image of juvenile delinquents and use that image to support our devaluation and discrimination of them.

■ Reacting to Juvenile Delinquency

The work of labeling theorists today goes beyond giving us a way of characterizing our responses to juvenile delinquency and a way of predicting what the effect of those responses will be. It also is encouraging us to think about how we can respond to juvenile delinquency in a way that avoids the negative effects of labels. Their thinking encourages us to consider two possibilities.

1. Labeling theorists suggest that we look beyond the offender and the offense for a greater appreciation of the context in which the offense occurred.

Instead of a focus that identifies the problem as inherent to the offender, labeling theory suggests that we take a broader look. As Cook and Laub (1998) suggest in their analysis of juvenile arrest rates, "Rather than a change in the intrinsic character of the youths, there may be something about the current social, economic, or physical environment that is more conducive to violence than in previous years. It is not that they are more vicious but rather that their circumstances promote an intensification of conflict" (p. 51).

2. Labeling suggests that we look for responses to juvenile delinquency that do not forever isolate and segregate the offender from conventional society.

Of those working today on reactions to offenders, John Braithwaite has taken us the furthest in examining how we can respond to offenders without causing more harm (Braithwaite 1989). Instead of reactions that stigmatize, Braithwaite calls for "reintegrative shaming." In reintegrative shaming, punishment "is followed by efforts to reintegrate the offender back into the community of law-abiding or respectable citizens" (p. 100). Reintegrative shaming does not mean that the offender is not punished, for the offender is expected to take responsibility for what he or she has done. After the punishment, however, the offender is accepted back into the community. Braithwaite believes that it is the acceptance of the offender back into the community of respectable citizens once he or she is punished that reduces the probability of developing a criminal self-concept, joining a deviant subculture, and re-offending.

The spirit of reintegrative shaming is shown most effectively in the idea of community conferences. According to Braithwaite and Daly (1994; see also Braithwaite and Pettit 1990), community conferences originated in New Zealand, where they now are the preferred method for dealing with juvenile offenders. The community conference works in the following manner. When an offense is committed, a juvenile justice coordinator calls a community conference. Those invited to the conference include the offender, the offender's family, supporters of the offender, the police, the victim, and victim supporters. The purpose of the conference is to discuss the harm caused the victim and the distress caused the offender's family. The purpose is also to instill a sense of shame in the offender. If the community conference works properly, the offender comes to feel remorse, understand that he or she can count on the love of his or her supporters, and agree to a plan of action to redress the harm and prevent further harm. The key to the community conference is the participation of both the victim and those who support the offender. The presence of the victim aids in getting the offender to understand the harm that was done. The presence of individuals who care about and support the offender helps to reintegrate the offender back into the community.

Programs that follow this logic in the United States include the increasing number of mediation or arbitration programs developing for juvenile offenders. A good example is the Juvenile Arbitration Program in Lexington County, South Carolina, which has been at work since 1983 (Alford 1997). Similar to community conferences, the guiding philosophy of the program is that the parties affected by a crime can sit down together and restore the balance of justice taken away by the crime. The purpose of the arbitration session is for all parties to forge a contract specifying just how justice can be restored. Typical components of the contract include having the juvenile pay restitution to the victim or do community service. Sometimes, the juvenile offender is asked to make restitution by paying back some of the intangible losses from the crime, for example, doing filing for a police officer to make up for the time the police involvement in the case took. Proponents of the program feel that it is especially suited for juveniles because it sends a message to them that they are responsible for their actions and that they can make up for the harm they have done.

The idea of restoring justice without stigmatizing offenders sounds most effective for property offenses. Community conferences, however, have been proposed as part of the plan for responding to violent crimes as well. In particular, Braithwaite and Daly (1994) discuss using community conferences in response to violence against women, particularly violence committed by intimates. Their plan includes arrest and prison as viable possibilities, but only after attempts to restore justice through community conferences have failed. The idea is that, with these particular acts of violence, community conferences empower victims and aid in the establishment of community control of crime in ways that arrest and prison do not.

■ Conclusion

As Tannenbaum suggested in 1938, our history is one of defining juvenile delinquents as different from juveniles who do not commit offenses. Although part of the reason why the juvenile justice system developed was to remove the stigma of a criminal label from juveniles, it has been limited in its success in reaching that goal. In fact, despite decreases in the juvenile arrest rate since 1994, fears over juvenile delinquency have led us to ways of responding to it that have taken us even further away from our initial goal.

Although there are valid criticisms of labeling theory, the basic argument behind this chapter is that this theory can provide us with a way of characterizing our present response to juvenile offending that leads us to think critically about what we are doing. It was argued here that many of our present reactions to juvenile delinquents can be characterized as forms of the dramatization of evil. Labeling takes us further than this, however, for it also encourages us to think about the effect of our reaction. Unlike any of the traditional criminological theories, labeling suggests to us the possibility that the effect of our present reaction to juvenile delinquency could be to increase, rather than decrease, the chance that a juvenile will re-offend. Finally, recent developments in labeling encourage us to think about new ways of responding to juvenile delinquency. The work of these new labeling theorists has led to the development of ways of responding to offending that control it without labeling offenders. Theorists such as Braithwaite who propose these new methods are working hard to encourage the communities to adopt these methods, giving them renewed power for dealing with crime.

STUDY QUESTIONS

1. Between the dramatizations of the act as evil and of the child as evil, which is the more harmful from the perspective of labeling theorists?

2. Think about recent changes in juvenile law in your state. Can these changes be categorized as a type of dramatization of evil?

3. What type of group, community, or society would be most able to use reintegrative shaming as a method of crime control?

4. Under what conditions do you think reintegrative shaming would be most effective at controlling crime?

5. How effective do you think community conferences are in dealing with property offenses? Crimes of violence?

REFERENCES

Alford, Susan. 1997. "Professionals Need Not Apply." *Corrections Today* 59:104-8.

Ball, R. A. 1983. "Development of Basic Norm Violation: Neutralization and Self-Concept Within a Male Cohort." *Criminology* 21:75-94.

Becker, Howard. 1963. *Outsiders: Studies in the Sociology of Deviance*. New York: Free Press.

Bennett, William, John DiIulio, and John Walters. 1996. *Body Count: Moral Poverty and How to Win America's War Against Crime and Drugs*. New York: Simon & Schuster.

Blumstein, Alfred. 1995. "Youth Violence, Guns, and the Illicit-Drug Industry." *Journal of Criminal Law and Criminology* 86:10-36.

Braithwaite, John. 1989. *Crime, Shame, and Reintegration*. New York: Cambridge University Press.

Braithwaite, John and Kathleen Daly. 1994. "Masculinities, Violence, and Communitarian Control." Pp. 189-213 in *Just Boys Doing Business?* edited by Tim Newburn and Elizabeth Stanko. London: Routledge.

Braithwaite, John and P. Pettit. 1990. *Not Just Desserts: A Republican Theory of Criminal Justice*. Oxford, UK: Oxford University Press.

Cook, Philip and John Laub. 1998. "The Unprecedented Epidemic in Youth Violence." Pp. 101-38 in *Crime and Justice: An Annual Review of Research,* edited by Mark Moore and Michael Tonry. Chicago: University of Chicago Press.

Dawson, Robert. 1996. *Texas Juvenile Law*. 4th ed. Austin: Texas Juvenile Probation Commission.

DiIulio, John. 1996. "Help Wanted: Economists, Crime, and Public Policy." *Journal of Economic Perspectives* 10:3-23.

Freedberg, Louis. 1989. "Death Penalty Decision Ends a Century of Adolescence." *Youth Law News,* July-August, 6.

Lemert, Edwin. 1951. *Social Pathology.* New York: McGraw-Hill.

Link, Bruce. 1987. "Understanding Labeling Effects in the Area of Mental Disorders: An Assessment of the Effects of Expectations of Rejection." *American Sociological Review* 52:96-112.

Link, Bruce and Francis Cullen. 1983. "Reconsidering the Social Rejection of Ex-Mental Patients: Levels of Attitudinal Response." *American Journal of Community Psychology* 11:261-73.

Link, Bruce, Francis Cullen, James Frank, and John Wozniak. 1987. "The Social Reaction of Former Mental Patients: Understanding Why Labels Work." *American Journal of Sociology* 92:1461-500.

Link, Bruce, Francis Cullen, Elmer Struening, Patrick Shrout, and Bruce Dohrenwend. 1989. "A Modified Labeling Theory Approach to Mental Disorders: An Empirical Assessment." *American Sociological Review* 54:400-23.

Maxson, Cheryl and Malcolm Klein. 1997. *Responding to Troubled Youth.* New York: Oxford University Press.

Office of Juvenile Justice and Delinquency Prevention. 1989. *Children in Custody.* Washington, DC: Office of Juvenile Justice and Delinquency Prevention.

Schur, Edwin. 1951. *Social Pathology.* New York: McGraw-Hill.

———. 1973. *Radical Non-intervention: Rethinking the Delinquency Problem.* Englewood Cliffs, NJ: Prentice Hall.

Schwartz, Ira. 1989. *(In)Justice for Juveniles: Rethinking the Best Interests of the Child.* Lexington, MA: Lexington Books.

Singer, Simon. 1996. *Recriminalizing Delinquency: Violent Juvenile Crimes and Juvenile Justice Reform.* Cambridge, UK: Cambridge University Press.

Tannenbaum, Frank. 1938. *Crime and the Community.* Boston: Ginn.

Wellford, Charles. 1975. "Labeling Theory and Criminology: An Assessment." *Social Problems* 22:332-45.

CASES CITED

Stanford v. Missouri, 492 U.S. 361 (1989).

Thompson v. Oklahoma, 487 U.S. 815 (1988).

Wilkins v. Missouri, 492 U.S. (1989).

New Directions in Theory

New Ideas, Applications, and Issues

CHAPTER 8

The Social Control of Corporate Criminals
Shame and Informal Sanction Threats

SALLY S. SIMPSON
M. LYN EXUM
N. CRAIG SMITH

In October 1996, Archer Daniels Midland Company (ADM), which calls itself the supermarket of the world, agreed to plead guilty to "anti-competitive conduct" (price-fixing) and to pay a $100 million fine, the largest ever levied against a corporation for criminal conduct. ADM had conspired with Japanese and Korean producers of lysine, a feed additive, to set prices and allocate sales among competitors. In addition, ADM engaged in similar conduct in the sales and distribution of citric acid (an organic acid used in foods and beverages to enhance flavor and/or preserve prepared foods). ADM was not charged with price-fixing and was exempt from prosecution in the high-fructose corn syrup product market because of its agreement to cooperate with the ongoing investigation. However, ADM has a history of price-fixing and other criminal behavior dating back to the 1970s. In several civil and criminal cases, ADM settled lawsuits or pleaded no contest to federal charges. Although ADM's chief executive officer (CEO) and president managed to avoid prosecution, division presidents Terry Wilson and Mark Whitacre, as well as Mick Andreas (vice chairman, executive vice president of ADM, and son of CEO Dwayne Andreas), were charged and found guilty of price-fixing. On July 9, 1999, each was sentenced to serve prison time for his participation in the conspiracy. (Simpson and Leeper-Piquero, forthcoming)

Every day, thousands of companies face similar opportunities and temptations yet manage to resist them. Why are some companies better corporate citizens than others, and how can society ensure that corporations act responsibly? What differentiates good from bad companies rests with the managers who run them and the cultural dictates of the organizations. Good corporate citizens are firms whose managers, when confronted with corporate criminal opportunities, will be guided by a sense of right and wrong, by their understanding of how others are likely to view their behavior, and by the extent to which they think the discovery of these acts would bring shame on their companies. Good corporate citizens are companies that encourage law-abiding behavior and respond appropriately to criminal misconduct. Being a good corporate citizen is important to society because of the extensive costs of bad citizenship. Corporate crime kills and injures more people yearly than does street crime. It adds billions of dollars to the costs of goods and services in this country, and it can shake the foundation of goodwill and trust in business when large-scale cases of corporate crime are revealed to the general public (Simon 1999).

Some companies are self-motivated to be good corporate citizens, whereas others narrowly define their interests and thereby callously or deliberately threaten the welfare of employees, customers, and society at large. Our goal in this chapter is to examine the problem of corporate crime and to explore one possible avenue for controlling it. We describe our use of Braithwaite's (1989) theory of shaming to account for why some companies and their managers conform to the law, whereas others do not. Finally, we speculate on whether public policy informed by shaming theory might help to control corporate crime.

■ Corporate Crime

At first glance, corporate crime appears easy to define. Corporate crime is criminal behavior by corporations. However, this definition does not suffice. First, although corporations are entities recognized in law as juridic persons (having the same rights and responsibilities as individuals under the law) and thus capable of criminal and victim status, they are collections of individuals. Therefore, corporations themselves are not capable of "thinking and acting." Instead, managers think and act on behalf of corporations. Thus, even though a company can be charged as an offender, the actual actor committing the crime is an individual (or a group of individuals).

All definitions of corporate crime originate with Sutherland's (1983) description of white-collar crime as "crime committed by a person of respectability and high social status in the course of his [or her] occupation" (p. 7; see also Sutherland 1940, 1949). In drawing scholars' attention to crimes by the wealthy and privileged, Sutherland noted that white-collar criminals tend not to be prosecuted and sanctioned within the criminal justice system. Rather, they are processed and sanctioned civilly or through regulatory agencies such as the Environmental Protection Agency (EPA).

Thus, the term *corporate crime* is somewhat of a misnomer because much of what is classified under this term is not prosecuted under criminal statutes. Still, offenses that fall under the purview of regulatory agencies and civil law also may be broadly defined as corporate "crime." Indeed, many civil and regulatory constraints on corporate behavior have criminal provisions (as does the EPA). In any case, given the difficulty of penetrating the corporate shell to find culpable parties or meeting the more rigorous standards of criminal prosecution, a civil or regulatory action might be more effective than a criminal prosecution. Clinard and Yeager (1980) acknowledge these realities in defining corporate crime as "any act committed by corporations that is punished by the state, regardless of whether it is punished under administrative, civil, or criminal law" (p. 16).

What most distinguishes corporate crime from other types of crime is that the corporate employee is committing the act primarily to benefit the company or to further organizational goals. An automobile executive who embezzles $1 million from her employer to finance a vacation home is committing a white-collar crime but not a corporate crime. If, however, she were to knowingly overestimate the company's quarterly earnings by $1 million to maintain the "fiction" of corporate profitability, then she would be participating in a corporate crime. When a chief financial officer (CFO) fails to file his or her own tax return, the CFO is committing a crime but not one that would count as a corporate offense. If the CFO fails to file a corporate tax return to avoid paying $500,000 to the Internal Revenue Service, then he or she is committing a corporate crime. In this chapter, we recognize the distinction between personal and company benefits when defining corporate crime.

■ Shaming as a Means of Crime Control

In his influential book, *Crime, Shame, and Reintegration*, Braithwaite (1989:56-58) explains why a model of punishment that emulates the family's functions will be more effective at controlling bad behavior than will a system based solely on punishment. He argues that people will adjust their behaviors in response to punishment only (1) when punishment is delivered by authorities who are respected and respectful and (2) when offenders or potential offenders have a stake in conventional society and care about how others view them. When these two conditions are met, punishment or its threat should effectively deter crime because miscreants will experience shame. Thus, punishment is more likely to deter future misconduct under the following scenario:

> In the presence of his wife, arresting officers listen politely to the suspect's story. After questioning him, they believe that there is enough evidence to arrest him, and they let their intentions be known. They read him his rights, and given that he has been cooperative, they choose not to put handcuffs on him. They tell his wife where they are taking him and what she needs to do next.

According to the theory, because the suspected offender is married (evidence of societal bonds) and treated with respect and dignity by criminal justice authorities, he will be more easily shamed than will an offender who has few ties to the larger society and who feels humiliated or unjustly treated by authorities.

Although Braithwaite's ideas about shame and punishment developed from his studies of white-collar crime, few studies have further explored the corporate crime-shame relationship beyond Braithwaite's (1989) original work (Braithwaite 1995; Fisse and Braithwaite 1983; Makkai and Braithwaite 1994; for an exception, see Levi 1998). Does shaming (or its threat) better deter crime when the object of shame is the corporation or when it is the responsible manager? And does shaming based in threats to informal systems of control (e.g., family, workplace) work better than threats based in formal legal sanctions (including civil, criminal, and regulatory interventions)? We felt that if we knew the answers to these questions, we might be able to point the way toward more effective remedies for corporate crime. The study we designed to test our hypotheses is described shortly, but first we explain Braithwaite's theory of shaming in greater detail.

□ Punishment and Shame

The shame-inducing aspects of punishment are far from new to the field of criminal justice. Placing offenders in stocks and pillory, branding adulterers with a scarlet letter A, and marching thieves and murderers through the public square on their way to execution were punishments intended to solicit public scorn and contempt. Such practices were used to minimize the status of the offenders by tearing down their reputations and, in some cases, were used to dehumanize so as to justify more brutal punishments (Andenaes 1974). When punishment became rationalized and more divorced from public scrutiny, its primary goals changed from such retribution to prevention, deterrence, and incapacitation. On the whole, the shift away from irrational and brutal punishments has been a positive development. However, Braithwaite (1989) argues that a consequence of this shift has been the uncoupling of shame from punishment, rendering deterrence less effective. In the current system, offenders are "determined" guilty or not guilty in a formal adversarial courtroom in which each side tries to prove guilt or innocence. Punishments are then rendered and served in relative anonymity.

Still, as Braithwaite (1989) notes, shaming is an element in contemporary punishment. Formal justice processing produces two types of shaming:

- *Disintegrative shaming:* The offender is isolated or humiliated. Defiance on the part of the offender is a possible result.
- *Reintegrative shaming:* The community conveys its disapproval of the offending act, but its reaction is tempered with forgiveness of the offender. Consequently, the offender is embarrassed or feels guilty about disappointing others and is deterred from future offending.

As Braithwaite suggests, reintegrative shaming is more effective if the goal of punishment is to encourage offenders to observe the community's norms: "The nub of deterrence is not the severity of the sanction but its social embeddedness. Shame is more deterring when administered by persons who continue to be of importance to us; when we become outcasts, we can reject our rejectors, and the shame no longer matters to us" (p. 55).

□ Shaming and Social Control

Braithwaite's (1989) theory of reintegrative shaming draws heavily from social control theory. Interdependency and communitarianism are key elements in Braithwaite's theory and, in social control theory, are gauges of one's bond to society (Hirschi 1969) and societal integration (Durkheim 1893):

- *Interdependency:* This is the extent to which individuals are enmeshed in relationships with others. Bonds reflect ties to others based on affection and caring as well as commitments to prosocial organizations and actions (Hirschi 1969).
- *Communitarianism:* This is the promotion of mutual concern and trust in a society through deeply embedded interdependencies. Communitarian societies, such as Japan, emphasize community over individual interests (egoism).

Interdependency and communitarianism are linked to shame and shame susceptibility in two ways: interdependent persons are more susceptible to shaming, and because individuals within communitarian societies are subject to extensive interdependencies, shaming is more widespread and potent in such societies.

Applying these concepts to corporate crime, we expected that persons who are more interdependent, as indicated by demographic characteristics (e.g., age) and social bonds (especially their attachments and commitments to significant others or institutions), would be more easily shamed and less apt to engage in corporate crime. Similarly, we anticipated that an individual's integration into a company is analogous to one's integration into society. In both situations, concern for the collective should enhance shaming. In other words, managers presumably care about the potentially negative impacts that their illegal acts could have on their employers.

■ Applying Shame Theory to Corporate Offending

To explore these issues, we designed a study using a survey. Among the participants were corporate managers along with M.B.A. students at a large urban university. We anticipated that the answers to the survey questions would help us to understand when managers are likely to violate the law and what types of controls inhibit offending. These were our expectations, drawing from Braithwaite's (1989) theory:

- Managers who are older, married, working, and female will be more interdependent than their counterparts and hence more susceptible to shaming.
- Managers who are attached and committed to significant others and conventional lines of activity will be more interdependent than their counterparts and hence more susceptible to shaming.
- Managers who strongly believe in the morality of the law will be more susceptible to shame than those who do not.

- Where defiance exists, shaming will be less effective (see also Sherman 1993).
- Public shaming will be more effective than private shaming.
- Shaming will be enhanced when shame is directed toward the offending managers *and* their companies.

If Braithwaite is right, then managers who are susceptible to shame will be less willing to engage in corporate crime than will managers who are insensitive to shaming.

The surveys described scenarios involving three types of corporate crimes: *price-fixing, environmental emission violations,* and *bribery.* Our goal was to accurately describe situations in which managers might be tempted to violate, or pressured into violating, the law. For example, a firm might be described as losing money or operating in a market that is declining. Similarly, a scenario might describe a manager who has been ordered by his or her supervisor to violate the law or a situation in which the depicted manager believes that the criminal act will be viewed positively by top management. The scenarios also provide descriptions of the types of controls that operate within the firms to discourage corporate criminal conduct. A firm might have an ethics code or mandatory ethics training. It might have random audits or a hotline to anonymously report corporate misconduct. The scenarios also indicate how well those corporate controls are operating. For example, a scenario might depict that a manager was reprimanded for engaging in a similar type of corporate crime. In another, the manager might be fired. In all instances, the manager is depicted as violating the law.

Each crime description is followed by a series of questions that ask about the ethics of the act, respondents' perceptions of the likelihood and consequences of its discovery (including shame) for the manager and the company, and how each respondent would act under similar circumstances. Because our primary interest is in learning about the conditions under which shaming is a successful punitive strategy, we explore the conditions under which respondents said that they, like the manager, would violate the law.

The characteristics of the sample respondents are described in Table 8.1. Most are male, in the their mid-30s, white, and of U.S. nationality. They are well educated (the majority hold some type of graduate degree or have one year of graduate studies), married, and have on average 12 years of business experience. Because these respondents tend to be seasoned managers, their responses to scenario conditions should give us a good understanding of why some managers will comply with the law whereas others will offend. Also,

TABLE 8.1 Characteristics of Survey Respondents ($N = 78$)

Respondent's gender	Male = 52 Female = 25 Missing = 1
Respondent's race	White = 71 Asian = 5 Hispanic = 1 Missing = 1
Respondent's age	Mean age = 35 years Range = 22-65 years
Respondent's education	B.S./B.A. degree = 24 One year of graduate school = 24 Graduate degree = 29 Missing = 1
Marital status	Married = 45 Single = 31 Divorced = 1 Missing = 1
Years of business experience	Mean experience = 12 years Range = 0-39 years
Nationality	U.S. = 60 Other = 11 Missing = 7

because the scenarios depict important characteristics of corporate cultures, we can learn what types of companies are susceptible to crime ("bad citizens") and which are not ("good citizens").

To understand whether corporate managers' behaviors are inhibited by the threat or experience of shame, it is important to identify which items on the survey correspond to Braithwaite's (1989) theory. From the vignettes, the following items indicate key ideas from the theory:

- corporate culture (act is common in firm/industry);
- defiance (illegal act challenges an unfair law);

- internal controls (ethics code, training, audits, and hotline); and
- operation of internal controls (firm takes no action, employee is severely reprimanded, or employee is fired).

We expect that when corporate cultures support illegal activity (i.e., managers are bonded to a corporate culture that encourages crime) or when managers feel that laws are unfair (i.e., defiance), the respondents should indicate that they would be more likely to commit corporate crime. On the other hand, when companies have effective internal compliance programs (i.e., those that take ethics seriously and respond appropriately to violators), corporate offending should be less likely.

Recall that Braithwaite's (1989) idea of interdependency suggests that persons who are embedded in interpersonal relationships, whereby they depend on others and others depend on them, will care more about what people think about them and thus be more susceptible to shame. If Braithwaite's theory is correct, then respondents who are older, female, and married (indicators of greater embeddedness) will be less likely to commit corporate crime than will younger, male, and single respondents. The survey also asked respondents to evaluate how likely and costly it would be if they were to be discovered to be engaging in corporate crime by their families, business associates, and friends. We expect that those who think that discovery is likely and consequential will indicate lower offending intentions than will those who estimate less certain and severe informal sanctions. Finally, social control theory predicts that persons with strong bonds to societal norms will be deterred from criminality. With this in mind, we asked respondents to rank the corporate offenses along three ethical dimensions of Reidenbach and Robin's (1990) Multidimensional Ethics Scale:

- moral equity (e.g., act is just/unjust, fair/unfair, morally right/wrong, acceptable/unacceptable to family);
- relativism (e.g., act is culturally or traditionally acceptable/unacceptable); and
- contractualism (e.g., act violates or does not violate an unspoken promise or unwritten contract).

If the act is perceived to be highly unethical within all of these dimensions, then the social control element of Braithwaite's theory predicts that the manager will not commit the crime.

■ **Survey Results**

In Table 8.2, we summarize our important findings by putting an asterisk next to the survey items that consistently predicted a manager's decision to engage in corporate crime. Items without an asterisk failed to affect the offending decision. Because the theory predicts interactions between inter-dependency and susceptibility to shame (i.e., shame works better for those who are more interdependent), we divided the sample of respondents into persons who can be classified as either low or high interdependency based on their social bonds to significant others.[1] We then tested the theory to see whether shaming deterred corporate crime better according to interdepen-dency levels. Results are reported in Table 8.3. Variables that predicted cor-porate offending intentions are noted with one asterisk. Theoretically inconsistent predictions are noted with two asterisks.

Looking first at results displayed in Table 8.2, the most consistent evi-dence in support of Braithwaite's (1989) theory is found in the public versus private shaming prediction (refer to the "Informal controls at the firm" entries). When an employee is severely reprimanded at work for his or her misconduct, the lesson learned appears more salient than if the same employee were fired or if the firm were to do nothing. This suggests that punishment that is public yet tempered with forgiveness (i.e., reintegrative) is a more effective deterrent than permissiveness (i.e., failure to punish) or punishment that is harsh (i.e., disintegrative). Yet, as demonstrated in Table 8.3, the effect is consistent regardless of ones' degree of interdependency. Persons who are low on interdependency as well as those who are high on interdependency take workplace reprimands seriously. Although this is not what Braithwaite's theory would predict, it might be that our measures of interdependency are biased toward the upper end (i.e., most respondents in our sample are highly interdependent people) and, therefore, we do not have the type of sample that would reveal the predicted differences.

Consistent with shaming theory, and as shown in Table 8.2, we find that older respondents are less likely to engage in corporate crime than are youn-ger respondents. However, when we examined whether this was related to one's level of interdependency (as the theory suggests), we found that it was not (Table 8.3). And none of the other indicators of interdependency identi-fied in the theory (i.e., sex, marital status) had an impact on offending.

Our study also challenges the idea that shaming the corporation is as important or effective as shaming the individual manager. At least according to our survey results, managers do not adjust their corporate offending

TABLE 8.2   Relationship Between Survey Items and Managers'
Offending Decisions: Consistent and Inconsistent Findings

Crime types
  Environmental Protection Agency
  Price-fixing * (+)
  Bribery * (+)
Characteristics of the company or industry
  Illegality is a common practice in the firm
  Illegality is a common practice in the industry
  The law is unfair
  The firm is experiencing declining sales and revenues
  The firm is experiencing growing sales and revenues
  The industry is economically healthy
  The industry is economically deteriorating
  The industry is losing ground to foreign competitors
  The act will save the company a small amount of money
  The act will save the company a large amount of money
  The act will modestly increase the firm's revenues * (+)
  The act will greatly increase the firm's revenues * (+)
Characteristics of the manager and/or manager's situation
  The manager is ordered by a supervisor to violate the law * (+)
  The manager decides to order an employee to violate the law
  The act might result in a promotion and salary bonus
  The act might result in increased co-worker admiration
  The act might result in a positive impression by top management
Informal controls at the firm
  Ethics code
  Mandatory ethics training
  Hotline
  Random audits
  No action taken against employee who acted similarly * (+)
  Employee severely reprimanded * (–)
  Employee recently fired
Perceived benefits of corporate crime by respondent
  Act is thrilling and/or will advance career * (+)
Ethics scales
  Moral equity * (–)
  Relativism * (–)
  Contractualism * (–)
Shame
  Sense of personal shame * (–)
  Sense of shame if tarnished reputation of firm
  Likelihood that act would tarnish reputation of firm

(continued)

TABLE 8.2 (Continued)

Feel bad if reputation of firm tarnished
Feel bad if personally shamed
Informal controls
    Scale including family, friends, and business associates as well as employment
        costs * (–)
Respondent characteristics
    Age * (–)
    Marital status
    Gender

NOTE: Variables followed by an asterisk (*) predict corporate offending. Variables followed by a plus sign (+) increase corporate offending. Variables followed by a minus sign (–) decrease corporate offending. Items left blank have no effect.

intentions even when their acts bring shame to their companies (refer to the "Shame" entries in Table 8.2). Most respondents reported that their actions would affect the reputations of their firms and that this could be seriously consequential (i.e., illegal acts by managers do have negative consequences for companies, and when illegality is discovered, firms' reputations might be jeopardized). Yet, this fact did not appear to affect the decision to engage in the criminal act. On the other hand, personal shame (i.e., feeling guilty if others found out what the managers had done) does matter. Thus, there is nothing in our findings to suggest that managers will act lawfully because their firms' reputations could suffer. Personal consequences (i.e., how the managers will be affected by the shame) are what drive these shaming effects, *not* concerns that the reputations of their firms could be damaged.

Another prediction of the theory that is not substantiated among this group of respondents has to do with the "defiance effect." Recall that Braithwaite (1989) predicts that persons who feel that laws are unfair or who believe that they are unfairly treated by legal authorities will not be "shamed" by punishment. Instead, they might become defiant, rejecting both the law and legal authority. Although we have only one measure that explores this possible effect (i.e., law is unfair), it does not have the positive effect on offending that the theory predicts. On the other hand, when we explored whether defiance depended on one's level of interdependency, we found that persons with fewer bonds were more defiant than those with stronger ties to family, friends, and colleagues. However, neither effect was statistically significant.

TABLE 8.3 Corporate Offending Intentions for Respondents Classified as Low and High Interdependency: Consistent and Inconsistent Findings

	Low Interdependency	High Interdependency
Bribery		
Manager is ordered		
Law is unfair		
Act will greatly increase revenue	* (+)	
Employee severely reprimanded	* (−)	* (−)
Employee fired		
Sense of personal shame		
Sense of shame if reputation of firm tarnished		** (+)
Likelihood act would tarnish reputation of firm		
Feel bad if reputation of firm tarnished	** (+)	
Feel bad if personally shamed	* (−)	
Moral equity (ethics)	* (−)	* (−)
Relativism (ethics)	* (−)	
Contractualism (ethics)	* (−)	
Bonds to significant others	* (−)	
Act thrilling or career advanced	* (+)	* (+)
Age		
Marital status		
Sex		
Religion		* (−)

NOTE: Variables followed by one asterisk (*) predict corporate offending. Variables followed by two asterisks (**) predict corporate offending in a theoretically inconsistent direction. Variables followed by a plus sign (+) increase corporate offending. Variables followed by a minus sign (−) decrease corporate offending. Items left blank have no effect.

A few other findings are noteworthy. First, looking at the types of crime that respondents considered, some corporate crimes seem more palatable than others. For example, respondents were somewhat more willing to fix product prices than they were to engage in bribery or environmental violations. However, only the former difference (between price-fixing and EPA offending) was substantial. There also is clear evidence that ethical reasoning drives managers' actions. When corporate criminal acts are thought to be fundamentally wrong, unacceptable to significant others, and violations of informal contracts, managers are much less likely to engage in them.[2] Furthermore, the survey results clearly demonstrate that social bonds are related to offending decisions. However, in an interesting twist, bonds (as measured by informal controls) are more of a crime-inhibiting influence for those who have fewer of them (Table 8.3). That is, persons who are classified as low on interdependency (i.e., they think that significant others are not as likely to discover the illegality or are not apt to respond negatively if discovered) nevertheless take these considerations into mind when making decisions on engaging in criminal acts.

Although it is clear that this study does not find strong support for Braithwaite's (1989) theory, there are several reasons to be cautious about these results. First, even though the vignette technique gives researchers a great amount of control over the conditions to which respondents are exposed, it also imposes conditions that might be arbitrary—not salient or meaningful to study participants. Thus, the technique trades researcher control for more detailed descriptions of factors that might affect managers' offending decisions but are not included in the study. Second, several of our measures simply do not capture the extent and richness of Braithwaite's concepts. For example, we do not measure communitarianism, and although multiple measures of concepts are preferable to single indicators, our indicator of defiance falls into the latter category. Last, as noted previously, this sample of respondents is not as variable on some of our key independent variables as we would like. For example, because most are relatively well integrated, there might not be enough poorly integrated respondents to accurately test Braithwaite's hypotheses about the interaction between shame and interdependency.

■ Policy Considerations

One goal of criminological theory and research is to inform criminal justice policy. Braithwaite (1989) suggests that his theory, as applied to corporate offenders, has several policy implications. One intervention that makes sense is for firms to incorporate internal systems of control that build on the ideas of interdependency and communitarianism. To the extent that managers are well integrated into a "team" in which ethical behavior is valued and ethical discussions are commonplace, deviations from this normative standard should be rarer and easier to discover when they do occur, and offenders should be more easily shamed if they transgress. As the theory reminds us, punishment does not have to be harsh to deter. This policy is consistent with our research results that show how reprimanding the miscreant produces greater deterrence than does firing the miscreant. It is reinforced by data showing that sanctions directed toward individuals are more effective than those directed against firms and that corporate crimes are less likely when the managers are embedded in relationships with significant others.

The theory and our findings also point to the importance of building compliance systems that reinforce managers' ethical standards. We found that managers were significantly less likely to consider committing corporate crimes when they believed that these acts were highly unethical. Given that ethical concerns often are treated as irrelevant and inappropriate subjects for discussion within corporate America (Kram, Yeager, and Reed 1989; Jackall 1988), it seems clear that open and frank communication about ethical standards is a must for firms that are serious about combating corporate crime. It also will give strength and recourse to employees who feel pressured into committing crime because they were ordered to do so by their supervisors.

The theory implies that sanctions directed toward firms will be as effective as those directed toward individual offenders. Braithwaite (1989) makes this argument for two reasons:

1. Firms that are punished for the misdeeds of employees will feel compelled to develop and implement internal compliance systems that will protect against future punishments.
2. Firms care about their good names. A soiled reputation and negative publicity are hard to overcome. Profits and employee morale are hurt. No good comes from bad publicity. Thus, firms will do whatever it takes to minimize exposure.

Although these reasons also seem compelling, our research suggests that different processes are at work. The fact that our respondents did not adjust their offending behaviors even if the firms suffered negative consequences suggests that corporate managers might be more self-interested than Braithwaite assumes. One of the current debates in the corporate sentencing literature centers around whether corporate crime sanctions (criminal or civil) should target the responsible actors or hold the corporations responsible for the acts of their employees. Our data suggest that the former might be a more effective crime control strategy.

In addition to informing policy, another goal of scientific theory is to test whether the theory has accurate predictions and to identify weaknesses. Although it certainly is too soon to suggest theoretical revisions to the theory, especially in light of the considerable research by Braithwaite and his colleagues that gave rise to the theory of reintegrative shaming in the first place, we might have identified some areas for further specification and elaboration. First, although the theory is touted as a "general theory," it might be that the theory is not as applicable to corporate offending as it is to other types of criminality. For example, most corporate managers are highly integrated into society and into their respective workplaces, yet many violate the law. The link between interdependency and offending might not work in the same way for this group of offenders. In fact, greater integration and dependency on workplace associates and socialization into organizational norms and values might actually increase the likelihood of corporate offending if the organizational culture promotes misconduct. (Recall that offending increased when a manager was ordered by his or her supervisor to violate the law.) We also failed to find the predicted interaction between interdependency and susceptibility to shame. For all of these reasons, it might make sense to reassess how and to what extent corporations and their managers differ from other types of offenders and to see whether these differences can be integrated into shaming theory.

Second, at what point, if at all, do self- and collective interests overlap? Or, to borrow a phrase from Braithwaite (1989), what is the individual-collective tipping point of shaming effects? This issue is particularly salient in the corporate crime field because most of our definitions of the phenomenon *assume* that managers and corporate officials operate to serve corporate interests. Yet, our results challenge this notion. When respondents thought that engaging in the corporate crime would be exciting (i.e., a sneaky thrill [Katz 1988]) or that it would advance their careers, offending proclivities went up *regardless* of level of interdependency. Also, the criminal offending of our managers was unaffected by firm-directed shaming. Future tests of the shaming theory should further explore these ideas so that the merits of this approach and relevant policy implications can be considered more carefully.

STUDY QUESTIONS

1. Why is defining *corporate crime* so difficult, and what are the issues that must be considered when defining it? Write a

definition of corporate crime that you think best addresses these issues.

2. Describe Braithwaite's theory of shaming. In your answer, be sure to distinguish reintegrative shaming from disintegrative shaming. According to the theory, who is more susceptible to shaming, (1) an offender who is young, single, and unemployed or (2) an offender who is older, married, and employed in a steady job? Why?

3. According to Braithwaite's theory of shaming, why would damage to the firm's reputation (i.e., shaming) be as important as damage to the offender's reputation in deterring corporate crime? Do the survey results discussed in this chapter suggest that shaming the company and shaming the manager are equally important? If not, which one appears more influential?

4. Our survey results suggest that companies that choose to fire corporate offenders might not deter as many future crimes as do those companies that choose to severely reprimand (but not fire) offenders. Using the principles of Braithwaite's theory of shaming, explain why adopting a policy of "reprimand but not fire" might deter more crime.

5. What policies or procedures would you recommend to reintegratively shame corporate offenders? How are these different from (or similar to) policies or procedures you might recommend to shame offenders of street crimes?

NOTES

1. The sample was divided into high- and low-interdependency groups using the mean value of the informal sanctions variable. This variable measures respondents' perceptions that their involvement in illegal acts would be salient to significant others (including family, friends, and business associates). Those who ranked above the mean were sorted into the high-interdependency group, whereas those who ranked below the mean were classified as low on interdependency.

2. Respondents for whom religion is important were substantially less likely to admit corporate offending tendencies than were their nonreligious counterparts. The effect is strongest among those who rank high on interdependency.

REFERENCES

Andenaes, J. 1974. *Punishment and Deterrence*. Ann Arbor: University of Michigan Press.

Braithwaite, J. 1989. *Crime, Shame, and Reintegration.* New York: Cambridge University Press.
———. 1995. "Corporate Crime and Republican Criminological Praxis." Pp. 48-71 in *Corporate Crime: Contemporary Debates,* edited by Frank Pearce and Laureen Snider. Toronto: University of Toronto Press.
Clinard, M. B. and P. C. Yeager. 1980. *Corporate Crime.* New York: Free Press.
Durkheim, E. 1893. *The Division of Labor in Society.* New York: Free Press.
Fisse, B. and J. Braithwaite. 1983. *The Impact of Publicity on Corporate Offenders.* Albany: State University of New York Press.
Hirschi, T. 1969. *Causes of Delinquency.* Berkeley: University of California Press.
Jackall, R. 1988. *Moral Mazes: The World of Corporate Managers.* New York: Oxford University Press.
Katz, J. 1988. *The Seductions of Crime.* New York: Basic Books.
Kram, K. E., P. C. Yeager, and G. E. Reed. 1989. "Decisions and Dilemmas: The Ethical Dimension in the Corporate Context." Pp. 52-76 in *Research in Corporate Social Policy and Performance,* vol. 11, edited by J. E. Post. Greenwich, CT: JAI.
Levi, M. 1998. "Shaming and the Regulation of Fraud and Business 'Misconduct': Some Preliminary Explorations." Paper prepared for the 12th International Congress on Criminology, Seoul, Korea.
Makkai, T. and J. Braithwaite. 1994. "The Dialectics of Corporate Deterrence." *Journal of Research in Crime and Delinquency* 31:347-73.
Reidenbach, R. E. and D. P. Robin. 1990. "Toward the Development of a Multidimensional Scale for Improving Evaluations of Business Ethics." *Journal of Business Ethics* 4:445-73.
Sherman, L. W. 1993. Defiance, Deterrence, and Irrelevance: A Theory of the Criminal Sanction. *Journal of Research in Crime and Delinquency* 4:445-73.
Simon, David R. 1999. *Elite Deviance.* 6th ed. Boston: Allyn & Bacon.
Simpson, S. S. and Nicole Leeper-Piquero. Forthcoming. "The Archer Daniels Midland Antitrust Case of 1996: A Case Study." In *Essays in Honor of Gilbert Geis,* edited by H. Pontell and D. Schichor. Englewood Cliffs, NJ: Prentice Hall.
Sutherland, E. H. 1940. "The White Collar Criminal." *American Sociological Review* 30:1-15.
———. 1949. *White Collar Crime.* New York: Dryden.
———. 1983. *White Collar Crime: The Uncut Version.* New Haven, CT: Yale University Press.

CHAPTER 9

Whither the Beast?

The Role of Emotions in a Rational Choice Theory of Crime

JEFFREY BOUFFARD
M. LYN EXUM
RAYMOND PATERNOSTER

To the nonexpert, criminal behavior might seem to involve intense levels of emotion and emotional arousal.[1] This is particularly likely to be true for violent crimes such as assault and rape, which appear to involve a heavy dose of emotional states (e.g., rage, righteousness, domination, anger, arrogance, lust). With a little careful thought, however, one could see that property crimes also are likely to be emotion-laden events for offenders, involving, for example, feelings of fear or risk, a sense of thrill, excitement/titillation, and anticipation. There also are less obvious emotional states that can motivate property crimes such as vengeance, anger, and sexual arousal (Katz 1988). Although somewhat evident to the untrained eye, historically emotions have not played an important part in criminologists' explanations of criminal offending. No small part of this neglect of the role played by emotions in crime has been due to strict disciplinary boundaries and scholars' (partially emotional) desire to first carve out and then protect their own intellectual turf.

A consideration of the causal role of human emotions in criminal conduct requires a focus on the individual as the level of analysis and the individual's internal psychological state as the subject matter. Such foci did not set well with many sociologists who first actively tried to capture the study of crime for their own discipline and who themselves steadfastly held to the belief that any cause of crime must be social, that is, supra-individual (Laub

and Sampson 1991). To them, the only appropriate level of analysis for criminological research was either the community (social disorganization) or
micro-level factors that were proximate but external to the individual (delinquent peers and their stable of "definitions"). As a result of the initial capture
by sociology of the study of crime, for decades crime scholars tended to
ignore the possible role played by offenders' emotions and emotional
arousal. In fact, this inattention to the part played by emotions in crime has
been so complete that it probably has been only in recent years that those
seriously interested in the study of crime have turned their attention, explicitly or implicitly, to offenders' emotional states. Perhaps no recent criminologist has as vividly captured the emotional quality of crime, both violent and
property, and has as clearly demonstrated the central role of emotions in
crime as has Jack Katz in his book, *Seductions of Crime* (Katz 1988).

Throughout Katz's (1988) explanations of different types of crime, we
can see the prominent role played by emotional states. For example, to Katz,
the typical homicide involves three distinct emotional levels or layers.[2] The
would-be killer first must work himself up to the emotional state where he
defines himself as defending the "good": "[the killer] must understand
not only that the victim is attacking what he, the killer, regards as an eter-
nal human value, but [also] that the situation requires a last stand in defense of his basic worth" (pp. 18-19). In other words, the killer must enter
the emotional state of being self-righteous—that even in the act of killing
(indeed, *by* the very act of killing), he is defending the good against evil. Self-
righteousness is not sufficient to propel someone into violence, however,
because an affront to good, even a personal affront, can be dealt with silently
by enduring humiliation. If, however, the humiliation is transformed into a
rage in which the impotence of humiliation is turned on its head (i.e., rage
against humiliation), then a violent, and often fatal, confrontation is more
likely. Where violence is made both more likely and more lethal is when self-
righteous rage is guided into what Katz calls a "practical project" (p. 32).
This practical project is not the simple death of the one causing the humiliation. In fact, as Katz clearly points out, the instigator's quiet demise might
actually frustrate this project. Rather, the objective of righteous rage is what
Katz calls "sacrificial violence"—transcending humiliation by obliterating
the victim. In other words, the victim is "wasted" or "blown away," and no
trace of the humiliating source is left.

Criminal offending also is at the service of strong emotions in the commission of property crimes. Picking up on an old theme by Cohen (1955),
Katz (1988) argues that most property crime (e.g., theft, vandalism) is

decidedly noninstrumental; things are not stolen because they are needed or desired in any strictly utilitarian sense. Rather, because an act is criminal, the object of the criminal act consequently is desired. Or, as Katz more eloquently puts it, "It is not the taste for pizza that leads to the crime; the crime makes the pizza tasty" (p. 52). In other words, items are attractive and assume value because of the crime; the value of the item does not lead to the crime. The question, then, is "Why are objects valuable in this sense?" The short answer Katz offers is that items that are the source of crime (e.g., theft, destruction) are forbidden objects and thus both emotion laden and seductive, and the taking of forbidden objects produces a euphoric or "sneaky thrill" (p. 53). Much like the righteous slaughterer, the property offender must pass through a series of emotional steps, from experiencing the seduction or magical obsession with the object, to controlling one's external emotions and "appearing calm," culminating in the euphoric thrill of "pulling off" the deed.

In short, as Katz (1988) eloquently illustrates, crime is a heavily emotional event. It would appear, therefore, that explanations of crime naturally would include the consideration of emotions as an important explanatory factor in criminal offending. Unfortunately, with few exceptions, criminological theorists have not incorporated the offender's emotional state into their explanatory schemes. This omission is unfortunate because it appears intuitive that emotions do have something to do with crime, and emotions as a topic of study can easily fit into most criminological theory. With this in mind, the purpose of this chapter is relatively modest. Rather than survey the entire field of criminological theory, we propose to examine one prominent criminological theory: rational choice theory. Our goal is to show how a consideration of emotions and offenders' emotional states is compatible with, and can enhance, a rational choice theory of criminal offending. It is our contention that if we can demonstrate that the consideration of human emotion plays an important role in a cognitive-based theory such as rational choice theory, then we will have opened the door for its inclusion in other theories of crime. We will rely on scholars following us to make the connection between emotions and these other theories of crime.

■ The Role of Emotion in Rational Choice Theory

As a theory of criminal offending, rational choice theory (or subjective expected utility theory) conceives of would-be offenders as rationally weighing the expected costs and benefits of criminal conduct before acting. The costs of criminal conduct include, among other things, the possibility and severity of discovery, capture, and legal sanctions; lost legitimate opportunities forsaken by criminal behavior; and various informal costs such as social censure, loss of the esteem and emotional support of loved ones, and any loss of self-respect. The benefits include considerations such as the perceived material gains of ill-gotten goods and any enhancement of respect that might accrue as a result of criminal behavior. It might appear at first blush that emotions and emotional arousal could have very little role to play in a theory of criminal conduct that seems to rely so heavily on cognition and rationality, however minimal that rationality might be. We would argue, however, that there are at least three important roles for emotions in rational conduct and, therefore, within a rational choice theory of crime.

First, the person's state of emotionality or arousal level is an important context or foundation on which rational conduct rests. That is, the rational contemplation of costs and benefits may require a "cool" head—a head not too hot because of intense emotional arousal or too cold because of a dysfunctional lack of arousal. Second, as Katz (1988) clearly points out, the "sneaky thrill" of minor property crime also might operate more generally such that the anticipated emotional consequences of criminal conduct is one of the benefits or utilities ("thrills") that are weighed in the process of rational decision making. Third, as a sizable body of criminological and psychological research can attest, the anticipated emotional costs associated with criminal behavior might serve to effectively reduce the likelihood of such behavior. We now examine each of these in more detail and then examine the empirical literature to determine whether the evidence supports a role for emotions in criminal conduct.

□ Emotional States and the Context of Crime

For instrumental considerations to affect would-be offenders' decisions to commit crimes, the intellect first needs to be engaged. There are times, however, when perceived self-interest might be bypassed and persons act with apparent disregard for their long-term utility. To cite a few examples, smokers continue to smoke even though they are aware of the fact that they run a very high risk of long-term health problems, the obese continue to overeat and fail to exercise even though they are fully cognizant of the fact that their lifestyle will shorten their lives, gamblers know that they have no long-term probability of winning, and drug addicts know that their habit is ruining their lives but seem unable to "control themselves." There are numerous forms of self-destructive behaviors, including criminal conduct, that reflect the very powerful and *excessive* influence of nonrational, emotional, and visceral factors. Moreover, Loewenstein (1996) argues that as the intensity of the visceral/emotional factor increases, so does its direct effect on behavior. In short, there are numerous times when the logic and predictions of rational choice theory fail, when a person's conduct is under the more direct control of emotional and visceral demands than the dictates of reason. There are, then, important limitations to fully rational control over conduct that must be acknowledged, and these limitations are due, at least in part, to the encompassing effect of emotional arousal.

Loewenstein (1996) refers to the condition when cravings and emotions, rather than self-interest, guide conduct as being "out of control." Persons are out of control

> from the action of *visceral factors* such as the cravings associated with drug addiction, drive states (e.g., hunger, thirst, and sexual desire), moods and emotions, and physical pain. At sufficient levels of intensity, these and most other visceral factors cause people to behave contrary to their own long-term self-interest, often with full awareness that they are doing so. (pp. 252-53, emphases in original)

Emotional arousal at the moment of a crime might be so acute, therefore, that would-be offenders find themselves out of control, and rational considerations are far less salient.

Three things occur when emotional intensity is high and people are out of control that short-circuits normal rational deliberation. First, as the visceral/emotional factors intensify, they narrow the content of the person's attention to those activities associated with the factor. For example, when under the influence of craving, addicts will do anything and give anything that will net them even a small amount of the drug. This, more than an appeal to rationality, would explain the conduct of a District of Columbia woman who allowed her young child to be sexually molested in exchange for cocaine. Goldstein (1994) relays a story of Charlie, a heroin addict/patient of his who had been "clean" for some time, had a job, and was rebuilding his life. Charlie reported that he was watching a television show about addiction that showed addicts shooting up. This caused him to develop an intense craving for heroin, and he rushed out of the house, located some of the drug, and shot up, thus relapsing. As Goldstein notes, when watching the behaviors associated with drug use, Charlie's attention was completely focused on obtaining heroin, to the exclusion of everything else: "it was as though he were driven by some external force he was powerless to resist, even though he knew while it was happening that it was a disastrous course of action for him" (pp. 220-21). Of course, drugs are not the only object that can produce a craving that thwarts rational conduct. One of Wright and Decker's (1994) burglars likens his criminal activity to an "addiction":

> It's like when you smoke a cigarette, you know, you want more and more from the nicotine. Well, from my experience, you can get bigger and better stuff the more times that you do it, and you can make more money. I'm addicted to money; I love money. So, I just keep doing [burglaries]. (p. 38)

In addition to a narrowing of the content of one's attention, being out of control has a second effect that short-circuits rational deliberation: it reduces a person's time horizon. Rational deliberation sways conduct when costs exceed benefits. The benefits of self-destructive conduct (e.g., smoking, drug use, overeating, crime) are, however, generally immediate, whereas the costs are more remote. Restraint works when individuals have a long time horizon, that is, when the long-term consequences of behavior are salient. One of the most powerful effects of intense visceral/emotional states is that a person's attention becomes much more restricted to the present rather than the future. Although an addict might well make the same no-use choice as a nonaddict when not under the spell of craving, the intense visceral demand of a craving will make the addict more present oriented and less able to resist the temptations of drugs. Similarly, when under the seductive spell of the object (i.e., an intense emotional state [Katz 1988]), a thief is more affected by the emotional immediacy of the theft than by any longer term material or utilitarian consequences. One of Katz's (1988) shoplifters described the narrowing of attention in the following terms:

> There we were, in the most lucrative department Mervyn's had to offer two curious (but very mature) adolescent girls: the cosmetic and jewelry department. . . . We didn't enter the store planning to steal anything. In fact, I believe we had "given it up" a few weeks earlier. But once my eyes caught sight of the beautiful white and blue necklaces alongside the counter, a spark inside me was once again ignited. . . . Those exquisite puka necklaces were calling out to me, "Take me! Wear me! I can be yours!" All I needed to do was take them to make it a reality. (p. 54)

The experience of this shoplifter—her craving for illicit jewelry "ignited" by the mere sight of the forbidden object—nicely illustrates a point by Goldstein (1994:222) about drug addition but is of much greater generality. As he puts it, the craving of an object is provoked not by its absence but rather by its presence. Any form of the proximity of an object (its smell, sight, or feel) can provoke a state of intense emotional arousal or craving that orients the person's attention on the present, thereby foiling more rational considerations.

Finally, intense visceral/emotional states can abort or severely hinder rational deliberations by narrowing the person's focus inward so that one's own needs have primacy to the neglect of the concern of others. Cravings, in other words, make one much more self-centered and selfish. Empirical work in the psychology of interrogation indicates that when individuals are deprived of sleep, food, or drink, they are more likely to satisfy their cravings by betraying family, friends, or comrades (Biderman 1960; Loewenstein 1996:275). More specifically, one of Miller's (1986) street hustlers reported that once she became addicted to dope, nothing else but the drug mattered:

> We got married and everything was going real well for us. But the dope got into the act, got into our lives. And soon after that happened, we ended up splitting up. It was just that there was nothing left for us. I mean, sexual desires weren't being met. We didn't care about each other as much as we did the dope. The dope always came first. (p. 112)

Intense emotional/visceral states can foil rational deliberation, then, because they have the effect of rendering social influence (e.g., informal social censure) less relevant.

It probably is quite clear that intense emotional states can thwart the process of rational decision making. Conventional wisdom warns to avoid getting "hot under the collar" and to "keep a cool head." So, it is likely that we all are aware of the fact that strong emotions can be quite harmful to our rational faculties and can keep us from making good decisions (i.e., those that are profitable or yield high utility). It probably is not so well understood, however, that the *absence* of emotion or arousal can be just as damaging to our rational thought processes. That is, just as intense emotional states can preempt rational deliberation, so too can overly subdued ones.[3] How can we be "too cool"? What possible good can emotional states provide rationality? After all, should we not separate our heads from our hearts and maintain the duality of mind and body suggested by René Descartes during the mid-1600s?

Important insights into the contribution that emotions make to rational thought have been made by neurologist Antonio Damasio and outlined in his book, *Descartes' Error* (Damasio 1994). Damasio studied patients who had been brain injured (i.e., damage to the frontal cortex) but who otherwise had maintained much of their rational faculties; the patients had language and memory, and they could perform calculations and abstract reasoning. Their injuries did, however, completely remove their capacity to feel emotions; they were cold, distant, socially shallow, and unfeeling. There was, in essence, no emotional arousal. Although fully capable of performing everyday life functions, Damasio's patients could not consider the consequences of their actions. Reward and punishment had no effect on the decisions they made; they were not affected by the costs and benefits of their actions. As a result, the decisions they did make were very poor. Damasio provides a good description of one of the brain-damaged and feeling-neutered patients:

> Patient A's emotional life seem impoverished. Now and then he might have a short-lived burst of emotion, but for the most part such display was lacking. There is no sign that he felt for others and no sign of embarrassment, sadness, or anguish at such a tragic turn of events [i.e., his life unraveling because of his poor "judgment"]. His overall affect is best captured as "shallow." (p. 56)

From examples such as these, Damasio (1994:56) argues that emotion is absolutely essential for the rational faculties because it allows us to filter and process information. It is an emotional state or feeling, he states, that allows us to immediately reject some course of action as bad for us and allows us to pursue information for a more limited set. In other words, without emotions to guide our conduct, rationality would not be optimal; in fact, it would break down, as in the patients with brain injuries that aborted their capacity to feel.

Descartes' "error," therefore, was in separating mind and body. It appears that whereas rationality is impaired when emotions are too strong (i.e., intense emotions, cravings, or "visceral states" can push a person out of control), it also is thwarted when emotional intensity is too weak. Far from being incompatible with rationality, some emotional intensity is necessary. It seems likely that rationality functions best when emotions are in a midrange (Loewenstein 1996). If so, then it seems incumbent on rational choice theorists to fully incorporate a consideration of persons' emotional states into their explanations of human conduct.

□ *Emotional States and the Benefits of Doing Crime*

There is a second emotional component to criminal conduct that rational choice theorists have not generally incorporated into their models of offenders' decision making. Whereas they have considered various material and social benefits that make criminal conduct more likely (e.g., the quick "score" of crime, the prestige in some social circles for being a "bad ass"), they have not generally considered the emotional effects of crime as a "benefit." That crimes can put offenders into pleasurable emotional states that constitute part of the allure of criminal offending cannot now be disputed. The thrill, risk, or emotional excitement of committing a crime is perceived by many offenders to be at least one reason why they engage in crime. For example, in his discussion of the seduction of shoplifting, Katz (1988) refers to the feeling of being "thrilled" by the act of stealing, and one of his shoplifters adopts a sexual metaphor in describing what her act came to mean to her: "The experience was almost orgasmic for me. There was a buildup of tension as I contemplated the danger of a forbidden act, then a rush of excitement at the moment of committing the crime, and finally a delicious sense of release" (p. 71). Sex is a powerful reinforcement and source of pleasure or benefit, and this shoplifter described the emotional consequences of her act as "delicious." The emotional and nonmaterial "thrill" or benefit of offending also was a prominent part of the motivation of Wright and Decker's (1994) burglars:

> I think [burglary] is fun. It's a challenge. You don't know whether you're getting caught or not, and I like challenges. If I can get a challenging [burglary, then I] like that. It's more of the risk that you got to take, you know, to see how good you can really be. I don't know if you ever stole anything in your life; it's a mixture of fear and anxiety and just excitement; it's adrenaline pumping through your body. . . . Even if we haven't cased out these houses as much as we would've liked to, [we just burglarize them]. But it's because we're up and our adrenaline is pumping and we want to just get it and get it done. (p. 58)
> . . . It's just a thrill going in undetected and walking out with all they shit. Man, that shit fucks me up. (p. 104)

The comments of this burglar are an example of how an act of crime allows the offender to penetrate a "sacred" area and not only defile it but also introduce chaos and what Katz (1988) calls a "moral stain" (p. 69). Katz relates a story of one of his female students who would break into persons' homes not to take anything but rather to feel the "magic" of being in a forbidden area and, most important, letting the occupants know that someone had entered the privacy of their home without permission by rearranging the furniture. The driving force behind the girl's actions, Katz states, was the "exotic sensations" she felt in touching objects in other persons' homes (p. 70).

The general point is that there are powerful psychic rewards of doing crime. It is thrilling and exhilarating; it allows some persons to feel a sense of power or control while permitting others to demonstrate mastery and the pride and self-respect that goes with a job well done. To the extent that there are these powerful nonmaterial and nonsocial rewards, rational choice models must incorporate them into their explanations of offenders' decision making.

□ Emotional States and the Costs of Doing Crime

In the previous subsection, we alluded to the fact that emotions or emotional states can constitute one of the benefits or pleasures of committing crimes. As such, we would expect that emotional arousal can increase a would-be offender's inclination to commit a crime. This clear picture is muddied by the fact that emotional states can just as likely be felt as uncomfortable or anxiety provoking rather than as pleasurable and thus would be included as a "cost" in a would-be offender's calculus. It is not at all unreasonable to think that, just as they can facilitate some crimes, strong emotional states felt by offenders can act as a deterrent and inhibit other crimes.

We do not have to think too long and hard to come up with a few examples of this possibility. Fear is a powerful emotion that can restrain would-be offenders from committing crimes in the first place or getting practicing offenders to quit. There are many possible sources of fear that would provide one of the costs of criminal offending. One source is the very act of committing crime itself. Many criminal offenses generate fear because such acts, by their very nature, involve a nontrivial amount of danger and personal risk. Cusson and Pinsonneault (1986) describe the "shock" that their robbers sometimes felt when committing armed robberies. This shocking and painful experience came in different forms. For one robber it was the experience of being shot at by police, for another it was witnessing his accomplice being fatally shot by police, and for a third it was nearly being killed by his crime partner (who tried to "rip him off"). In each instance, the shock generated a sufficiently painful emotional state that it led to the robber quitting crime.

In their discussion of residential burglars, Wright and Decker (1994) refer to the fact that, to eventually commit burglaries, offenders not only must know how to commit the offense but also must be able to manage their fears. A failure to manage their anxiety and apprehension would lead potential burglars to call off their "capers." This is reminiscent of Matza's (1964) suggestion that repeated acts of delinquency require offenders not only to overcome the rudimentary technical skills—what he calls the behavioral component of delinquency—but also to manage their fears, avoid being "chicken," and overcome the apprehensive component:

> If drifting boys are too scared, too apprehensive, about repeating an old offense because they recall the fear they experienced the last time, the will to crime is obviously discouraged. Thus, it is important that they be prepared by past experiences to manage, and in large measure discount, the apprehensiveness they normally feel upon entering the infraction. (p. 186)

More generally, fear as a cost of crime is intentionally generated by the criminal justice system. In this case, fear is created by the possibility of discovery, apprehension, and punishment. Fear is an uncomfortable emotional state that the legal system deliberately attempts to invoke in persons to persuade them that crime is more costly than are conventional alternatives. Offenders' accounts of their deliberative process in deciding to commit crimes tend to suggest that fear of formal sanctions is a formidable consideration. The burglar-turned-novelist, Malcolm Braly, eloquently conveys the feelings of anxiety and fear during his final burglary that could drive even an experienced "career criminal" out of the business:

> I went broke and convinced myself it would be a small risk to take something easy, just enough for food and rent, and I was out in the night, prowling a nursery and garden supply house, when the lights of a squad car washed over me, and I was sure they had spotted me crouched there in the underbrush. I bolted in an instant panic to run stumbling and frequently falling across a large empty lot, expecting at any moment to see spotlights ahead. I would be snared from the darkness like a terrified rabbit. (Braly 1976:43)

Finally, fear of crime comes from other sources besides the inherent dangerousness of criminal activity and the workings of the state. A source of fear that, as a cost of crime, might inhibit criminal intentions can come from family members and even oneself. Grasmick and Bursik (1990) argue that offenders and would-be offenders can perceive that crime is costly because significant others in their lives might find out and terminate their relationships. The potential of social embarrassment, then, constitutes another emotional cost of crime. In addition, a powerful emotion is shame or self-punishment, and feelings of shame can be triggered when offenders feel that they have let themselves down. Both shame and informal rebukes by significant others can serve as powerful costs of crime. Shover (1996) provides a few very vivid examples of how the careers of thieves can be terminated when the social costs of crime become too high and continued when self-respect is so eroded that self-rebuke carries no weight:

> When I reached the age of 35 [years,] it just seemed like my life wanted to change. I needed a change in my life, and I was tired of going to jail. I wanted to change my life and stay out of here. And by meeting the woman that I met, it just turned my life completely around. . . . When I met her, it just seemed like something in my life had been fulfilled. (p. 126)

> I started living with this woman, you know, and my life suddenly changed. . . . I was contented, you know, bein' with her. . . . I cared about her, you know. I wanted to be with her, you know, that was it. . . . And, hey, I just found enjoyment there.

> It . . . gets to the point that you get into such as desperation. You're not working, you can't work. You're drunk as hell, been that way two or three weeks. You're no good to yourself, and you're no good to anybody else. Self-esteem is gone, [and you're] spiritually, mentally, physically, [and] financially bankrupt. You ain't got nothing to lose.

In sum, in addition to forming the background or context of rational thinking and providing a powerful incentive to crime, emotionally charged states also provide an important cost of crime that enters into offenders' and would-be offenders' rational calculus.

■ The Empirical Status of Emotional Arousal and Crime

A sizable body of literature has studied emotions as costs and benefits within a rational choice framework. For example, Grasmick and Bursik (1990) felt that the traditional focus on formal legal sanctions as deterrents contributed to the disappointing results of the deterrence doctrine. They proposed a broader conceptualization of the sources of potential costs of crime to include shame and embarrassment, both arguably sources of physiological and emotional discomfort. Using a cross-sectional randomly selected sample of adults, the authors found that both threats of shame and legal sanctions inhibited self-reported intention to commit petty theft, tax cheating, and drunken driving. The anticipated effects of embarrassment, however, were not found.

Bachman, Paternoster, and Ward (1992) examined the effect of perceived threat of shame in relation to sexual offending in a sample of university students. These authors tested the effects of contextual aspects of the offense, formal and informal sanctions (including shame), and moral beliefs on the self-reported likelihood to engage in sexual assault as described in a hypothetical scenario (a short story describing the commission of a crime). Results reveal that moral beliefs and threats of formal sanctions do influence the likelihood of assault but that shame does not. However, the authors conclude that several measurement issues might account for this null finding. In particular, participants were asked to estimate the threat of informal sanctioning dependent on being arrested, whereas Grasmick and Bursik's (1990) measure of shame was not dependent on legal sanctions. Similarly, Grasmick and Bursik asked participants to rate their own likelihood of experiencing self-imposed shame, whereas Bachman et al.'s (1992) participants were asked to estimate the likelihood of the "scenario male" experiencing shame as a result of committing the assault. Thus, the null findings for threats of shame might be due to the failure of participants to place themselves fully in the scenario male's shoes and imagine their own feelings in response to the act.

Evidence from the Bachman et al. (1992) study suggests that the anticipated pleasure associated with the sexual assault also can increase the risk of offending. Although not explicitly conceptualized as a test of the effects of emotional benefits on offending, the study found that participants' self-reported likelihood of sexual assault was increased if the female in the story first allowed the scenario male to "kiss and/or fondle her." Although this is discussed as a contextual factor by the authors, it is plausible that the participants responded to their own perceived pleasure and emotional arousal derived from the consensual sexual activity depicted in the story. Thus, the participants rating their likelihood to act as the scenario male did might have been responding more to the perceived emotional (i.e., sexual pleasure) benefit depicted in the scenario. This is indirect evidence that perceived pleasure derived from a criminal act can influence the likelihood to offend. In a similar study of sexual forcefulness, Loewenstein, Nagin, and Paternoster (1997) found support for the inhibitory effect of perceived threat of shame on self-reported likelihood to both force sex and coax a woman into removing her clothes. In addition, the authors report that those participants who expected that engaging in the behavior of the scenario male would be "fun" reported a higher likelihood of engaging in sexual forcefulness.

Paternoster and Simpson (1996) examined the potential inhibitory effects of shame as well as the impact of an emotional benefit (i.e., how thrilling the act would be) on corporate offending. Business students and professionals were given four separate corporate crime scenarios and asked to rate the likelihood that they would act accordingly. The authors found that the perceived threat of shame and guilt significantly reduced the self-reported likelihood of engaging in instances of corporate crime. They also report that participants were more likely to engage in offending if they found the act potentially "thrilling."

Tibbetts and Herz (1996) examined possible gender differences in the effect of shame and pleasure on the likelihood of offending among college students. They report that perceived shame, independent of detection, was significantly and negatively correlated with the likelihood of both shoplifting and drunk driving among males and females. Similarly, the effect of perceived pleasure derived from offending was significantly and positively correlated with both crimes.

In general, there seems to be a relatively consistent body of research demonstrating the inhibitory effects of shame on the likelihood of committing a diverse selection of criminal offenses. Similarly, several studies have demonstrated the positive impact of the expected pleasure derived from crime on the likelihood of engaging in the acts. These emotional elements of crime might be particularly salient within a subset of people with certain predispositions or personality traits. For example, Nagin and Paternoster (1994) found that participants who were more present oriented and self-centered were more likely to view crime as "fun" and less likely to be deterred by the potential losses of social/emotional bonds (see also Longshore, Turner, and Stein 1996; Nagin and Paternoster 1993; Piquero and Rosay 1998; Piquero and Tibbetts 1996).

In addition to comprising part of the costs and benefits of doing crime, we have alluded to the fact that emotions and emotional states also might serve as moderators of rational thinking. This seems especially true with respect to sexual arousal. Several authors have proposed models explaining the development of sexually coercive behaviors that include a sexual arousal component (e.g., Barbaree and Marshall 1991; Hall and Hirschman 1991). In addition, numerous reports within the fields of psychology and criminology have tested the role of sexual arousal in sexual violence (Abel et al. 1977; Loewenstein et al. 1997; Malamuth 1981; Quinsey, Chaplin, and Upfold 1984). This research has studied the direct effects of arousal (the satisfaction of which is a form of emotional benefit) on the likelihood of sexual aggression and examined the possible indirect effects of arousal on the rational decision-making process.

Using an experimental design, Loewenstein et al. (1997) randomly assigned undergraduate males to view either sexually arousing or sexually neutral photographs. Participants then read a dating scenario in which the female consents to sexual foreplay but not to sexual intercourse. Participants were later asked how likely they would be to pressure the woman in the given situation to have sex. Results indicate that those exposed to sexually arousing photographs report a greater likelihood of sexual aggression, suggesting a direct effect of arousal. The indirect impact of sexual arousal on offending likelihood also has been widely studied (Bachman et al. 1992; Bouffard and Exum 1997; Check and Malamuth 1983; Loewenstein et al. 1997; Malamuth and Check 1980a, 1980b; Malamuth, Heim, and Feshbach 1980; Porter and Critelli 1994). For example, research suggests the potential for sexual arousal to mediate the processing of information, particularly perceptions of the victim's pain and pleasure, that might be expected to inhibit sexual aggression among individuals whose heads are "cooler" (Malamuth and Check 1980a, 1980b; Malamuth et al. 1980). Bouffard and Exum (1997) also report that male participants' trait-level arousability diminishes their perceptions of victims' pain, which in turn increases their likelihood of sexual aggression.

Arousal in general (as opposed to sexual arousal) also has been found to attenuate the potential costs of crime. For example, Cochran, Wood, and Arneklev (1994) examined the effect of low arousal and need for stimulation on self-reported delinquency. Controlling for measures of social control and demographic factors, they found that a high need for stimulation diminished the inhibitory influence of religiosity on assaultive behaviors. Similar results were found for theft but not for substance abuse. Hagan, Gillis, and Simpson (1985, 1990) found that a "taste for risk taking" is strongly related to delinquency, controlling for gender and social class. McCarthy (1996) also reports that risk seeking and an "affinity for danger" predict both drug selling and theft among homeless youths in Toronto. Andrews and Bonta (1994) categorize various risk factors for criminality and conclude that risk seeking (presumably the result of low emotional arousal) is one of the "major" predictors of crime. Finally, the extensive work of Hare (1998) and his colleagues has resulted in a substantial accumulation of knowledge about the relationships among low physical/emotional arousal, punishment, and various criminal behaviors (traditionally assessed as it occurs among samples of psychopaths). Thus, just as too much arousal can lead to deviant behavior, so too can too little arousal.

■ Policy Implications

There are scant direct policy implications that come from a greater understanding of the role of emotions in crime in general and rational choice theories of crime in particular. This is not because we think that the actual role played by emotional arousal is weak or limited to only a few specific crimes. Rather, we think that it is because the criminal justice system and criminal justice policy cannot do much to influence human emotions. To suggest that a target of criminal justice policy should be to decrease the emotional pleasures of crime (and increase the pleasures of not engaging in crime) and increase the emotional costs of crime (and increase the emotional benefits of not engaging in crime) is not to say very much that we already do not know or have tried to do. The brute fact is that most emotional factors are beyond the reach of criminal justice policy.

We can, however, make one modest recommendation based on what we know about the role of emotions in behavior generally. The problem of getting would-be criminals to more vigorously consider the costs of crime and the benefits of not engaging in crime is analogous to the problem that health practitioners have in getting homosexual men to consider the risk of AIDS infection and take the appropriate cautions. The risk of AIDS is present in unprotected sexual activity and has a high severity; it also is preventable if condoms are used. Much like the would-be criminal who might maintain that he or she considers the benefits and costs of offending, individuals might rationally consider the costs and benefits of unprotected sexual activity and anticipate that, when in the "heat of the moment," they will protect themselves. Unfortunately, research suggests that people in an emotionally "cool" state often are unable to anticipate very accurately what they would do in an emotionally "hot" state. Although we might think that we will act rationally (and protect ourselves from either AIDS or the temptations of crime) when not in the situation, we find ourselves unprepared to deal with the issues when deeply involved in the situation and emotionally "hot." In other words, people cannot accurately anticipate the intensity of the "heat of the moment" and are unable to deal with it.

Treatment programs in the criminal justice system can provide some service by providing some insight into this problem of hampered rationality by forcing offenders to recall the emotional feelings they had at the times when they were contemplating crimes and how they responded to it. Research by Gold (1993) with male homosexuals shows that when participants were asked to vividly recall sexual encounters in which they did not use condoms and relate the justifications they employed at those times, as well as how rational they now thought those justifications were, they were less likely to engage in unprotected sex in subsequent encounters. There might be some promise, then, of teaching persons to anticipate the power and strength of their emotions so that they are better prepared to deal with them when they arise.

■ Summary

In sum, we would argue that emotions play a very important role in criminal conduct and that they should have a prominent role in criminological theory. In this chapter, we have attempted to illustrate that rational choice theories of criminal offending can easily accommodate a more commanding position of emotions in their models. We also have briefly reviewed the literature on rational choice theory with an eye to suggesting that a more concerted effort to consider the role of human emotions in criminal conduct might pay substantial empirical dividends. What also is clear is that scholars have only scratched the surface with respect to both exploring the theoretical link between emotions and criminal conduct and empirically examining that link. A great deal more theoretical and empirical work needs to be undertaken in this area.

STUDY QUESTIONS

1. What are the different ways in which emotions and emotional arousal are related to the decision to commit criminal offenses?

2. Have you ever been in a situation where you were "out of control" and did not consider the consequences or implications of your actions?
3. If some offenders are "out of control" but not necessarily insane, should they have diminished criminal responsibility?
4. Are emotions relevant only for violent crimes such as rape and assault?
5. What are the most powerful emotions involved in the commission of criminal acts? Are these same emotions involved in other destructive, but not necessarily criminal, acts?
6. What other theories of crime are compatible with a consideration of offenders' emotional states?

NOTES

1. Throughout this chapter, we adopt a very general definition of *emotion:* a short-lived state of mind characterized by physiological reactions to, and psychological assessments of, specific events and stimuli. We recognize that such a basic definition does not fully capture the complexity of human emotions. For this, we recommend Power and Dalgleish (1997) and Izard (1977).
2. The male pronoun is used because the majority of homicides, at least in this country, are committed by males. However, Katz (1988, pp. 47-51) argues that women construct impassioned murders in ways equivalent to men, albiet in distinctive styles.
3. Loewenstein (1996) repeatedly alludes to the fact that rational deliberation and the rational control over one's conduct are achieved when visceral/emotional states are in a midrange: "At low levels of intensity, people seem to be capable of dealing with visceral factors in a relatively optimal fashion. . . . At low levels of visceral factors, people generally experience themselves as behaving in a rational fashion. At extremely high levels, such as the level of sleepiness that causes one to fall asleep at the wheel, decision making is seen as *arational*— that is, people don't perceive themselves as making decisions at all" (pp. 273, 289, emphasis in original).

REFERENCES

Abel, Gene G., David H. Barlow, Edward B. Blanchard, and Donald Guild. 1977. "The Components of Rapists' Sexual Arousal." *Archives of General Psychiatry* 34:895-903.

Andrews, Donald and James Bonta. 1994. *The Psychology of Criminal Conduct.* Cincinnati, OH: Anderson.

Bachman, Ronet, Raymond Paternoster, and Sally Ward. 1992. "The Rationality of Sexual Offending: Testing a Deterrence/Rational Choice Conception of Sexual Assault." *Law and Society Review* 26:343-72.

Barbaree, Howard E. and William L. Marshall. 1991. "The Role of Male Sexual Arousal in Rape: Six Models." *Journal of Consulting and Clinical Psychology* 59:621-30.

Biderman, A. D. 1960. "Social-Psychological Needs and 'Involuntary' Behavior as Illustrated by Compliance in Interrogation." *Sociometry* 23:120-47.

Bouffard, Jeffrey A. and M. Lyn Exum. 1997. "Predicting Sexual Coercion From Deviant Arousal and Perceptions of the Victim." Paper presented at the annual meeting of the American Society of Criminology, San Diego.

Braly, Malcolm. 1976. *False Starts: A Memoir of San Quentin and Other Prisons.* Boston: Little, Brown.

Check, James V. P. and Neil M. Malamuth. 1983. "Sex Role Stereotyping and Reactions to Depictions of Stranger Versus Acquaintance Rape." *Journal of Personality and Social Psychology* 45:344-56.

Cochran, John K., Peter B. Wood, and Bruce J. Arneklev. 1994. "Is the Religiosity-Delinquency Relationship Spurious? A Test of Arousal and Social Control Theories." *Journal of Research in Crime and Delinquency* 31:92-123.

Cohen, Albert. 1955. *Delinquent Boys: The Culture of the Gang.* New York: Free Press.

Cusson, Maurice and Pierre Pinsonneault. 1986. "The Decision to Give Up Crime." Pp. 72-82 in *The Reasoning Criminal: Rational Choice Perspectives on Offending,* edited by Derek B. Cornish and Ronald V. Clarke. New York: Springer-Verlag.

Damasio, Antonio R. 1994. *Descartes' Error: Emotion, Reason, and the Human Brain.* New York: Putnam.

Gold, R. 1993. "On the need to mind the gap: On-line versus off-line cognitions underlying sexual risk-taking. Pp. 227-52 in *The Theory of Reasoned Action: Its Application to AIDS Preventive Behavior,* edited by D. Terry, C. Gallois, and M. McCamish. New York: Pergamon.

Goldstein, Avram. 1994. *Addiction: From Biology to Drug Policy.* New York: Freeman.

Grasmick, Harold G. and Robert J. Bursik. 1990. "Conscience, Significant Others, and Rational Choice: Extending the Deterrence Model." *Law and Society Review* 24:837-61.

Hagan, John, A. R. Gillis, and John Simpson. 1985. "The Class Structure of Gender and Delinquency: Toward a Power-Control Theory of Common Delinquent Behavior. *American Journal of Sociology* 90:1151-78.

―――. 1990. "Clarifying and Extending Power-Control Theory. *American Journal of Sociology* 95:1024-37.

Hall, Gordon C. Nagayama and Richard Hirschman. 1991. "Toward a Theory of Sexual Aggression: A Quadripartite Model." *Journal of Consulting and Clinical Psychology* 59:662-69.

Hare, Robert D. 1998. "Psychopaths and Their Nature: Implications for the Mental Health and Criminal Justice Systems." Pp. 188-212 in *Psychopathy: Antisocial, Criminal, and Violent Behavior,* edited by Theodore Millon and Erik Simonsen. New York: Guilford.

Izard, Carroll E. 1977. *Human Emotions.* New York: Plenum.

Katz, Jack. 1988. *Seductions of Crime: Moral and Sensual Attractions in Doing Evil.* New York: Basic Books.

Laub, John H. and Robert J. Sampson. 1991. "The Sutherland-Glueck Debate: On the Sociology of Criminological Knowledge." *American Journal of Sociology* 96:1402-40.

Loewenstein, George. 1996. "Out of Control: Visceral Influences on Behavior. *Organizational Behavior and Human Decision Making Processes* 65:272-92.

Loewenstein, George, Daniel Nagin, and Raymond Paternoster. 1997. "The Effect of Sexual Arousal on Expectation of Sexual Forcefulness." *Journal of Research in Crime and Delinquency* 34:443-73.

Longshore, Douglas, Susan Turner, and Judith A. Stein. 1996. "Self-Control in a Criminal Sample: An Examination of Construct Validity." *Criminology* 34:209-28.

Malamuth, Neil M. 1981. "Rape Fantasies as a Function of Exposure to Violent Sexual Stimuli. *Archives of Sexual Behavior* 10:33-47.

Malamuth, Neil M. and James V. P. Check. 1980a. "Penile Tumescence and Perceptual Responses to Rape as a Function of Victim's Perceived Reactions." *Journal of Applied Social Psychology* 10:528-47.

———. 1980b. "Sexual Arousal to Rape and Consenting Depictions: The Importance of the Woman's Arousal." *Journal of Abnormal Psychology* 89:763-66.

Malamuth, Neil M., Maggie Heim, and Seymour Feshbach. 1980. "Sexual Responses of College Students to Rape Depictions: Inhibitory and Disinhibitory Effects." *Journal of Personality and Social Psychology* 38:399-408.

Matza, David. 1964. *Delinquency and Drift.* New York: John Wiley.

McCarthy, Bill. 1996. "The Attitudes and Actions of Others: Tutelage and Sutherland's Theory of Differential Association." *British Journal of Criminology* 36:135-47.

Miller, Eleanor. 1986. *Street Woman.* Philadelphia: Temple University Press.

Nagin, Daniel and Raymond Paternoster. 1993. "Enduring Individual Differences and Rational Choice Theories of Crime." *Law and Society Review* 27:467-96.

———. 1994. "Personal Capital and Social Control: The Deterrence Implications of a Theory of Individual Differences in Criminal Offending." *Criminology* 32:581-606.

Paternoster, Raymond and Sally Simpson. 1996. "Sanction Threats and Appeals to Morality: Testing a Rational Choice Model of Corporate Crime." *Law and Society Review* 30:549-83.

Piquero, Alex R. and Andre B. Rosay. 1998. "The Reliability and Validity of Grasmick et al.'s Self-Control Scale: A Comment on Longshore et al." *Criminology* 36:157-73.

Piquero, Alex and Stephen Tibbetts. 1996. "Specifying the Direct and Indirect Effects of Low Self-Control and Situational Factors in Offenders' Decision-Making Model: Toward a More Complete Model of Rational Offending. *Justice Quarterly* 13:481-510.

Porter, James F. and Joseph W. Critelli. 1994. "Self-Talk and Sexual Arousal in Sexual Aggression." *Journal of Social and Clinical Psychology* 13:223-39.

Power, Mick and Tim Dalgleish. 1997. *Cognition and Emotion: From Order to Disorder.* East Sussex, UK: Psychology Press.

Quinsey, Vernon L., T. C. Chaplin, and D. Upfold. 1984. "Sexual Arousal to Non-Sexual Violence and Sadomasochistic Themes Among Rapists and Non-Sex Offenders." *Journal of Consulting and Clinical Psychology* 52:651-57.

Shover, Neal. 1996. *Great Pretenders: Pursuits and Careers of Persistent Thieves.* Boulder, CO: Westview.

Tibbetts, Steven G. and Denise C. Herz. 1996. "Gender Differences in Factors of Social Control and Rational Choice." *Deviant Behavior* 17:183-208.

Wright, Richard T. and Scott H. Decker. 1994. *Burglars on the Job: Streetlife and Residential Break-ins.* Boston: Northeastern University Press.

Understanding Illicit Drug Use
Lessons From Developmental Theory

PAUL MAZEROLLE

Illicit drug use is one of the more common deviant behaviors in which adolescents engage. Unfortunately, illicit drug use is associated with numerous negative consequences. For example, drugs have been linked to educational problems, delinquency, reduced productivity, and domestic violence (Office of National Drug Control Policy 1998:15-18). Drug-related deaths increased by 42 percent between 1990 and 1995 (p. 12). The annual societal costs associated with illegal drugs are estimated to be approximately $62 billion (p. 12). Clearly, better ways of preventing and reducing drug use need to be developed. One of the best ways in which to achieve such a goal is to develop an improved theoretical understanding of illicit drug use.

Many of the current theories of illicit drug use are inadequate for understanding drug-using behavior. Most of the traditional theories offer static descriptions of why people use drugs and do not fully account for the way in which drug-using behavior changes over time. In short, traditional theories do not fully account for the factors involved in initiating, escalating, and ceasing drug use.

In this chapter, I examine how developmental theories can more completely explain illicit drug-using behavior. The chapter is divided into four sections. I first discuss some drug-using patterns drawn from survey information collected in the United States. Next, I examine current information on how drug use develops over time. Third, I describe contemporary developmental theories applied to the illicit drug use context. Finally, I close the chapter by identifying some interventions aimed at preventing and reducing drug-using behavior that are based on these developmental theories.

■ Trends in Illicit Drug Use

Approximately one-third of Americans age 12 years or over have used illicit drugs during their lifetimes. Just over 10 percent have used illicit drugs during the past year, and about 6 percent have used them during the past month. As Exhibit 10.1 shows, marijuana is the drug of choice, with cocaine and nonmedical therapeutic drugs (e.g., tranquilizers) representing the second largest category of use.

The fact that approximately one-third of the U.S. population reports illicit drug use in their lifetimes is significant. However, the prevalence of illicit drug use is substantially lower than the lifetime use of alcohol (82 percent) and cigarettes (72 percent).

Trends in prevalence of illicit and licit drug use among different age groups, shown in Exhibit 10.2, reveal a number of interesting patterns:

- Among most age categories, illicit drug use was much lower during the mid-1990s than it was during the late 1970s. However, illicit drug use increased noticeably after 1992 for the youngest (12-17 years) and oldest (35+ years) age categories.

- Trends in the use of any illicit drug appear to be driven by marijuana use patterns. Marijuana trends mirror the patterns for any illicit drug. Despite the diversity of illicit drug use, the majority of use is limited to marijuana.

- Cocaine use is much lower than marijuana use, generally declined through the 1990s, and is most evident among persons who were ages 26 to 34 years during the mid-1990s.

- Use of legal drugs (e.g., alcohol), although much higher than use of illicit drugs, has remained stable across most age groups and declined among individuals ages 12 to 17 years.

These data on drug use are drawn from perhaps the most comprehensive self-report survey of drug use in the United States, the National Household Survey on Drug Abuse (NHSDA). This cross-sectional survey provides information on the prevalence of illicit drugs, alcohol, and tobacco for the civilian noninstitutionalized population age 12 years or over in the United States. In 1995, data on drug-using behavior was gathered from more than 17,000 respondents. Information from the NHSDA is especially helpful for identifying general trends in drug use. However, keep in mind that certain groups are overlooked including persons who are homeless, incarcerated, or recently arrested. These individuals are at high risk for using drugs. Furthermore, self-report surveys of drug use rely on respondents' willingness to

(Text continues on page 186)

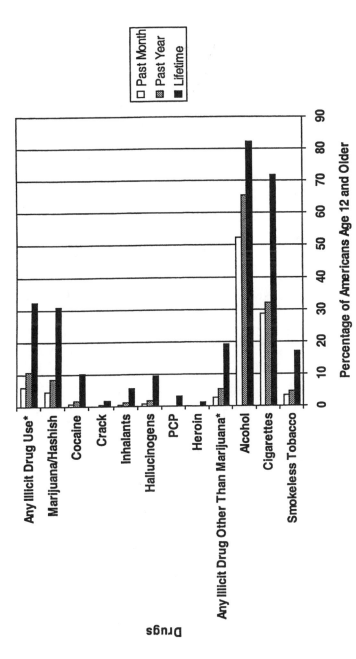

Percentage of Americans Age 12 and Older

Legend:
- ☐ Past Month
- ▨ Past Year
- ■ Lifetime

Exhibit 10.1. Estimated Numbers of Users of Illicit Drugs, Alcohol, and Tobacco in the U.S. Population Age 12 Years or Over: 1995

SOURCE: Substance Abuse and Mental Health Services Administration, *National Household Survey on Drug Abuse: Main Findings*, 1995.
*Any illicit drug indicates use at least once of marijuana or hashish, cocaine (including crack), inhalants, hallucinogens (including PSP and LSD), heroin, or any prescription-type psychotherapeutic used nonmedically. Any illicit drug other than marijuana indicates use at least once of any of these listed drugs, regardless of marijuana use; marijuana users who also have used any of the other listed drugs are included.

Any Illicit Drug

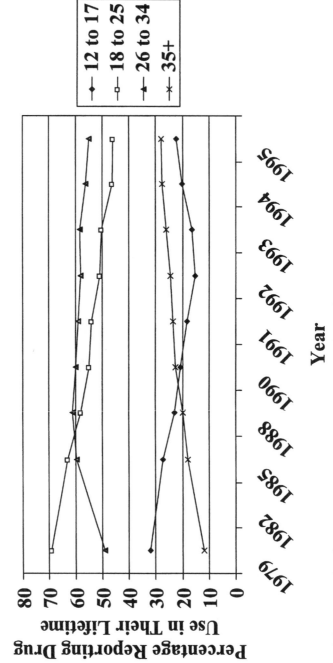

Exhibit 10.2. Trends in Percentage Reporting Drug Use in Their Lifetimes, by Age Group: 1979-1995

SOURCE: Substance Abuse and Mental Health Services Administration, *National Household Survey on Drug Abuse*, 1979-1995.

Marijuana / Hashish

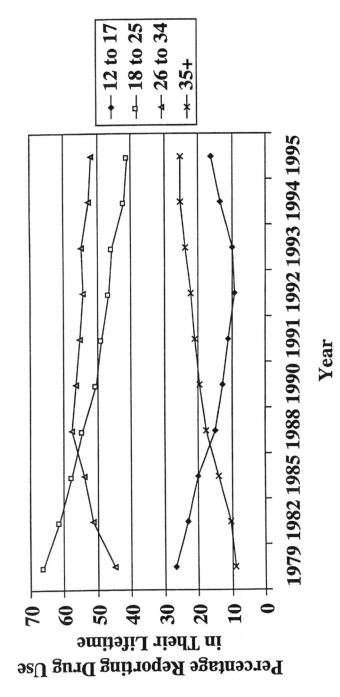

Exhibit 10.2. (Continued) Trends in Percentage Reporting Drug Use in Their Lifetimes, by Age Group: 1979-1995
SOURCE: Substance Abuse and Mental Health Services Administration, *National Household Survey on Drug Abuse*, 1979-1995.

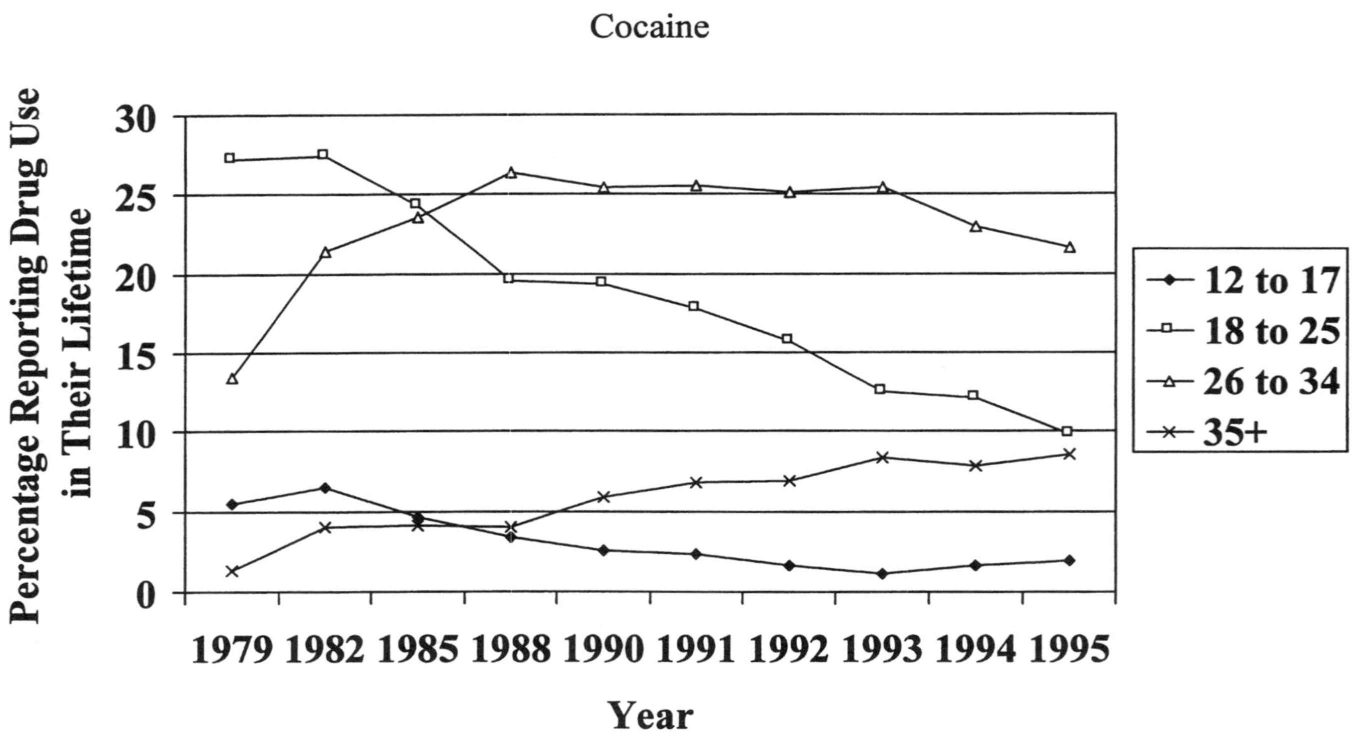

Cocaine

Exhibit 10.2. (Continued)   Trends in Percentage Reporting Drug Use in Their Lifetimes, by Age Group: 1979-1995
SOURCE: Substance Abuse and Mental Health Services Administration, *National Household Survey on Drug Abuse*, 1979-1995.

Alcohol

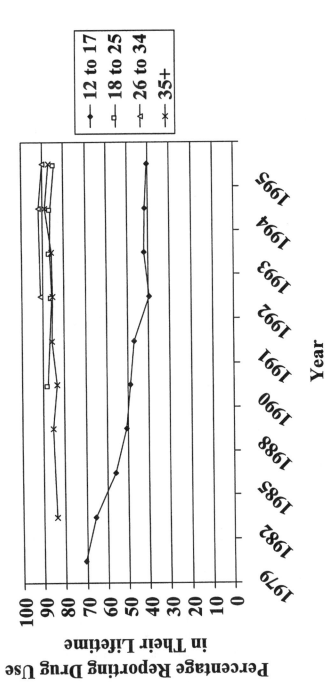

Exhibit 10.2. (Continued) Trends in Percentage Reporting Drug Use in Their Lifetimes, by Age Group: 1979-1995
SOURCE: Substance Abuse and Mental Health Services Administration, *National Household Survey on Drug Abuse, 1979-1995.*

accurately report their behavior. Of course, some degree of under- and overreporting occurs. However, improvements in the accuracy of the information about drug use are continually being explored. Aside from subjecting samples drawn from the general population to drug urinalysis screening, self-reports are the most practical method for capturing this information.

Reliable information on drug use is critical for developing valid theories of drug use as well as successful interventions aimed at preventing or reducing drug use. In addition to the more immediate public health and public safety considerations, reliable information on drug use is useful for uncovering the developmental nature of drug-using "careers," a topic I discuss in the next section.

■ Developmental Nature of Drug-Using Careers

Researchers often examine drug-using careers to identify distinctive patterns. Coombs (1981) observes, for example, that several developmental stages underlie drug-abusing careers including the initiation, escalation, maintenance, discontinuation, and renewal of use. Similar terms (e.g., initiation, frequency, persistence, and desistance of offending behavior) also are used to describe criminal careers more generally (Blumstein, Cohen, and Farrington 1988; Blumstein et al. 1986). Career perspectives are beneficial for identifying unique features of illicit drug use. These approaches allow researchers to examine whether predictors of drug use initiation differ from predictors of persistence or desistance. Uncovering this type of information on drug use is important because interventions can then be tailored to address specific aspects of drug use. Interventions aimed at delaying the onset of drug use could, therefore, differ from efforts focusing on stopping drug use after it has begun. In short, examining different aspects of drug-using careers offers enormous potential for designing effective interventions.

As mentioned previously, drug-using behavior tends to follow clear lines of progression from minor drug experimentation toward more serious substance abuse. Of course, not all users of soft drugs progress to use more serious drugs; in fact, the overwhelming majority of marijuana users, for example, do not move toward more serious drugs (Akers 1992). Still, among serious drug users, there appears to be a progression in which minor drug use (e.g., alcohol) leads to marijuana use, which subsequently leads to more serious substances (e.g., cocaine) (Kandel and Yamaguchi 1993).

TABLE 10.1   Drug Use Histories: Average Ages at Onset and
Percentages of Sample Involved

	Average Age at Onset (years)	Percentage Involved
Alcohol		
First use	7.1	100.0
First high	8.0	98.8
First regular use	8.9	61.4
Marijuana		
First use	9.9	100.0
First regular use	11.0	100.0
Cocaine		
First use	11.6	98.4
First regular use	12.4	94.5
Heroin		
First use	12.1	58.7
First regular use	11.9	19.7
Prescription depressants		
First use	12.3	86.2
First regular use	12.8	51.6
Speed		
First use	12.4	50.0
First regular use	12.7	4.7
Crack		
First use	12.8	96.9
First regular use	13.3	84.3

SOURCE: J. A. Inciardi and A. E. Pottieger. 1991. "Kids, Crack, and Crime." *Journal of Drug Issues* 21:257-70. Reproduced by permission of *Journal of Drug Issues.*

Examining the mean age of onset for different types of drugs illustrates how drug use follows a sequential ordering from less serious to more serious substances. Information on average onset ages for different types of drugs used by high-risk street youths in Miami, Florida, is reported in Table 10.1 (Inciardi and Pottieger 1991). Mean onset ages for various drugs increase as illicit substances become more serious. The mean age for first alcohol use is just over 7 years, whereas the mean ages for first marijuana and first cocaine use are 9.9 and 11.6 years, respectively. The high-risk nature of this sample, criminally active street youths, accounts for the relatively young average onset ages. However, the fact that these youths use licit substances (e.g., alcohol) prior to progressing to more serious drugs (e.g., cocaine) illustrates that drug use follows a developmental progression.

Recognizing that drug use follows a sequential pattern indicates that certain drugs function as gateways toward more serious substances. Substances typically identified as gateway drugs include alcohol, cigarettes, and marijuana. Gateway drugs can be thought of as important milestones from which serious substance users already have passed. Evidence supports the idea that drug use progresses through various stages along predictable patterns. For example, Yu and Williford (1994) find that using alcohol and cigarettes increases the likelihood of marijuana use for both males and females. Further research has revealed that "pack-a-day" smokers are three times more likely to drink alcohol and from 10 to 30 times more likely to use illicit drugs (depending on the drug) compared to nonsmokers (Torabi, Bailey, and Majd-Jabbari 1993). Based on a recent longitudinal study, Kandel, Yamaguchi, and Chen (1992; see also Kandel and Yamaguchi 1993) report that drug use follows predictable patterns through four stages: alcohol or cigarettes, marijuana, other illicit drugs, and medically prescribed drugs. The researchers correctly point out, however, that gateways are not the same as "stepping-stones." These progressions merely identify facilitative, as opposed to deterministic (or inevitable), relationships. Clearly, most users of alcohol do not progress to more serious drugs (e.g., cocaine). However, some alcohol users do, and they tend to follow predictable, but not inevitable, developmental patterns. In fact, a recent study finds that, despite the fact that the alcohol–marijuana–other illicit drug use sequence is the most typical pattern observed among serious drug users, it accounts for only about one-third of all drug use sequences (Mackesy-Amiti, Fendrich, and Goldstein 1997).

Previous explanations of drug use have not always considered key developmental features of illicit drug use. A better understanding of why individuals begin to use drugs, why they persist, why they increase their use, and why they ultimately cease using is critically important for designing effective interventions. Available theories of drug use, therefore, must consider the developmental aspects of drug use. In the next section, I discuss how recent developmental theories can be used to help us better understand illicit drug-using behavior.

■ Developmental Theories and Illicit Drug Use

Traditional sociological theories fail to offer a comprehensive explanation for illicit drug use. These approaches commonly take a static view of drug use, focusing on initial influences such as strain or stress (Agnew 1992; Merton 1938), weak social bonds (Hirschi 1969), and drug-using peers (Akers 1992; Sutherland 1939). These theories fail to explain why drug use might progress, escalate, or persist over time.

Drug use is perhaps the most explicitly developmental of all deviant behaviors. For example, persons rarely use cocaine before using alcohol or marijuana. They rarely become intravenous drug users before experimenting with numerous other substances. In short, serious drug use usually represents the end point after a series of milestones have been reached. Understanding this developmental process and the characteristics associated with it is an important challenge for researchers, theoreticians, and policymakers.

Developmental theories have emerged during recent years offering important statements about the causes of criminal behavior and illicit drug use. Developmental theories provide "dynamic" (as opposed to "static") explanations of behavior. Dynamic approaches identify how processes causing drug use change over time. Developmental theories of drug use recognize how behavior is shaped over the life course including the processes that affect the initiation, escalation, and ultimate termination of drug use. Despite differing in content, many developmental theories recognize the progression of drug-using behavior over time, the reciprocal consequences of drug use, and how important life events (e.g., marriage) systematically shape the likelihood of the persistence or cessation of drug use.

In this section, three developmental theories are discussed and applied to illicit drug-using behavior. It is important to recognize that many developmental theories actually build on earlier theories. In most instances, for example, developmental theories integrate, reconceptualize, and extend previous theories to examine the developmental mechanisms involved with illicit drug use.

□ Social Developmental Model

The Social Developmental Model (SDM) emerged in 1985 from the work of J. David Hawkins and Joseph Weis (Hawkins and Weis 1985; see also Catalano and Hawkins 1996). The theory represents a general model of human behavior that accounts for both prosocial and antisocial outcomes such as drug use. The approach integrates dominant propositions from well-known criminological theories. Specifically, the SDM examines risk and protective factors for antisocial behavior that are drawn from social control, social learning, and differential association theory. Dominant themes from these theories include how bonding to prosocial and antisocial persons influences behavior as well as how specific experiences, interactions, and reinforcements affect prosocial and antisocial outcomes.

The SDM holds that individuals learn to be deviant or prosocial from various socializing influences. According to the model, socialization depends on perceived opportunities for social interaction, levels of social interaction, skills required for behavioral involvement and interaction, and perceived rewards for prosocial or "problem" behavior. Together, these mechanisms lead to the development of a social bond that reflects the values and context of one's socializing influences. If primary social influences are deviant, then individuals will become bonded to deviant others. In other words, persons become deviant or prosocial because of the primary norms and behavior held by persons to which they are bonded.

A full presentation of the SDM is displayed in Exhibit 10.3. The model identifies two distinct paths leading to antisocial behavior. The prosocial path (shown at the top of the exhibit) inhibits antisocial behavior, whereas the antisocial path directly promotes antisocial behavior such as drug use. The model begins with the premise that individuals must perceive opportunities for prosocial or antisocial interactions. Perceptions of opportunities and individual skills for social interaction and involvement give rise to participating in these activities. Taking part in prosocial and problematic activities leads to perceptions of the rewards associated with these behaviors. Three distinct outcomes can then occur. First, individuals can participate directly in antisocial behavior. Second, individuals can become attached and committed to antisocial or prosocial others. Third, individuals can perceive opportunities for prosocial or antisocial behavior in the future. The final stage includes an individual's belief systems. Holding strong beliefs in the moral validity of the law (e.g., against drug use) insulates individuals from drug use, whereas holding pro-drug-using attitudes gives rise to drug-using behavior.

The model is developmental in nature because it examines how risk and protective factors evolve over time to influence behavior, both prosocial and antisocial, across different contexts. The model specifies behavioral outcomes and risk and protective factors across four distinctive periods: preschool, elementary school, middle school, and high school contexts.

Three applications of the SDM to drug use have been conducted recently. In one study, Catalano and his colleagues (1996) use data from the Seattle Social Development Project (SSDP), a longitudinal study that includes information collected from more than 800 youths drawn from 18 elementary

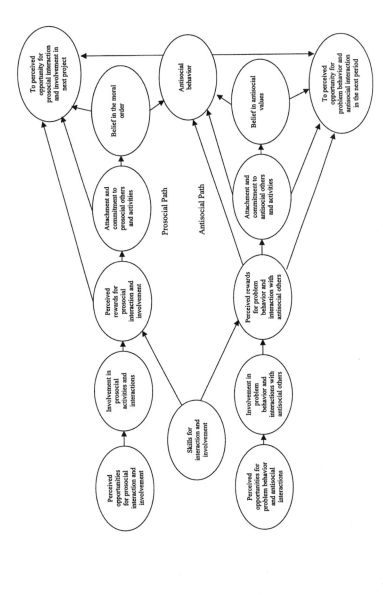

Exhibit 10.3. Social Developmental Model of Antisocial Behavior

SOURCE: R. Catalano, R. Kosterman, J. D. Hawkins, M. Newcomb, and R. Abbott, "Modeling the Etiology of Adolescent Substance Use: A Test of the Social Developmental Model," *Journal of Drug Issues*, 1996, vol. 26, pp. 429-55. Reproduced by permission of *Journal of Drug Issues*.

schools to assess whether measures consistent with the SDM and assessed during the early adolescent years (ages 13 and 14 years) are related to illicit drug use at ages 17 and 18 years. With few exceptions, their findings reveal that measures developed to assess the SDM are predictive of adolescent substance use.

Also using data from the SSDP, O'Donnell, Hawkins, and Abbott (1995) examine the processes that accentuate drug use and delinquency among boys previously identified as aggressive during childhood. Their results indicate that certain factors buffer or stifle the development of drug use including holding norms against substance use, avoiding antisocial peers, and being bonded to and achieving success in school. In short, these factors allow O'Donnell and her colleagues to differentiate between previously aggressive boys who did and did not become involved in substance use during early adolescence.

Finally, a recent study by Fleming et al. (1997) uses information collected from adolescents whose parents are participating in methadone treatment programs to examine a key premise of the SDM—that the relationship between parental bonding and adolescent drug use depends on the drug-using status of parents. As mentioned previously, the SDM holds that strong bonds to prosocial others inhibit drug use, whereas strong bonds to drug users promote drug use. Using data collected from 165 parents and 208 children, Fleming and colleagues assess the impact of parental drug use on the relationship between parental bonding and adolescent substance use. Their results reveal that parental bonding and parental drug use are only weakly related to adolescent substance use. Interestingly, however, their results indicate that bonding to parents is inversely related to substance use among offspring of abstaining parents but is positively related to substance use among offspring of current drug users, a finding that is consistent with the SDM. In short, parental drug use appears to be an important influence on adolescent drug use, and parental bonding does not function as a protective factor under these circumstances.

The SDM offers a comprehensive approach for better understanding illicit drug use. Drug use originates through the combination of opportunities, interactions, and socialization with drug-using affiliates, be they parents or peers. The theory, as well as recent research, suggests several avenues for designing interventions for reducing illicit drug use. Three factors appear most prominent: fostering attachment with prosocial institutions such as schools, reducing exposure to drug-using peers, and encouraging abstinence of drug use among parents. Fostering protective influences (e.g., school bonding) and limiting exposure to certain risk factors should significantly reduce the likelihood of illicit drug use among adolescents.

□ Sampson and Laub's Age-Graded Theory of Informal Social Control

Sampson and Laub's (1993) recent age-graded theory of informal social control offers a comprehensive explanation of developmental trajectories of delinquency and drug use over the life course. Building on the social control theory of Hirschi (1969), Sampson and Laub (1993) argue that there are strong relationships among early childhood antisocial behavior, delinquency, and adult criminality, but there also are important events and conditions that alter and redirect criminal pathways. Their theory of informal social control comprises three separate themes. First, they recognize that structural factors affect the development of social bonds. They argue, for example, that structural conditions (e.g., poverty) diminish the quality of parenting and other family processes and, together with weak ties to school, jointly increase delinquency. Second, they argue that there is much stability in antisocial behavior across the life span. For example, one of the strongest predictors of future crime and drug use is previous participation in these activities. In short, they observe that adult deviance relates strongly to previous deviant activity during adolescence and early childhood. Third, the development of informal social capital during adulthood can alter criminal trajectories toward conformity. They argue that developing strong social ties to a spouse (i.e., having a strong marriage) and developing employment commitment and stability can lead to an investment in conformity even among individuals who were seriously antisocial during adolescence and young adulthood. Sampson and Laub's full developmental model is displayed in Exhibit 10.4.

A number of studies have examined key themes derived from Sampson and Laub's theory (Laub, Nagin, and Sampson 1998; Sampson and Laub 1988, 1990, 1993). However, most of the research has focused on understanding processes of change and *desistance* from criminal behavior. Research has been conducted, for example, on how ties to a spouse and employment stability redirect criminal trajectories toward desistance (Sampson and Laub 1993). Whereas Sampson and Laub's own research has not focused specifically on illicit drug use, their general theory applies to that behavior. Moreover, a number of drug-related studies have examined desistance and are related conceptually to Sampson and Laub's theory. For

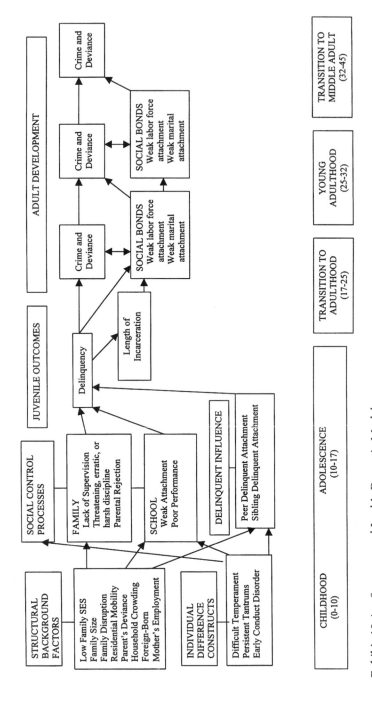

Exhibit 10.4. Sampson and Laub's Dynamic Model

SOURCE: R. Sampson and J. Laub, *Crime in the Making: Pathways and Turning Points Through Life* (Cambridge, MA: Harvard University Press, 1993). Reproduced by permission of Harvard University Press. Copyright © 1993 by the President and Fellows of Harvard College.

SES = socioeconomic status.

example, White and Bates (1995) compare cocaine users to cocaine stoppers (defined as no use during the past year) and find that stoppers are more likely to be married, have children, experience negative effects associated with drug use, and be less exposed to drug-using friends. Similarly, Esbensen and Elliott (1994) examine factors related to desistance from drug use for individuals ages 11 to 30 years (Elliott, Huizinga, and Menard 1989). According to their study, getting married and becoming a parent increases the likelihood of desisting from marijuana use; persons experiencing the birth of a first child are more than twice as likely to desist from marijuana use compared to those not having a first child. In addition, the authors find that a reduction in attitudes favoring delinquency and exposure to drug-using peers also is associated with cessation of marijuana use.

Further research on desistance from marijuana use was reported recently by Warr (1998). Using data from a nationally representative sample of youths (Elliott et al. 1989), Warr examines whether exposure to deviant peers *or* being married is more important in fostering desistance. In initial statistical models, Warr finds marriage to be related to desistance; however, in subsequent analyses, he observes that the effects of marriage vanish when the influences of deviant peer affiliations are considered. Warr's research suggests that the drug-reducing effects of marriage also might contribute to desistance by limiting exposure to deviant affiliations and opportunities. Although these results appear consistent with social learning theory (Akers 1992), they do not disprove Sampson and Laub's hypothesis that a good marriage redirects criminal (and drug-using) trajectories. Reducing one's affiliations with deviant peers is perhaps an effect or outcome of the significance of social ties to a spouse. However, the specificity of this temporal relationship has not yet been examined.

Finally, research by Chen and Kandel (1998) identifies the anticipatory effects of life events on marijuana cessation. Using a representative sample of more than 700 marijuana users, the authors find cessation of use to be associated with age, gender, use status, and the development of important social roles. For example, being a late starter, a social user, and an infrequent user is associated with desistance from marijuana use. Moreover, marriage and becoming pregnant are associated with desistance (especially for women), and most of these effects are anticipatory. For example, Chen and Kandel find that cessation from marijuana use is most pronounced for men one month prior to their marriages and for women nine months prior to the births of their first children. The effects of these life events—in particular, how they are anticipated—are important for reducing marijuana use.

Moreover, these results are consistent with Sampson and Laub's theory that ties to social institutions can redirect criminal and drug-using trajectories toward desistance.

Sampson and Laub's (1993) age-graded theory represents an important extension of social control theory (Hirschi 1969) because it better specifies the processes of stability and change in offending careers. Their theory represents a general model of deviant behavior and, therefore, applies to the drug-using context. Perhaps the most important aspect of their theory rests with better understanding the developmental sequences leading to the stability of offending behavior as well as the processes that redirect criminal and drug-using trajectories. An important issue, however, concerns whether these processes of stability and change apply to all drug users. It could be, for example, that only some offenders follow this pathway to delinquency and drug use. Some offenders might have distinct developmental trajectories. Our next developmental theory examines this issue in more detail.

□ Moffitt's Dual Taxonomy of Offending

Do drug users follow similar pathways to illicit drug use? Do some persist over time and others desist at much earlier stages? Why does drug use peak during late adolescence? These are just some of the questions that a recent developmental theory allows us to ask about the nature of drug-using behavior.

Psychologist Terrie Moffitt's developmental theory holds that there are two typologies of offenders, each with its unique features and explanations for their offending behavior (Moffitt 1993). According to her theory, the two typologies, termed *adolescent limited* and *life course persistent* offenders, have distinct age-crime curves that magnify particular aspects of their antisocial behavior. The adolescent limited typology captures both the upsurge of delinquency during adolescence and the remarkable downswing soon thereafter as adulthood approaches. According to Moffitt, the causal forces leading to adolescent limited offending include an expanding maturity gap that magnifies the differences between adolescents' biological maturity and their social maturity. Many adolescents become frustrated because they are limited from legitimately having the adult privileges, resources, and responsibilities they so strongly desire. Given this situation, adolescent limited offenders become susceptible to negative influences of delinquent peers. Through a process of social mimicry and observational learning, adolescent limited offenders engage in delinquent behavior including illicit drug use. In

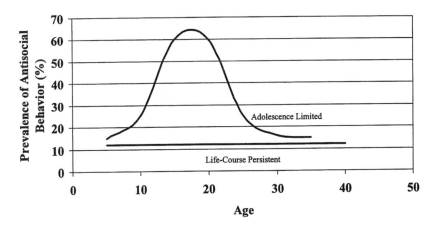

Exhibit 10.5. Moffitt's Dual Taxonomy of Antisocial Behavior
SOURCE: T. Moffitt, "Adolescent Limited and Life Course Persistent Antisocial Behavior: A Developmental Taxonomy," *Psychological Review,* 1993, vol. 100, pp. 674-701. Reproduced by permission of T. Moffitt and the American Psychological Association.

sum, becoming frustrated by one's adolescent status and being exposed to delinquent peers jointly contribute to the huge upsurge in delinquent activity during adolescence. Importantly, however, for this group of offenders, change (i.e., desistance) is likely because as maturation occurs, adult roles become available (Exhibit 10.5).

Moffitt's (1993) life course persistent typology recognizes that a small number of individuals (about 6 percent [especially males]) are at risk for early delinquent behavior, substance abuse, and other age-inappropriate behaviors (e.g., early smoking, sexual intercourse). These offenders exhibit antisocial tendencies during early childhood that become amplified in certain familial and structural contexts (e.g., poor neighborhoods, families with ineffective parental management). According to Moffitt, the origin of early antisocial tendencies are neuropsychological deficits in infants that affect temperament as well as cognitive abilities. These deficits are thought to occur, in part, because of the behavior of women who consume large quantities of alcohol or drugs, have poor nutritional habits, and/or become exposed to toxic agents (e.g., lead) while pregnant. The combination of initial antisocial tendencies (e.g., difficult temperament, neuropsychological risks) and structural (e.g., poverty) and familial (e.g., lax parenting) deficits contributes to the formulation of an antisocial personality. Life course persisters have limited academic success and, due to their antisocial interactional styles, often are marginalized in the elementary school environment. As a result of their accumulating deficits, life course persistent offenders are at risk for early involvement in delinquency, drug use, and other antisocial behaviors.

According to Moffitt (1993), life course persisters represent the minority of all offenders, comprising approximately 20 percent of that population. Moreover, life course persisters are at great risk for escalation to serious criminal activity such as violence and chronic offending, persistence in crime into adulthood, substance abuse, and employment and relationship problems. The antisocial behavior of life course persistent offenders continues through the life span and manifests across numerous contexts. In sum, life course persistent offenders are antisocial in their conduct as children, get involved in delinquency at an early age, and progress into more serious forms of crime, including substance abuse, over time.

Although Moffitt's (1993) theory was not developed specifically to examine drug use, it has implications for better understanding this behavior. One implication of her theory is that there are perhaps (at least) two distinct groups of drug users. One group begins experimenting with drugs at an early age and subsequently progresses toward more serious drugs over time, leading to substance abuse. This pathway, although of great concern in terms of public health and safety issues, does not reflect the majority of drug users. By contrast, the majority of drug use is confined to the period of adolescence and young adulthood in a way that is consistent with Moffitt's adolescent limited typology. For this group, drug involvement does not usually progress beyond marijuana use.

Moffitt's (1993) theory leads us to expect substantial overlap between serious delinquent conduct (e.g., early initiation, violence) and serious substance use. In fact, recent studies support this relationship. For example, van Kammen and Loeber (1994) find that initiation of drug use and/or drug dealing is associated with an increase in person-oriented offenses such as violence and carrying weapons. Moreover, White and Hansell (1998) find both marijuana and cocaine use to be associated with increases in violent behavior. In addition, recent evidence on the consequences of early age at onset for substance use by Zhang, Wieczorek, and Welte (1997) reveals that early substance use, defined as use prior to 13 years of age, is related to persistence in substance use, associating with delinquent peers, and engaging in deviant activities. Finally, in a study using data from the Minnesota Twin Family Study, Elkins and her colleagues (1997) find persistent antisocial behavior (consistent with Moffitt's [1993] life course persistent typology) to be related to low IQ, personality deficits, and substance abuse.[1]

Consistent with Moffitt's (1993) theory, past research suggests that antisocial personality disorders are strongly correlated with alcohol and drug problems (Helzer and Pryzbeck 1988; Hesslebrook 1991). In a recent study, Biderman and his colleagues (1998) examine whether attention deficit hyperactivity disorder (ADHD), a disorder that overlaps with some of the neuropsychological risks identified by Moffitt's life course persister typology, is related to drug use. Their results reveal that ADHD is associated with a twofold increase in substance use. Through detailed comparisons, the authors find that ADHD youths also are much more likely to transition from alcohol use to drug use and are significantly more likely to persist in their drug use than are non-ADHD youths.

It is perhaps an overstatement to suggest that drug use, even among lower risk adolescent limited offenders, does not have negative consequences. Although Moffitt's (1993) theory leads us to expect that life course persistent offenders should have more negative consequences associated with their substance use, a recent study by Nagin, Farrington, and Moffitt (1995) calls this observation into question, at least for one outcome. Their study examines the relationship between illicit drug use and job instability for different offender groups including adolescent limited and life course persistent offenders. Using data from the Cambridge Study in Delinquent Development (Farrington and West 1990), Nagin and his colleagues (1995) find that drug use is *not* related to job instability among the most serious offenders, the life course persisters. For these offenders, job instability already is very high; therefore, illicit drug use does not additionally contribute to this outcome. However, a strong relationship exists between illicit drug use and job instability for adolescent limited offenders, and this finding is observed at ages 18 and 32 years. Across these two age periods, adolescent limited offenders who use illicit drugs have substantially more employment problems than do adolescent limited offenders who do not use drugs. In short, illicit drug use appears to have negative consequences (in terms of job stability) even for adolescent limited offenders.

In summary, Moffitt's (1993) theory represents an important contribution that surely enhances existing knowledge about developmental trajectories of offending behavior. Despite its recency, a number of research studies have emerged to test some of the core statements of the theory. Many of the previous tests have not focused specifically on the implications of the theory for understanding drug use. More research will need to be conducted to examine whether there are distinctive drug-using typologies with unique natural histories and developmental courses.

■ Interventions Against Illicit Drug Use: Developmental Applications

What implications do developmental theories have for designing effective interventions aimed at preventing and reducing illicit drug use? Surveying developmental theories of drug use suggest a number of promising opportunities. For example, the SDM (Catalano and Hawkins 1996) identifies a number of targets for implementing drug use interventions including efforts that foster attachment with prosocial institutions (e.g., schools), reduce exposure to drug-using peers, and encourage abstinence of drug use among parents. Broadly speaking, efforts that encourage protective conditions and reduce susceptibility to deviant influences, especially from drug-using peers, appear most promising.

Sampson and Laub's (1993) age-graded theory of informal social control identifies a number of opportunities for developmentally appropriate interventions. First, during the early childhood years, the authors identify parent training programs as useful efforts for fostering improved socialization of youths at risk for delinquent conduct (Laub et al. 1995). Second, during adolescence, programs that encourage ties to conforming institutions (e.g., schools, the wider community) are appropriate. Laub et al. (1995) identify community service/volunteerism programs, youth mentoring, and community service centers as interventions holding much promise for reducing the risks for delinquency and drug use through adolescence. Finally, during adulthood, their theory recognizes that ties to spouses and employment stability function to reduce criminal trajectories. Obviously, programs cannot feasibly be developed that encourage marriage. However, to the extent that serious offenders, including drug-using offenders, have opportunities to develop better interpersonal and employment skills that allow them to function more successfully in these contexts, cessation from drug use and crime should increase.

Finally, Moffitt's (1993) theory, with its distinct typologies of offenders, identifies two broad areas for developmental interventions against drug use. For the most serious offenders, interventions must begin early in the life course, when children are very young and before their primary socialization experiences have been completed. Interventions that encourage improved parental management (especially to handle and socialize children with difficult temperaments) and that foster cognitive development hold the most promise. By contrast, efforts at reducing drug use among offenders whose drug-using patterns are more discrete (e.g., during adolescence) should focus on enhancing individual resistance skills against the negative influences provided by drug-using peers. Moreover, interventions that foster belief in the value and special qualities of adolescence and reduce the glamorization of drug-using peers will go far toward reducing drug use among this age group.

Before closing this chapter, it is perhaps useful to emphasize various conditions that should be considered prior to developing and implementing drug use interventions. They include the following.

First, given that certain drugs function as gateways to more serious substances, interventions need to target the early stages of drug-using sequences to limit progression to more serious substances.

Second, interventions need to be contextualized to the varying aspects of drug-using careers including why people initiate, escalate, and persist with this behavior. Given the probable asymmetry between the predictors of initiation and desistance (Esbensen and Elliott 1994; Uggen and Piliavin 1999), interventions aimed at preventing the onset of drug use should differ from interventions that focus on other dimensions such as the frequency, escalation, or cessation of drug use.

Third, interventions need to be informed by the most recent empirically supported aspects of theories that account for the dynamic nature of illicit drug use.

Fourth, drug use interventions need to be age graded to fit appropriate developmental contexts. Interventions targeting children must differ from interventions targeting adults. Moreover, there are important developmental contexts even within narrow age ranges that need to be considered when designing interventions. Recent evidence reveals that exposure to stress and negative coping responses (e.g., drug use) are consistently higher among youths in the 11th grade than among youths in the 10th and 12th grades (Mazerolle et al. 1999). Programs aimed at preventing illicit drug use should consider the specific nature of certain developmental contexts.

Fifth, drug use intervention programs need to be subjected to systematic evaluations to determine what works, what does not work, and what needs to be done differently to reduce drug use over the life course.

A number of themes have been covered in this chapter, ranging from static and dynamic explanations of drug use to the developmental dimensions of drug-using careers. One observation that can be drawn from this discussion is that illicit drug use is not a simple phenomenon that is easily understood and preventable. Rather, drug use is an exceptionally complex behavior with overlapping relationships to other forms of deviance as well as considerable heterogeneity among types of drug-using careers. Ultimately, our ability to better understand, prevent, and control illicit drug use will rest with new advances in theories of drug-using behavior. Developmental theories appear to hold much promise in furthering us along this pathway.

STUDY QUESTIONS

1. What are the differences between static and dynamic theories of drug use?
2. What types of life events alter drug use pathways? Why?
3. How do different developmental theories explain desistance from drug use?
4. Why does drug use follow certain developmental patterns?

NOTE

1. Although there is evidence to suggest that early drug use leads to serious crime and violence in the future, the majority of the research supports the view that early antisocial behavior and violence leads to future substance abuse, a view that is consistent with Moffitt's (1993) theory. Refer to a recent comprehensive review by Wagner (1996) for further evidence regarding these relationships.

REFERENCES

Agnew, R. 1992. "Foundation for a General Strain Theory of Crime and Delinquency." *Criminology* 30:47-87.

Akers, R. 1992. *Drugs, Alcohol, and Society: Social Structure, Process, and Policy.* Belmont, CA: Wadsworth.

Biderman, J., T. Wilens, E. Mick, S. Faraone, and T. Spencer. 1998. "Does Attention-Deficit Hyperactivity Disorder Impact the Developmental Course of Drug and Alcohol Abuse and Dependence?" *Biological Psychiatry* 44:269-73.

Blumstein, A., J. Cohen, and D. Farrington. 1988. "Criminal Career Research: Its Value for Criminology." *Criminology* 26:1-35.

Blumstein, A., J. Cohen, J. Roth, and C. Visher. 1986. *Criminal Careers and "Career Criminals."* Vol. 1. Washington, DC: National Academy Press.

Catalano, R. and D. Hawkins. 1996. "The Social Developmental Model: A Theory of Anti-social Behavior." Pp. 149-97 in *Delinquency and Crime: Current Theories,* edited by J. D. Hawkins. New York: Cambridge University Press.

Catalano, R., R. Kosterman, J. D. Hawkins, M. Newcomb, and R. Abbott. 1996. "Modeling the Etiology of Adolescent Substance Use: A Test of the Social Developmental Model." *Journal of Drug Issues* 26:429-55.

Chen, K. and D. Kandel. 1998. "Predictors of Cessation of Marijuana Use: An Event History Analysis." *Drug and Alcohol Dependence* 50:109-21.

Coombs, R. 1981. "Drug Abuse as Career." *Journal of Drug Issues,* Fall, 369-87.

Elkins, I. J., W. Iacono, A. Doyle, and M. McGue. 1997. "Characteristics Associated With the Persistence of Antisocial Behavior: Results From Recent Longitudinal Research." *Aggression and Violent Behavior* 2:101-24.

Elliott, D., D. Huizinga, and S. Menard. 1989. *Multiple Problem Youth: Delinquency, Substance Abuse, and Mental Health Problems.* New York: Springer-Verlag.

Esbensen, F. and D. Elliott. 1994. "Continuity and Discontinuity in Illicit Drug Use: Patterns and Antecedents." *Journal of Drug Issues* 24:75-97.

Farrington, D. and D. West. 1990. "The Cambridge Study in Delinquent Development: A Long-Term Follow-Up of 411 London Males." Pp. 115-38 in *Criminality: Personality, Behavior, and Life History,* edited by Hans-Jurgen Kerner and G. Kaiser. New York: Springer-Verlag.

Fleming, C., R. Gainey Brewer, K. Haggerty, and R. Catalano. 1997. "Parent Drug Use and Bonding to Parents as Predictors of Substance Use in Children of Substance Abusers." *Journal of Child & Adolescent Substance Use* 6:75-86.

Hawkins, J. D. and J. Weis. 1985. "The Social Developmental Model: An Integrated Approach to Delinquency Prevention." *Journal of Primary Prevention* 6:73-97.

Helzer, J. and T. Pryzbeck. 1988. "The Co-occurrence of Alcoholism With Other Psychiatric Disorders in the General Population and Its Impact on Treatment." *Journal of Studies on Alcohol* 49:219-24.

Hesslebrook, M. 1991. "Gender Comparison of Antisocial Personality Disorder and Depression in Alcoholism." *Journal of Substance Abuse* 3:205-20.

Hirschi, T. 1969. *Causes of Delinquency.* Berkeley: University of California Press.

Inciardi, J. A. and A. E. Pottieger. 1991. "Kids, Crack, and Crime." *Journal of Drug Issues* 21:257-70.

Kandel, D. and K. Yamaguchi. 1993. "From Beer to Crack: Developmental Patterns of Drug Involvement." *American Journal of Public Health* 83:851-55.

Kandel, D., K. Yamaguchi, and K. Chen. 1992. "Stages of Progression in Drug Involvement From Adolescence to Adulthood: Further Evidence for the Gateway Theory." *Journal of Studies on Alcohol* 53:447-57.

Laub, J. H., D. Nagin, and R. Sampson. 1998. "Trajectories of Change in Criminal Offending: Good Marriages and the Desistance Process." *American Sociological Review* 63:225-38.

Laub, J. H., R. Sampson, R. Corbett, and J. Smith. 1995. "The Public Policy Implications of a Life-Course Perspective on Crime." Pp. 91-106 in *Crime and Public Policy: Putting Theory to Work,* edited by Hugh D. Barlow. Boulder, CO: Westview.

Mackesy-Amiti, M., M. Fendrich, and P. Goldstein. 1997. "Sequence of Drug Use Among Serious Drug Users: Typical and Atypical Progression." *Drug and Alcohol Dependence* 45:185-96.

Mazerolle, P., E. Cauffman, A. Piquero, L. Broidy, and D. Espelage. 1999. "Exposure to Stress and Conflict Among High School Aged Youth: Do Coping Responses Vary for Males and Females?" Paper presented at the annual meeting of the Academy of Criminal Justice Sciences, Orlando, FL.

Merton, R. 1938. "Social Structure and Anomie." *American Sociological Review* 3:672-82.

Moffitt, T. 1993. "Adolescent Limited and Life Course Persistent Antisocial Behavior: A Developmental Taxonomy." *Psychological Review* 100:674-701.

Nagin, D., D. Farrington, and T. Moffitt. 1995. "Life-Course Trajectories of Different Types of Offenders." *Criminology* 33:111-39.

O'Donnell, J., J. D. Hawkins, and R. Abbott. 1995. "Predicting Serious Delinquency and Substance Use Among Aggressive Boys." *Journal of Consulting and Clinical Psychology* 63:529-37.

Office of National Drug Control Policy. 1998. *The National Drug Control Strategy 1998.* Washington, DC: Government Printing Office.

Sampson, R. and J. Laub. 1988. "Unraveling Families and Delinquency: A Reanalysis of the Gluecks' Data." *Criminology* 26:355-80.

———. 1990. "Crime and Deviance Over the Life-Course: The Salience of Adult Social Bonds." *American Sociological Review* 55:609-27.

———. 1993. *Crime in the Making: Pathways and Turning Points Through Life.* Cambridge, MA: Harvard University Press.

Substance Abuse and Mental Health Services Administration. Various years. *National Household Survey on Drug Abuse,* 1979-1995. Rockville, MD: U.S. Department of Health and Human Services.

Sutherland, E. 1939. *Criminology.* Philadelphia: J. B. Lippincott.

Torabi, M., W. Bailey, and M. Majd-Jabbari. 1993. "Cigarette Smoking as a Predictor of Alcohol and Other Drug Use by Children and Adolescents: Evidence of the 'Gateway Drug Effect'." *Journal of School Health* 63:302-6.

Uggen, C. and I. Piliavin. 1999. "Asymmetrical Causation and Criminal Desistance." *Journal of Criminal Law and Criminology* 88:1399-422.

van Kammen, W. B. and R. Loeber. 1994. "Are Fluctuations in Delinquent Activities Related to the Onset and Offset in Juvenile Illegal Drug Use and Drug Dealing? *Journal of Drug Use* 24:9-24.

Wagner, E. 1996. "Substance Use and Violent Behavior in Adolescence." *Aggression and Violent Behavior* 1:375-87.

Warr, M. 1998. "Life-Course Transitions and Desistance From Crime." *Criminology* 36:183-215.

White, H. Raskin and M. Bates. 1995. "Cessation From Cocaine Use." *Addiction* 90:947-57.

White, H. Raskin and S. Hansell. 1998. "Acute and Long-Term Effects of Drug Use on Aggression From Adolescence Into Adulthood." *Journal of Drug Issues* 28:837-58.

Yu, J. and W. R. Williford. 1994. "Alcohol, Other Drugs, and Criminality: A Structural Analysis." *American Journal of Drug and Alcohol Abuse* 20:373-93.

Zhang, L., W. Wieczorek, and J. Welte. 1997. "The Impact of Age of Onset of Substance Use on Delinquency." *Journal of Research in Crime and Delinquency* 34:253-68.

CHAPTER 11

The Routine Activity Approach as a General Crime Theory

MARCUS FELSON

A *paradigm* is a fancy word for a general theory or framework that organizes a field of study (Kuhn 1962). Every science needs one to keep from
going to pieces. Criminology lacks one. For example, a recent survey of
criminologists found that no more than 17 percent agreed with any one general theory of crime (Ellis 1999). Indeed, criminologists dispersed their votes
among 22 general theories. They did not even apply the same theories to
serious and persistent offending that they applied to delinquency and minor
offending. Some people will insist that criminology is a "multiple-paradigm"
field, but that violates the very idea of a paradigm as a single road map for scientific exploration.[1]

That does not mean that everyone in a discipline needs to agree on every
matter, but nearly everyone must agree about the basic concepts and ideas
organizing their field of study. Interestingly, criminologists do agree substantially about four basic crime correlations:

1. Family life discourages crime participation.
2. Males commit more crimes than do females.
3. Persons ages 12 to 25 years are disproportionate offenders.
4. As socioeconomic status rises, crime participation declines.

Criminologists disagree about which of these correlations to emphasize
and how to put them together into a general theory. Adherents to each theory criticize the competition for neglecting one of the four correlations. A

major problem faced by traditional crime theories is that all four of these correlations are overstated. Males commit relatively more crimes, but females are all too active in crime. Youths have no crime monopoly, and those who are older have extra employee theft opportunities. Crime occurs within families, and good parents can have bad kids. The income-crime correlation is not that strong. One never should hitch a paradigm to correlations as weak as these. This is why criminologists need a new general theory. What criteria should we use to develop it?

■ Making Crime Explanation Coherent

Criminology already has plenty of facts and ideas. Our problem is to figure out which of these facts and ideas are central and which are peripheral. For example, it is tempting to exaggerate race differences in offending and to forget that nations lacking racial differences still have crime. The race issue, although very important for the operations of the criminal justice system, can become a distraction for studying the origins of crime itself.

Which facts and ideas should we use to forge a general science of crime? To make these difficult decisions, I suggest that we adopt from more successful sciences the following five standards of scientific coherence.

The "touch-it" standard. Find highly tangible explanations at the outset. Take advantage of the physical world and our five senses to state the first principles in very down-to-earth terms. For example, Harvey figured out the human circulatory system by considering flows of blood among specific organs in a definite order, and Galileo dropped objects from the Tower of Pisa and watched when they hit the ground.

The "near-and-far" standard. Find explanations that work as well at micro and macro levels, in different settings and eras, internationally, and for all types of crime (Brantingham and Brantingham 1984). A good explanation should help us to understand crime for the individual, neighborhood, town, city, metropolis, and nation as well as for the hour, day, week, month, year, decade, millennium, and epoch. For example, a physiologist can study submicroscopic and microscopic flows of blood as well as those visible with the naked eye. He or she can link capillaries to small blood vessels, to large vessels, to the largest vessel, the aorta. Labs can study blood flows by the second, minute, or hour. Good science is universal for all nations and ethnic groups. This point inspired

Gottfredson and Hirschi (1990) to state their "general theory of crime." A general theory does not neglect variations among individual cases or localities; it merely puts these variations into a common framework.

The "few-to-many" standard. Find a few scientific rules with many ramifications. If one's list of first principles gets too long or complex, then he or she is going to get lost. This is why Newton stated only three laws of thermodynamics. Darwin boiled about 1,000 pages of observations down to a single principle of natural selection. Scientists call this process "Occam's razor," cutting away at confusion and getting to the point on principles while elaborating on facts and derivations.

The "exactly how" standard. Find clear *mechanisms,* that is, exactly *how* something leads to more or less crime (Pawson and Tilley 1997). Scientists want to know the direction in which blood flows, exactly what animals eat, how chlorophyll works, and how organisms live and die. Criminologists must find out exactly what burglars look for and how they break in. Even one's armchair speculations should say exactly how he or she *thinks* something happens. I would rather be precisely wrong than vaguely right.

The "fit-the-facts" standard. Learn everything possible about specific crimes, their settings, their modus operandi, and how they are prevented. Make sure that the explanations are consistent with these facts (see, e.g., Clarke 1997). Modify the explanations as more facts come in. If explanations need to be contorted to fit the facts, then it is time for a new paradigm.

We can learn from the more successful sciences how to formulate a general theory for criminology. Fortunately, these five standards for coherent crime explanation apply to one extant general theory of crime: the routine activity approach to crime analysis.

■ The Original Formulation of the Routine Activity Approach

The routine activity approach began by describing how a direct contact predatory offense occurred (Cohen and Felson 1979). Such an offense was predatory because it had, at a minimum, one offender and one target of crime. Direct physical contact between the offender and target also was required. The original formulation excluded threats from a distance, suicide, drug sales, and fights in which both participants were offenders. A direct contact predatory offense in the original formulation had three minimal elements:

- a likely offender;
- a suitable target; and
- the absence of a capable guardian against the offense.

During the era of its formulation, the routine activity approach differed greatly from other crime theories because it treated the offender as relatively less significant. The routine activity approach also defined the target of crime distinctly from the victim. The best guardian against a crime is neither a police officer nor a security guard. The best guardian is someone close such as a friend or relative. Guardianship against crime depends on someone's *absence*. Two presences (offender and target) and one absence (guardian) make the best crime setting. The convergence of these three conditions invites a criminal act to occur.

A suitable crime target might include a wallet, a purse, a car, or a human target for personal attack. A target's suitability for attack is determined by four criteria, summed up by the acronym VIVA:

- Value
- Inertia
- Visibility
- Access

The value of the target is defined from the offender's viewpoint, depending on what the offender wants. Find out what property someone might like to steal or vandalize or who an offender might prefer to attack or even kidnap. Usually, the offender would be discouraged if a target were high in inertia. For example, a heavy appliance is too difficult to carry out of a home, and a large or muscular person is difficult to outmuscle. Usually, an offender is drawn to a target more visible to him or her such as money flashed in a bar or someone who unwittingly invites an attack. The offender's access to a street or building renders its contents and people more subject to his or her illegal action.

The routine activity approach started with crime conditions right there. It considered how a criminal act occurs or fails to occur at specific times and places. Without the convergence of minimal elements for crime, a direct contact predatory criminal act would be virtually out of the question. Such immediate conditions are set in place from the routine activities of the surrounding community. The transportation system, the structure of work and household, and the technology and production of goods—in short, the everyday *macro*-level organization of the community and society—lead to *micro* convergences of conditions more or less favorable to crime.

Consider how a residential burglary occurs. A burglar tries to find a suitable household that is empty of guardians or within which the guardians are asleep or indisposed. The burglar seeks a place containing valuables easy to remove. Easy access and visibility draw the burglar further. The larger community structure offers the burglar crime opportunities by producing more lightweight but valuable goods and getting people out of their homes for work, school, or leisure. While they are out, the burglar goes in.

■ Applying the Five Standards of Coherent Science to the Routine Activity Approach

The routine activities explanation for crime holds up quite well when tested against the five standards of scientific coherence. Following the *touch-it standard,* the routine activity approach is highly tangible, emphasizes the physical world, and considers physical convergences in its core requirements. Its image of the offender takes into account the offender's use of the five senses to carry out crime. Following the *near-and-far standard,* the routine activity approach works at both the micro and macro levels, in different settings and eras, internationally, and for different types of crime (Felson 2000). It shows how offenders, targets, and guardians move into and out of potential crime settings. The routine activity approach also uses a few clear and simple principles. Simplicity is not the same as simple-mindedness. Indeed, very diverse findings, difficult problems, and complex information can be absorbed within its few and simple principles. For example, the many features of home, neighborhood, and household activities could be summed up in one principle: the offender must find the target with nobody there to stop the offender from attacking it. Indeed, routine activity analysis brings forth many nuances of criminal acts, still maintaining coherence by deriving all this from a very few rules, in accordance with the *few-to-many standard.* It starts at a very simple level before it elaborates. If one gets lost, one can just go back to the few fundamentals to find his or her way once more.

The routine activity approach also seeks clear mechanisms, examining which features of daily life lead to more or less crime. Its adherence to the *exactly how standard* is well illustrated elsewhere (Felson 1998). For example, the old theories state vague and inexact hypotheses, for example, "Social disorganization creates crime." By contrast, the routine activity approach details mechanisms such as the following:

- Tough guys can seize local abandoned houses for their own illegal uses. For example, they can set up drug houses.
- Failed local businesses leave streets unsupervised and dangerous.

The routine activity approach also helps us to understand why some forms of "social disorganization" do not give us more crime and might even produce less:

- Shabby paint on buildings might be ugly, but it probably does not itself contribute to more crime.
- Graffiti in subways probably does not lead to more robberies.
- Extreme deterioration of a neighborhood might cause vice crimes to decline by scaring away customers.

The *fit-the-facts standard* of scientific coherence is reflected in the growing convergence between the routine activity approach and several studies of crime specifics, settings, modus operandi, broken windows theory (Kelling and Coles 1996), and prevention. Relatively recent work is devoted to such convergences (Clarke and Felson 1993; Felson 1998; Felson and Clarke 1999).

Burglary offers us many cogent examples of how the routine activity approach follows all five standards of scientific coherence. A burglar follows the touch-it standard using his or her senses to determine crime opportunities and risks and to put criminal acts into motion. In accordance with the near-and-far standard, a burglar responds to specific and local crime opportunities while also benefiting from new transport systems that help the burglar get to additional crime settings. Specific routine factors assist the burglar (e.g., more lightweight goods, more cash in homes or businesses). The few-to-many standard also is very relevant; the burglar can consider a few aspects of his or her targets, such as VIVA (discussed earlier), to decide whether or not to break in. The burglar might seek easy access and lightweight things to carry away. These minimal elements have elaborate applications when considering what streets lead to a crime target, different types of buildings, the timing of commercial burglary versus residential burglary (weekend for the

TABLE 11.1 How to Modify Criminological Concepts to Meet
Scientific Standards, Using the Routine Activity Approach

Vague Criminological Concept	More Precise and Useful Statement
Criminogenic social roles	More time away from home brings more offending and less guardianship
Differential association	An offense is easier to carry out with help from friends
Social strains	Nearly empty streets invite muggings
Shaming and social control	Keeping an eye on the likely offender discourages further misbehavior
Marxist materialism	Study who owns what, who watches what, and which things are easy to steal
Offender emotions	Learn the timing and settings for emotional outbursts of crime
Labeling, secondary deviance	Find out exactly how one offense sets up another in time and space
Racial inequality	Find out how easily burgled housing is distributed by race

(the near-and-far standard). Perhaps it makes most sense to specify emotional acts in space and time and the proximate conditions leading up to an emotional outburst.

Notwithstanding these criticisms, the crime theories other than routine activities that are applied and explained in this book raise valid issues. Their most general strength is an intuitive feel for society's structures and processes that tend to generate crime. Their most general shortcoming is a failure to formulate tangible principles and mechanisms, precisely what the routine activity approach does offer. Table 11.1 shows how each of the principles and intuitions represented by the eight other crime theories discussed in this book could be strengthened with more precise language. Do not talk about criminogenic social roles; instead, specify activity patterns that expose people to specific crime risks. Do not get caught in the rhetoric of Marxism or anti-Marxism; instead, find out who owns what, where they keep it, and how readily it can be stolen or vandalized.

■ Conclusion

Crime is complex, and criminology is difficult. Most theories have not been able to find their way through all this complexity or to find the elusive secret of individual disposition to commit crime. These theories failed because they tried to predict the unpredictable—what each individual is going to do next. It is much more promising to work with tangible processes and incidents. Five standards of scientific coherence provide us with the tools for progress. The routine activity approach uses these tools well and places the crime incident at the center of inquiry. Crime is a physical act, and we must not forget it.

NOTE

1. During a scientific revolution, two paradigms do battle for a brief period until the new one wins. Criminology today lives in a "pre-paradigm state," that is, theoretical chaos. Although many paradigms might exist over the total history of a science, they cannot live together simultaneously. Moreover, an old paradigm might have made good sense in its day given what was then known. But as new information comes along, so does a new and better paradigm. There is no turning back. For example, today's astronomers could not return to Ptolemy's image of the universe even if they wanted to. It just would not work.

REFERENCES

Brantingham, P. J. and P. L. Brantingham. 1984. *Patterns in Crime.* New York: Macmillan.
Clarke, R. V., ed. 1997. *Situational Crime Prevention: Successful Case Studies.* 2nd ed. New York: Harrow & Heston.
Clarke, R. V. and M. Felson. 1993. "Introduction: Criminology, Routine Activity, and Rational Choice." In *Routine Activity and Rational Choice: Advances in Criminological Theory,* vol. 5, edited by R. V. Clarke and M. Felson. New Brunswick, NJ: Transaction Books.
Cohen, L. E. and M. Felson. 1979. "Social Change and Crime Rate Trends: A Routine Activity Approach." *American Sociological Review* 4:588-608.
Ellis, Lee. 1999. "Criminologists' Opinions About Causes and Theories of Crime and Delinquency." *The Criminologist,* July/August, 1, 5.
Felson, M. 1998. *Crime and Everyday Life.* 2nd ed. Thousand Oaks, CA: Pine Forge.
———. 2000. "The Routine Activity Approach: A Very Versatile Theory of Crime. In *Explaining Crime and Criminals,* edited by R. Paternoster. Los Angeles: Roxbury.
Felson, M. and R. V. Clarke. 1999. *Opportunity Makes the Thief: Practical Theory for Crime Prevention.* Police Research Series, No. 98. London: Home Office, Policing and Reducing Crime Unit.
Gottfredson, M. and T. Hirschi. 1990. *A General Theory of Crime.* Stanford, CA: Stanford University Press.
Kelling, G. L. and C. Coles. 1996. *Fixing Broken Windows: Restoring Order and Reducing Crime in Our Communities.* New York: Free Press.
Kuhn, T. S. 1962. *The Structure of Scientific Revolutions.* Chicago: University of Chicago Press.
Pawson, R. and N. Tilley. 1997. *Realistic Evaluation.* Thousand Oaks, CA: Sage.

INDEX